LINCOLN COLLECTOR

CARL SANDBURG

Lincoln Collector

The Story of Oliver R. Barrett's

Great Private Collection

NEW YORK

BONANZA BOOKS

1960

This edition published by Bonanza Books,

a division of Crown Publishers, Inc.,

by arrangement with Harcourt, Brace and Company.

Designed by Robert Josephy

PRINTED IN THE UNITED STATES OF AMERICA

CONTENTS

ILLUSTRATIONS

ix

between pages 144 *and* 145

Proof from unfinished engraving of young Mary Todd
Photograph of Lincoln from unretouched negative discarded by Hesler
Brady portrait of Lincoln at time of Cooper Union speech
Hesler photograph of Lincoln in Springfield, June 3, 1860
Carte-de-visite-sized photograph of Lincoln by Hesler, June 3, 1860
Mary Todd Lincoln, widow
William Wallace Lincoln in Washington
Early photograph of William Wallace Lincoln
Tableware Mary Lincoln presented Usher Linder for Mrs. Linder
Lincoln's hunting-case watch, closed and open
Attest by Dennis F. Hanks to whom Lincoln gave watch
The President's seal, and the right hand of Lincoln molded from life

Foreword

W HAT IS IT collectors do when they collect? Where would history and biography be unless there were collectors? What do collectors do for and to each other? Is the collector's life mostly humdrum or can it be filled with the quaint and droll, even excitement and drama? What is the difference between the mere hobbyist and the truly impassioned collector? Does the true collector meet adventures, unexpected follies and humiliations, heartbreak one day and breathtaking elation the next, satisfactions like the hunter who has run down and bagged his game? Are collectors "just plain folks" or do they belong among "queer people"? Can there be such cases as one collector coming to another and saying with utter sincerity, "I can't sleep nights. I want that 'Auld Lang Syne' manuscript in Burns's handwriting"? These and many other related questions get their answers amid these pages in the life story of the most picturesque and tireless of collectors in the Lincoln field, his story interweaving with others of the collector breed, no two ever alike.

Lincoln Collector is an album of Americana, a folio of American portraits and scenes. Lincoln perhaps is foremost but the folks he came from, the American people and traditions from which he drew strength and wisdom, the forces that suckled him, they are here in more than equal measure. Why, in his obscure speech opening the second chapter, did he term the Declaration of Independence "that immortal emblem"? Why do those neglected words of his in 1858 have high meaning now, not only for this country, but for the whole world? Why in the same chapter have we included an 1864 comic biography of Lincoln that Lincoln himself possibly enjoyed reading for its horseplay and clowning? Because laughter is ever part of the American genius and our book is not intended for solemn duffers and patriotic stuffed shirts.

We have included a mystery story written by Lincoln, wherein he, a lawyer for the defense, reports how after much howling and hullabaloo they saw the supposed murdered man walk into the courtroom alive and well. We present an authentic portrait of the most fascinating braggart and scalawag known to Lincoln's boyhood and youth, his stepbrother John D. Johnston.

We meet Robert E. Lee in two different pools of his personality through the medium of two candid letters. We meet John Brown and his handwriting and see him confess he would be willing to give death to an entire generation of men, women, and children toward bringing an end to slavery. We glimpse the youth Jefferson Davis with a romantic soft heart in a love letter to Zachary Taylor's daughter, with whom he later eloped. We meet another Jeff Davis much later giving the detailed circumstances of his being taken prisoner by Federal forces. We get intimately acquainted with the seventeen-year-old Ulysses S. Grant at West Point in a long quizzical boyish letter to a cousin back home in Ohio. We meet a reprint of the New York *Herald* two-column editorial of April 17, 1865, on Abraham Lincoln's "place in history," which many will incline to rate as possibly the most adequate appraisal given Lincoln in his own generation. We learn, too, in an abrupt peremptory letter of General William Tecumseh Sherman why he refused to write for a charity bazaar the sentiment "The pen is mightier than the sword."

The foregoing may properly preface a book that is Lincolniana as well as Americana, presenting Lincoln in a series of different frames, revealing the people, the times, the speech and lingo, of the generation who knew Lincoln and that he knew. We may gather in degree how the tumultuous American nation of this present momentous hour grew from an America that *was*.

Carl Sandburg

Flat Rock
North Carolina

LINCOLN COLLECTOR

I. The Collector

When the materials which go into the making of a biography are filtered through the mind of the author, something is invariably lost. A significant phrase from a letter, a paragraph perhaps, fits the biographer's immediate need; the balance of the document is rejected. Proper proportion—itself an approach to fidelity—and the necessity of keeping the finished sketch within readable limits make selection inescapable. Nevertheless, valuable lights on character are frequently sacrificed in the process. Letters are bits of self-portraiture, sometimes more effectively done, more convincing, than anything from the pen of another can possibly be. Often a few paragraphs which a newspaper writer struck off as part of a day's routine have an authentic ring that defies duplication.

—PAUL M. ANGLE

THERE was the artist who was asked why he didn't draw the pelican. "Why should I? There it is as God made it—the pelican. Go look at it! What more is there to say?"

And the Lincoln Collection of Oliver R. Barrett, which represents toil, pursuit, and sagacity of more than half a century—you tell what is in it, if you can, and there is no need to say more. To enumerate and describe every last item would tire the reader, weary the printers, and bring exasperation to the proofreaders. This is an attempt at presenting many of the notable items with collateral data, an endeavor to answer in a limited compass a query often heard among students of Lincoln, "What precisely is there to the Barrett Collection?"

Both eminent scholars of proved worth and narrow gradgrinds gnawing small bones have had help and contributions from the willing and patient Barrett. Randall, Beveridge, Tarbell, Hertz, Barton, Warren, Thomas, Bas-

3

ler, Donald, Townsend, W. C. Ford, Paul Angle, David Mearns, to name only a few offhand, have written and spoken their acknowledgments of time and materials obtained from Barrett, the present writer saying in a 1939 preface, "The collector's flair leading Barrett since he was a boy has resulted in a mass of source materials wherein are many items that would have probably been lost for historical purposes but for the sagacity and method by which they were sought out."

Many kinds of paper here—heavy parchment and vellum engrossed—legal cap—letter and note paper—scrap—newsprint of the later era now beginning to disintegrate—rag paper of the previous generation, tough and fibrous and good for centuries to come with its register of handwriting or printing—quiet paper that whispers its tender message, or groaning, roaring paper that for those of imagination carries its own grief or elation of a vanished hour and day. Paper, if you please, sir or madam, as soundless as hushed footfalls on silent snow.

In the course of preparing this book for the printer, the manuscript was submitted for suggestions and criticism to Benjamin P. Thomas, the author of *Portrait for Posterity*, a stormy and tumultuous volume reporting the successive waves of Lincoln biographers across eighty-four years. Among his notes Thomas wrote: "The Barrett Collection is so full and basic that a pretty good life of Lincoln could be written from it alone, whereas no present-day life could be written without it. Barrett's generosity has enriched the Lincoln story." This feeling or viewpoint is to be found in the forewords, acknowledgments, or footnotes in more than twoscore biographies or special works on Lincoln.

About the year 1886, some twenty years after the death of Abraham Lincoln, it happened that the thirteen-year-old boy Oliver R. Barrett began what was to become a massive and diversified collection of Lincoln letters, documents, relics, and related source materials. In his home town of Pittsfield, Illinois, there was the memory of Colonel D. H. Gilmer, who had volunteered for the war, received his commission from President Lincoln, fought in several battles, and met his death in combat at Chickamauga. In line with an announced appointment policy of preference for a veteran or his dependents, President Lincoln appointed Colonel D. H. Gilmer's widow to be postmaster at Pittsfield. The daughter, Lizzie Gilmer, could remember that as a girl swinging on the front gate she saw the visiting lawyer and politician Abraham Lincoln come out of the Gilmer house. And Lincoln took hold of Lizzie, swung her high in the air, kissed her, and put her back on the gate to go on swinging. So that became a tradition, and likewise the story of another Pittsfield woman, Susan Scanland, who freely gave her opinion of Lincoln—"The laziest man there ever was, good for nothing except to tell stories." Susan had fixed a turkey dinner for Lincoln and other menfolks, and six o'clock came and half-past six, and the dinner went cold, because Lincoln was spinning yarns for a crowd of men at a drugstore.

At a meeting of a Lincoln group in Chicago, Barrett told how, as a boy in Pittsfield, his interest in Lincoln was first deeply awakened. In a grade classroom, the one Negro pupil sat alone in a front seat, a double seat. And when a boy or girl whispered, the teacher thought it proper to make such guilty boy or girl, as a punishment, sit beside the Negro girl, who was always smiling, had big gleaming eyes, didn't mind at all. One day the teacher called out, "Ollie Barrett, you sit down beside this girl," pointing toward the Negro pupil. He took the seat as ordered and heard the snickering of boys who sent spitballs and pieces of chalk against his neck and head. Going to the back of the room for a drink of water, as the rules permitted, the Barrett boy suddenly was out the room, slammed the door, and ran home to tell his mother and get sympathy. His mother gave him a hug, talked long with an arm around him, told him about Lincoln, about slavery and emancipation and the terrible war. She explained for him how there were ladies in Pittsfield who didn't like Mr. Lincoln because when he came to town he would tell stories and keep the men from coming home to dinner on time. Then the mother told the boy she would fix it with the teacher—and if Ollie was a good boy she would take him to Springfield. He kicked himself on the shins—he was going to have his first ride on a railroad train, the choo-choo cars. Spring came and the mother did take her boy to see the capital, the tomb, and the old Lincoln home.

The custodian of the tomb then was one John Carroll Power, and in Barrett's recollection, "It was almost a personal charge he had there, a very unusual man, a very positive and determined man." On a busy day Power would usher in first one group and then another, 25 cents a head, point to the sarcophagus and to various relics, with explanations and descriptions. Here the boy saw for the first time the dress of the actress Laura Keene and heard that the dark stain on the fabric was the blood of Lincoln. From this somber moment Power turned to telling of the robbers or ghouls who had tried to steal the body of Lincoln and who escaped from the clutches of Power and of waiting detectives. The ghastly and grotesque elements are recited in detail in Lloyd Lewis's *Myths after Lincoln*.

"My boyish mind wandered away," Barrett once reminisced, "and I looked around and saw a pair of old Congress gaiter shoes on a glass shelf, and I got to thinking and wondering, imagining Lincoln treading around the White House wearing those shoes." Later he heard Mr. Power say, "Now there are the shoes belonging to one of the robbers that night," adding that once a smart schoolteacher had asked him, "Well, if you could get the shoes off the robber, why didn't you get the robber?" Mr. Power told her, "We will come to that later." And later Mr. Power did explain to young Barrett and his mother that the tomb robbers took off their shoes and hid them in bushes so as to sneak in quietly, detectives finding the shoes after the robbers vanished.

In reverence and quiet the boy and his mother sat on the hillside sloping up from the tomb, the mother leading the boy on in a deepening interest in the man whose moldering bones lay enclosed at the foot of the hill. They then went to the plain two-story corner house where Abraham Lincoln and his family had lived. In charge there they met Osborn H. Oldroyd, who was later to go to Washington and establish a museum in "the house where Lincoln died." They found Oldroyd widely informed, kindly, and he took them upstairs and down, pointing to beds, chairs, tables, cabinets, relics, giving young Oliver a few souvenirs.

Then back to Pittsfield, only sixty-odd miles from Springfield, and having its own Lincoln associations. Here were men and women who could remember the little red-headed "printer's devil" who later became the editor of the weekly *Pike County Free Press*, young John G. Nicolay. In his mother's autograph album young Barrett found a poem written by Nicolay:

FRIENDSHIP

Many are the ships that sail
O'er the changeful sea of Life,
Wooing every gentle gale,
Daring every tempest strife.
Ships of every form and kind,
Ships of every taste and mind,
Shall I tell *my* choice to thee?
Friendship is the ship for *me*.

Pittsfield, January 25, 1853
—Jno. G. Nicolay

Later Nicolay was to be private secretary to President Lincoln and co-author of an immense biography of Lincoln. Here the other coauthor, then a boy, John Hay, came from near-by Warsaw to attend a small seminary school in Pittsfield and to strike up an acquaintance with Nicolay that was to last far beyond their association as secretaries to Lincoln in the Executive Mansion in Washington. Here, too, Milton Hay, an uncle of John, had practiced law, and later sold his home to young Barrett's grandfather and moved to Springfield, his law office near that of the Lincoln & Herndon firm. John remained to complete his term at the Thompson Academy.

After arriving home from Springfield, and sensing Oliver's newly whetted interest, the mother took the boy up to the attic of their house. Here he saw bullet molds, candle molds, a hoop skirt that boys had used for a tent, grants of land to the boy's grandfather, documents signed by Presidents of the United States. His hands came on an envelope marked "verry Precious," and he told his mother someone must have taken out whatever in the envelope was "Verry Precious." But the mother showed him the letter in the handwriting of Robert Burns. A niece of Burns had given the letter to Oliver's father.

Then they opened a trunk made of deerskin, the hair turned outside, the inside of the trunk lined with copies of the *Christian Evangelist*. Inside the boy saw something like one million used postage stamps. The boy's father during years of duty with the Freedman's Aid Society had laid by all used postage stamps that had come his way, having heard that when he got a million, they would bring a small fortune. Then, when he learned that used postage stamps would bring him little or nothing in the open market, he put his million of them up in the attic. The boy Oliver found that many of the stamps in the trunk were rare and brought good prices; he managed to sell them, and with this income bought autographs and letters. In Pittsfield and elsewhere the boy sought and gathered Lincoln letters, tokens, handbills, newspapers, and miscellany bearing on Lincoln and his times. At the local hotel he lay in waiting and snared autographs from stars on the lyceum lecture course—Mary A. Livermore, organizer of battlefield hospitals and the Sanitary Fairs, John B. Gough, the sworn foe of alcohol, and other names of the hour. The boy worked out a form letter:

Pittsfield, Ill.
Nov. 31, 1887

Dear Sir or (Miss):
A youth am I of 14 years
Suppressing all my doubts and fears
I take my pen in hand
To write this note as best I can
Asking you as a favor kind
Please, to return the enclosed with some verses signed.
If not too much this asking be
Please send when convenient to me.
Thanking you for so kindly reading this
And hoping nothing is amiss
I now will close and finish this in prose.

Very truly yours,

Ollie Barrett.

Among other items the boy sought and found was a letter of the War Governor, Richard Yates, to President Lincoln recommending the appointment of Oliver's father, the Reverend George Johnson Barrett, to be a chaplain in the Union Army. The father had come West and, after brief service as a missionary among the Indians, had become a circuit rider, later serving as presiding elder of the district of the Methodist Church having headquarters at Jacksonville, Illinois, where in 1873 Oliver was born.

State of Illinois
Executive Department
Springfield Oct. 13. 1863

To any Colonel of an Illinois Regiment of Volunteers
Dear Sir.
I have requested Rev. Mr. Barrett to call upon you with a view to his being elected a Chaplain of your Regiment. He is a minister of the very first abilities, a truly able and eloquent man, of the best moral character, and in every respect the kind of man, I am willing to vouch for, to make you a good Chaplain. I sincerely hope you will have him elected and thereby oblige,

Your humble servt,

Rich. Yates, Govr

The persistence and pertinacity of the young collector Barrett was first brought out publicly in *The Diary and Letters of Rutherford B. Hayes,* Vol. IV, p. 436, where this passage occurs, as written in 1889:

January 22. Tuesday.—All sorts of droll requests reach me. I have this morning a letter as follows, in a boyish handwriting:—

Pittsfield, Ill., Dec. 28.

To the person to whom this letter is addressed:

DEAR SIR, MADAM, ETC.:—I enclose you a portion of my autograph book and would be very much obliged if you would sign your name on one page and then addressing an envelope to the next person after you on the opposite page, enclosing this letter and the book. If you will, you will greatly oblige

Your obedient servant,

Oliver Barrett

On the opposite page is written (with addresses):—O. W. Holmes, Oliver Optic, E. E. Hale, E. Eggleston, S. L. Clemens, Charles Dudley Warner, Mrs. Harriet Beecher Stowe, L. P. Morton, Gen. W. T. Sherman, Rev. Mr. Howard Crosby, Rev. Mr. T. DeWitt Talmage, George W. Curtis, Rev. Theo. Cuyler, Mr. and Mrs. R. B. Hayes, Miss Frances E. Willard.

The strange result makes it all interesting. All of the list have responded to the lad's request favorably. Mark Twain grumbled of course in characteristic phrase, but General Sherman, O. W. Holmes, and all came down handsomely; E. E. Hale and Dudley Warner in the true spirit.

Doctor Hale writes:—"I am glad to do what you wish"; and sends on with the note:—

"Dear Eggleston:—The above is forwarded by dear Doctor Holmes to me. I now forward to you. Please pass it on, till the trick shall come 'nigher-nigher.'"

Edward Eggleston forwards with the words:—"Dear Clemens:—Pass the thing along. I hope it'll get back to him safely.—E. Eggleston."

Mark Twain signs "Truly yours," and on the envelope in pencil writes:—"Pass the damned piece of impudence to Warner."

Charles Dudley Warner signs "Yours sincerely," and on the envelope:—"Passed on in an unruffled spirit to Mrs Stowe. C. D. W."

Mrs. Stowe passed it on to Levi P. Morton, writing: "Dear Sir:—Please pass this little boy's book along. H. Beecher Stowe."

It was "passed by Mr. Morton to General Sherman"; by him "to Rev. Mr. Talmage"; "by T. DeW. Talmage to Rev. Dr. Cuyler"; by Dr. Cuyler to George William Curtis, with the note: "I hope you will add a name that all men honor"; by Mr. Curtis to Dr. Crosby with the phrase, "I follow my leader"; and by Dr. Crosby to me with the injunction, "Keep up the boy's ball." We sign today "with best wishes" and send on, adding: "Passed by Mr. and Mrs. Hayes to Miss Frances E. Willard, with kindest regards."

The good thing about this is that such busy persons as have here given time to make a boy happy seem to have made themselves happy in doing it. You will, I am sure, go and do likewise.—R. B. H.

Thus a small boy in a Midwestern country town had reached a wide circle of interesting, prominent Americans who accommodated him with autographs and enjoyed doing so. In his home town he set out on a canvass and got enough subscriptions to the *Youth's Companion* to win him a small printing press. He set type and ran off a circular: "WANTED, Letters of Famous Men." He sent this circular to postmasters over a wide area, requesting them to put it where post-office patrons would see it. Meantime, of course, he continued selling to stamp-collectors from the million in his father's deerskin trunk, and with the proceeds buying more autographs and letters.

One book the boy often took from a shelf was titled *Europe through American Spectacles*, and he always turned to the place where it said that the Reverend George J. Barrett of Illinois and the U.S.A. was in Italy, and told of a town where a crowd, beggars, lazzaroni, began following the stranger from America. After a time Mr. Barrett grew tired of the way they near-jostled him, pointed at him, and jabbered at him in words he couldn't understand. Mr. Barrett stopped in his tracks. He put the fingers of one hand in his mouth. Before their eyes he snatched out his teeth. They gaped. They turned and ran—as though next he would snatch off his head—probably possessed of the Devil. And soon as they were gone Mr. Barrett opened his mouth and put his teeth in again.

One cousin of Lizzie Gilmer's father was Meriwether Lewis, of the unforgettable team of Lewis and Clark, who had crossed the continent and reported to President Jefferson what the country was like. Scores of distinguished men had exchanged letters with Meriwether Lewis, and the time had come when Lizzie Gilmer burned all of these letters, first cutting off the signatures. When Lizzie Gilmer died, she willed to Oliver Barrett her library and the library of her distinguished father.

The young collector, a high-school graduate at seventeen, had been advertising in country weekly newspapers for old letters and autographs. He had worked out another form letter, paying boys at school a penny a letter to copy it, sending these to notables everywhere asking for autographs and old letters.

Two determinations had been moving the young fellow: first, to be a collector, second, to be a lawyer. The going was not so easy as he would have liked. His strong-willed grandfather wanted him to be a farmer and his lovable mother had her deep wish that he should become a preacher. Once before a Lincoln group in Chicago Barrett gave this reminiscence:

"When I was a boy, my grandfather, the stern old Puritan type, had his mind made up that I was to be a farmer. My mother thought I should be a preacher. I heard my grandfather tell so many reasons why it would be bad for me to be a preacher that I agreed with him, and my mother said so many reasons why I shouldn't be a farmer that I agreed with her.

"In those days I didn't know that anyone else in the world had thought about collecting autographs. I was getting everything I could in the county and the state. Finally, I think I traded a *Youth's Companion* for a *Golden Days* of one of the boys. In that was an advertisement from an autograph dealer. I sent for the catalogue. That was the first time I knew autographs could be bought. It happened I had a good bank account for the reason that my grandfather, in his efforts to undermine my mother's efforts, would give me a young calf and then I would fatten it and could keep the proceeds, providing I taught the calf to drink, and so on. He would give me a pig, and as soon as that got to weigh enough, I would sell it and that money was mine. This was to encourage me to be a farmer. He had a crib full of corn and he allowed me to sell it out to the farmers for chicken feed at 25 cents a bushel, and all that went into my bank account. When I got that catalogue from the autograph dealer, I figured how far that money would go, and I sent for the autographs, and when they came my grandfather was very mad and said I was done, and I would find out that I wouldn't get the farm, and that it would be no better than I deserved if Mother made me a preacher. From that time on he left me alone, and I was glad, because I could argue my mother out of my being a preacher easier than I could my grandfather out of my being a farmer."

The Pittsfield youngling struck up a correspondence with the Boston poet and essayist Oliver Wendell Holmes. The elder enjoyed the points and queries put to him, took time to answer the boy and wish him well, took time to write for the boy two verses of "The Last Leaf," a poem that Lincoln knew "by heart" and recited aloud.

Their good mother never gave a moment of pain or anxiety to her children. When parsons came to court the widow, "Sister Barrett," her offspring knew their mother lived for them alone. The parsons whom they suspected had come to woo remained to pray. The little band gathered in a semicircle in the parlor with their foreheads pressed to the seat of a chair to listen to a lengthy prayer to save the souls of the "poor fatherless children and their widowed mother." They knew that as soon as the services were over would come a dinner of fried chicken and peach ice cream with which the parsons were always treated before they were dismissed.

One evening home came the boy's sister saying she had for the last time attended a Methodist midweek prayer-and-experience meeting and from then on would attend the Congregational Church, as she did thereafter. She reported one trustee standing up and in the course of his testimony in a high-keyed voice declaring, "Sister Ellen Barrett, yes, she's got the grace of Almighty God but she needs it, indeed she needs it, for she's got the worst children in Pittsfield!" Years later when the grown man went to the church alone, and sat before a stained-glass window with the letters in Gothic "Ellen Watson Barrett," he meditated on time and what a vapor it is.

The boy was going to be a lawyer. One day the mother saw this was definite. She gave him for a Christmas present a four-volume set of *The Lives of the Chief Justices of England* by Lord Campbell. She promised him if he read those four volumes, and also the Holy Bible from cover to cover, he would then get for his own to keep a ten-volume set of the *Lives of the Lord Chancellors and Keepers of the Great Seal of England*. The day came when he told her he had done all the required reading, "only I may have skipped a few begats in the Bible." So there he was, sunk deep in the lore of law and the courts at an early age. It was many years later that Barrett's name was signed to law-journal articles on Sir Edward Coke, Thomas Erskine, John Philpot Curran, Rufus Choate, and more great lawyers of other days. The mother's loving eye had seen what direction he was headed in and gave him just the right help. Far more than she realized, however, was the lighted devotion she had kindled in him around the name and life of Lincoln. She had deepened these motives of his when he was reading Kent and Blackstone in a lawyer's office. As to collecting she was never convinced; very kindly and gently she demurred to it. They discussed it many times. He saw an interrelation between lawyer and collector and quoted for her from the Scottish poet and novelist Sir Walter Scott, who was also a lawyer: "A lawyer without history or literature is a mechanic, a mere working mason; but if he possesses some knowledge of these, he may venture to call himself an architect."

While reading in a law office, Barrett took his first whirl at the realities of life in the American selling game. He would knock on any door and ask if they had ever heard of *The Life of Phineas T. Barnum, the Showman*, written by no less a person than Mr. Barnum himself—and later *In Darkest Africa* by Henry M. Stanley, who at one point in the book said, "Dr. Livingston, I presume?" From books he shifted to the unparalleled Underwood & Underwood Stereoscopic Photographs, quitting suddenly one day when his whole sample outfit, stereoscope and views, was eagerly purchased by a woman who had suddenly received a large insurance payment on the accidental death of her husband.

In 1896 Barrett graduated in the law class of the University of Michigan and entered on a lifelong practice of law. There was an interlude. In April of 1898 he enlisted in the Fifth Illinois Volunteers. Next November, having advanced from private to corporal, his muster-out papers read: "Battles and engagements—None; Skirmishes—None; Wounds—None."

Once in early practice in the lower courts of Peoria County, Illinois, Barrett's client was Jack Armstrong, a farmer whose uncle, Duff Armstrong, years ago had been freed of a murder charge. In that famous case Lincoln produced an almanac as evidence there was no moon nor bright moonlight by which witnesses could see what they said they saw. In the case of Duff's nephew, the landlord, following a procedure called "distress for rent," had gone to Jack Armstrong's farm, loaded on wagons and hauled away for rent payment crops, a piano, and other chattels. The time of this, as established by witnesses, was 4:38 P.M. and thereafter. Barrett rose and pointed attention to the old English law which says that such a seizure of property, for rent payment, must take place between sunrise and sunset. Next Barrett produced an almanac showing that sunset on that day occurred at 4:35 P.M.—wherefore the landlord was three minutes later than the law allows! Barrett's almanac saved Jack Armstrong's crops and piano as Lincoln's almanac saved Jack's uncle's neck. All of which the old *Chicago Inter-Ocean* considered a fine Midwestern folk tale, and one Sunday gave it a whole page.

The foregoing incident, curiously enough, neither Barrett's son Roger nor the present writer ever heard Barrett tell until one night in March 1949 when he talked it off as something by the way before going to bed. Why did it take him so long to get to telling it to us? Roger and I talked about that. We decided that so many odd and interesting things have happened to him and around him that he just naturally can't get to telling them all.

At times Barrett has come near being lured into a political career. In the end he managed to push away nominations for office and hold to law practice and collecting. After leaving Peoria for Chicago a limerick came to him:

> There was a young lawyer named Barrett,
> Who at law was a regular ferret;
> But one client said, "Please don't take shirt off my back—
>   I can't spare it!"

His Lincoln collection continued to be more than healthy recreation and fascinating byplay—it became an absorbing passion. "Human instinct is such that every person is a collector of some sort or other," Barrett once philosophized before a group of Lincoln students and collectors. "Some collect books. Others collect money—and yet others children. In this world you gather whatever you like best, if you can. Whatever you like most, whatever you give most of your time to, that makes you, in a sense, a collector. Personally, I have collected in a great many lines, but I have always come back and felt most interested in the collection of letters and manuscripts of poems."

Across years, then, the correspondence of Barrett ranged far and wide. When he heard of a Lincoln letter or a paper or a relic having Lincoln associations, he would write his inquiries about it. Whether it was a farmer who had found a letter that his father, a Union soldier, had received from Lincoln, or whether it was a well-known item in the hands of an experienced and sophisticated collector, Barrett would gather his information about it, what condition it was in, whether it might be sold, whether sometime it was going to be put up at auction. In the course of time it became widely known that the attorney Barrett welcomed at his office anyone who had material bearing on Lincoln or on actions, events, characters, that interwove with the life of Lincoln. It would make a considerable story by itself, the variety of Lincoln folk and kin who came on one errand and another to Barrett's office.

One of these, a man of national reputation, twice happened to come to the Barrett office, without a previous appointment, on days when Barrett was engaged in a trial and couldn't possibly see his caller. What the caller wanted particularly was President Lincoln's gold watch chain. The caller was chairman of the board of the Pullman Company, Robert Todd Lincoln, eldest son of President Lincoln. He made offers to Barrett of Lincoln documents to be given in exchange for the gold watch chain of his father. From Charles Moore, chief of the Manuscripts Division of the Library of Congress, came a letter to Barrett advising an exchange "if you want to make the heart of an old man very happy." An exchange was agreed on, but before its conclusion Robert T. Lincoln died.

The watch chain had been part of the estate inherited by Mrs. Lincoln. The chain is a curious specimen of goldsmith's craft, many strands of fine-spun gold being intricately woven, the mesh so fine that the fingers of one hand can roll the chain into a ball. The English playwright John Drinkwater, struck with admiration of the keepsake, told Barrett he would try to find a goldsmith who would make him a replica of the chain, Drinkwater later reporting that the goldsmiths he interviewed were baffled, saying: "There used to be men doing that kind of work but we don't know of any nowadays. A machine to reproduce it would be of prohibitive cost." This token was presented to Lincoln by a California delegation that called at the White House and gave it to him as a specimen of what fine metal and workmanship they had in their state. The chain shows plainly in several Lincoln photographs, looped through the second buttonhole from the top of the vest. The new watch chain replaced one of silver links that Lincoln gave to Dennis Hanks, who many years later sold it to a man who sold it to Barrett.

The catalogues came, year by year. A ton or two of catalogues have passed through Barrett's hands across the years. He has been heard to say, "I can't live without catalogues." He scrutinized the items listed. He discussed with other collectors what was being offered. He attended important auctions in New York and Philadelphia, most often made his bids through others, sometimes getting precisely what he wanted. He followed journals that covered the field of Lincolniana. He shaped his own library of basic Lincolniana, became familiar with the books and periodicals, well known or obscure, essential to a knowledge of Lincoln's life and personality. He became familiar with the controversies and moot points regarding Lincoln's course of action or policy in many varied situations. What he sought out anxiously and keenly, to bring later into his collection, was often based on his sense of history, an accurate instinct as to why the letter or the document held importance.

Barrett tells of a Chicago lawyer who heard that a man would live longer if he had a hobby like collecting. He decided he would collect. But what? "Ah," ran his thought, "I will collect every United States coin minted in the year I was born." The years went by and he had a box full of coins earmarked by the important number of the highly significant year in which he first saw the light of day, his mother being present. The time came when he found nobody was interested in his particular numismatic gyrations, nobody cared, including himself. He began searching for somebody born in the same year as himself, on whom he might unload his collection at a profit.

More soundly based was a butterfly collector who caught Barrett's interest. The man had words for his enthusiasm: "I have run a mile before now, at breakneck speed, over bushes and fences, through swamps and forests—and all for one butterfly; and I would gladly do it again to experience the same pleasure that I did while panting on the ground and holding the insect between my fingers. The man who cannot get enthusiastic over some subject—be it a gorgeous butterfly, a sparkling jewel, a magnificent waterfall, a frightful storm, an eloquent lecture, a dimpled child, a lovely woman—must lead an exceedingly dull and uninteresting life."

The collector's wife often comes in for discussion among collectors. To be happy, her hobby must be a husband who has a hobby. This sentiment has been heard where collectors forgather. For some years after his marriage Barrett had a system when bringing home an armload of books or manuscripts. He laid them gently and quietly outside the front basement window. Later at night he would go to the basement and, as casually as you please, bring his new acquisitions upstairs as if from his old basement stock. This smuggling system came to an end when a law partner, in retaliation for a practical joke, repaid in kind and told how the system worked—and it ended. The collector was forced to devise new methods.

In the story of how this Lincoln Collection came to be gathered, it would not be permissible to omit mention of the foremost candy man of the Midwest, Charles Frederick Gunther, born March 6, 1837, in Wildberg, Württemberg, Germany. He was five years old when his family sailed for America and settled in Somerset County, Pennsylvania. At eleven he was riding a daily mail route through mountains, twenty-five miles each way, his pay 25 cents a day. He went to schools, public and private, and when the family moved to Peru, Illinois, in 1850, he began at fourteen to earn his own living. He worked in a country store, then a drugstore, later became a bank cashier with his name on the window. Out of Peru associations he saw chances for the ice business in the South. On starting for Memphis in 1860 he told friends, "The South needs ice." He was working on his plans for more and better ice in the South when the war broke. The Confederates pressed him into service and appointed him purchasing agent of the Confederate ship *Rose Douglas*. Union forces took him prisoner; late in the war he was exchanged, and headed back to Peru, Illinois.

Over the South and the Midwest he traveled for a large candy firm at Chicago, never failing to attend with enthusiasm the reunions of old comrades in the Confederate Army. Then in 1868 he began on his own the manufacture and sale of candies made from German recipes known to his family. One biographical sketch of Gunther has the statement, "His invention of the caramel set millions to munching." This of course is apocryphal in its allegation that across the recorded progress of mankind this candy remained an unrealized dream until C. F. Gunther in Chicago presented a munching mankind with its first caramel. Nevertheless the name of Gunther did come to stand supreme with a host of candy buyers and eaters.

Then the Chicago fire wiped out Gunther's shop and store. Word came to him that Marshall Field, the merchant and financier, wanted to see him. Field told him the city of Chicago must go on, and offered him a loan of money for a fresh start in business.

Gunther opened his new shop and store on a site near McVicker's Theatre and was on a road leading to fortune. He was short and stocky, with a round face wearing mustache and chin beard, later a goatee. People liked his cheerful face and twinkling eyes. He was lighted with enthusiasms, not merely well known for his candies but with a reputation as a collector. A born antiquarian, he was like many a historian having difficulties on the border line that separates antiques and junk, genuine relics and trash. Word got around, "Gunther will buy anything," which was not quite true and yet in a sense correct. With reference to the Civil War and its documents, letters, relics, it did seem at times that Gunther would buy anything. Far and wide people had heard of his interest and his readiness to buy in this field. Into his possession came papers brought North by soldiers of service in captured Southern cities. This, however, was but one phase of Gunther's collecting. On one of his many journeys abroad with Mrs. Gunther, it was told, when in Egypt he acquired an assortment of mummies, and wishing no delay in transport, he reserved sleeping-car berths for his cargo of ancient dehydrated Pharaohs.

By 1889 his building at the corner of Quincy and State streets had become known as worth the time of sight-seers. It was on the west side of the street, a narrow six-story building topped with a big sign: "Gunther's Candy." The larger part of the building was a whatnot holding treasures, holding also miscellany, bric-a-brac, and helter-skelter curiosities. When in Richmond, Virginia, they wrecked that house of horrors known as Libby Prison and brought it to Chicago to reassemble the pieces, it was mainly at the instigation and promotion of Gunther. It stood there on Wabash Avenue near Twelfth, one of the sights of Chicago for many years. Wrecked after the World's Columbian Exposition, on the former site of the old reassembled Confederate prison came the Coliseum, where the Republican Party national conventions and the Bull Moose convention nominated candidates.

Time came when Gunther had an eight-story building, one floor filled with miscellany, crammed with humpty-dumpty boxes and chests. He proposed to his collector friend, Oliver R. Barrett, "Buy the whole kit and caboodle." Barrett said that all he would like to take care of would be letters, documents, papers of interest to him and of pertinence to the rest of his collection. Across the years, from then on, Barrett carried on his labors amid the immense accumulations of Gunther, searching and sifting in the loot of battlefields and the dusty findings from garrets and closets brought to the candy man who would "buy anything."

Years back it had been that Barrett and Gunther, two collectors, lawyer and candy man, were walking along Michigan Avenue on a summer evening and Gunther said: "Someday I am going to have a big building and have my collection there. On the front there would be just one word 'Gunther,' and people would wonder what it is, and that is all I want to be remembered by." Another day he said to Barrett, "I want people to ask, 'Who is Gunther?' And get the answer 'He's the old Dutchman who made good candy.'" Besides buying from people who came to him in Chicago, Gunther had made twenty-seven trips abroad, at all points adding to his collection.

The day came when he telephoned Barrett saying he had offered his collection to the city of Chicago and couldn't get anyone interested, that they didn't know a Washington letter from a Lincoln one, that he was discouraged, that his family would sweep it out in the alley—and he again wanted to sell Barrett the whole works. Barrett said it would take a lifetime to go through it, and he wanted only autographed letters, documents, manuscripts. Gunther liked Barrett. Hadn't he heard Barrett say that he would be glad to get any autographed letters Gunther was willing to part with? That in itself was a gesture of appreciation which Gunther at that time could do with. For more than twelve years many were the nights and holidays that Barrett spent among the boxes, chests, packing cases, with a Gunther assistant named Benjamin Franklin Stoneberger and known as "Stoney." Out of a case might come an Indian battle-ax, a head-hunter's dried head, a petrified alligator, an oyster shell into which somehow had fallen an old-fashioned denture around which the shell had grown—or letters signed "Benedict Arnold," "George Washington," or mementos of Napoleon, Josephine, Michelangelo.

One Saturday Gunther telephoned Barrett to come see him and Barrett went over to hear Gunther: "I know you like Lincoln, but I like Washington better because he treated the Germans better than Lincoln. Washington treated Von Steuben and others better. I would rather let the Lincoln go first. I have picked out twenty letters, all long. I have my taxes to meet today." Barrett was waiting. Gunther went on, "Take those twenty Lincoln letters." And Barrett went away with a great windfall for one day.

In another session when Barrett saw a manuscript in the handwriting of Robert Burns—the verses of "Auld Lang Syne"—he said, "I want this 'Auld Lang Syne.'" Gunther replied, "I know how you feel. I went over to England and I got it and I had to pay a lot of money."

Barrett: "I want it now. You know how it *feels* to have it, and I *don't* know how it feels."

Gunther: "I will sell you this 'Auld Lang Syne' and you write out the receipt and put in the receipt that any time I want it, I can buy it back at the same price."

Barrett took it home. A week later Gunther was on the phone and saying: "Bring back the 'Auld Lang Syne.' You know, I haven't been able to sleep. I hear the waves of Lake Michigan pounding at night and I think about it. I walk down Michigan Avenue thinking about it, and now it is gone and I am not going to last many years. Let me have it back."

Barrett brought back the manuscript. Years passed. Then one day Barrett stood before Gunther and said, "I can't sleep, and I want that 'Auld Lang Syne.'" Gunther smiled. They were brothers. Gunther said, "You just double the price and I will let you have it, and you can take it along." And in the passing of time Barrett would not have been surprised on any day to hear Gunther say, "I want that 'Auld Lang Syne.' I can't sleep."

Across many years ran the friendship of Barrett with Henry C. Folger, whose memory lives green in a white building on Capitol Hill, Washington, D.C., where is housed with taste and discretion the greatest collection of Shakespeare material in the world. Folger collected. He was a director of the Standard Oil Company of New York and collected Shakespeare like a demon and an angel. He pursued Shakespeare with the same flair that Barrett hunted Lincoln. The two men could meet on a common ground of enthusiasm. After Folger had come to his decision to make a free gift of his greatest of Shakespeare collections for public use in all time, Barrett's small collection of Shakespeare quartos and a huge vellum document of Shakespeare's father John went into the Folger accumulations.

The loyalty of Folger to his collection ran deep. Once when Barrett called Folger stepped out from a meeting of the directors of the Standard Oil Company of New York and in an adjoining room held his conference with the fellow collector from Chicago. Others present during the one-hour conference included a physician near the door—anxious about a heart condition of Folger, having instructed Barrett that he should beware of any undue excitement to his patient—and a secretary on immediate call. Also for possible service there was a Negro guard and doorman.

One little spoken communication that day as between collectors was Folger's: "I now have over fifty first folios." He then told of their being safely in storage vaults and of his intention to have his acquisitions assembled in one building available to the public. They told each other what they had and needed. As Barrett put it: "Folger said he wanted Shakespeare, I wanted Lincoln. I let him have my Shakespeare and I bought Lincoln items I wanted."

For years Barrett has held in security an authenticated sword of Gustavus Adolphus, awaiting the day when he might trade it with some big Swede having a Lincoln item.

Another time a death in a family brought into Barrett's collection a document he had long sought. It had occurred to Barrett that many more letters had been written by Lincoln to Horace Greeley than had come to light in publication. Greeley had been one of the most incessant of letter-writers to Lincoln and many of his long epistles had brought immediate and pointed replies from Lincoln. "Where are these replies of Lincoln?" asked Barrett. He went to Chappaqua, New York, the old home of Greeley, and interviewed Greeley's daughter, Mrs. Clendennin, the wife of an Episcopal rector. From her he learned that there had been a fire in the house that had burned all of her Lincoln letters except one, at that time on loan to a neighbor. The First World War was then going, her daughter's husband with the U.S. Armed Forces, and Mrs. Clendennin couldn't think of selling the letter. She led Barrett to a corner of the room, pointing to the Lincoln letter in a frame on the wall, and with a pleasant smile: "I could never sell that. It's got to go to my daughter." It was an abrupt, peremptory Lincoln letter. Greeley had written to Lincoln of "confidential" information he had of two Confederate ambassadors in Canada waiting and ready to cross over from Canada and talk peace terms and end the war slaughter. Greeley believed the "ambassadors" had full power from their government to negotiate, and told Lincoln of his belief. The affair was involved. After various outcries from Greeley, Lincoln sent John Hay to New York with a letter to Greeley. In a hotel parlor Hay delivered the letter to Greeley, who read in part:

I am disappointed that you have not already reached here with those Commissioners, if they would consent to come, on being shown my letter

Washington, July 15 . 1864.

Hon. Horace Greeley
    My dear Sir

    Yours of the 13th
is just received; and I am disappointed that you have not already reached them, with those Con-
missioners, if they would consent
to come, on being shown my letter to you of the 9th Inst.
Show that and this to them;
and if they will come on the
terms stated in the former, bring
them. I not only intend a sincere effort for peace, but I intend that you shall be a personal witness that it is made.

       Yours truly
       A. Lincoln

Letter of Lincoln to Horace Greeley

to you of the 9th Inst. Show that and this to them; and if they will come on the terms stated in the former, bring them. I not only intend a sincere effort for peace, but I intend that you shall be a personal witness that it is made.

The peace negotiations of Greeley proved much of a farce. Mrs. Clendennin mentioned that another Lincoln collector, Judd Stewart, had made offers for the letter. Barrett said, "If you ever want to sell it just send it C.O.D. for double his offer." Barrett thanked her, she had been kindly, and on leaving he heard her say she would let him know of any development in regard to the letter.

Thus the matter stood as the years passed till the day Barrett received a letter from the Rev. Clendennin saying: "Now that our dear daughter has gone over to the better country we have decided to part with Lincoln's letter." Now they could meet Mr. Barrett's wish and let him have the letter.

Worthington Chauncey Ford, man of books, delver in documents, a great seeker and craftsman in basic historic materials, came occasionally to see Barrett in Chicago. Barrett at times called on Ford at the Massachusetts Historical Society in Boston; he had his last visit with Ford in the Danish legation in Paris, France, in 1938, not long before the death of Ford. Letters between the two were many, and they had fellowship. Ford, we might say, was a document scout. Having located papers of special interest, he would help at guiding them to safety and usage in institutions or collections. "He had a super-collector's instincts," Barrett has said, "caring little about personal possession but endlessly active and ingenious in tracking down basic data, whether in public archives or private collections, both in America and Europe. His elaborately informative annotation of *The History of Plimouth Plantation* by William Bradford is regarded at present as definitive."

Once when it was evident that certain historic telegrams and letters of Lincoln, offered for sale, had been abstracted from government records, Ford made arrangements with authorities that he would be assured immunity from any attempt on the part of the government to reclaim them. Joyfully Ford told Barrett of this feat, adding that he had found a donor to provide that the documents, upward of two hundred, be installed as part of the Lincoln Collection at Brown University.

Ford died on the last ship leaving France for America on the outbreak of war, having earlier sent to Barrett a massive and formidable manuscript of about 1400 typewriter size sheets written on both sides, all of it in the same clear meticulous script so unmistakably that of Worthington Ford. Three notebooks cover events of 1865. Ford intended to carry on the Beveridge biography of Lincoln from where it ended in the year 1858, this following naturally from the editorial work he did after the death of Beveridge. In America and in Europe, amid public archives, private collections, newspaper files, he transcribed materials for future use, resulting in a colossal aggregate of source material on Lincoln covering the years 1858-60. He wrote from Paris January 27, 1935, to Barrett: "You understand that these books are wholly yours, to do with them what you wish—the paper basket, your Lincoln lot or some distribution. The material contains much that is excellent, but such material is after all my selection, and another would have made a different one. . . . Take the lot and dispose of them to your liking. . . . It was much sport in gathering the material and it gave me much information, but I am not in a position to use it and am greatly pleased to have you to turn to."

The English craftsman in paper, Austin J. Cross, stayed many days that ran into many weeks at the Barrett house, in varying periods. "I have had my lifetime with paper," said the wiry and elderly master workman. He could make any kind of a repair or restoration of paper. He could split, bevel, inlay, and make paper behave.

"He had every kind of a knife you ever saw," says Barrett, "each one just as sharp as a whisper. He could bevel edges so as to make two thicknesses of paper join and hold neatly and firmly. You might see that there was joining but you couldn't feel it with your fingers, so smooth was the work. He would estimate the thickness of the paste so as to have the joining exact. I have seen him take a newspaper sheet with a muslin cloth pasted on each side. When the paste was dry he would make a slight split along the top of the newspaper sheet. Then with a quick movement he would tear the two muslin backings apart and on each muslin sheet would be a split half of a newspaper page. You could lay the two side by side or mount them as you chose. If necessary Mr. Cross could again split each half, the print then looking as if it were on cobwebs. Mr. Cross warned against glue or mucilage; they leave discolorations or difficulties in removal. He always used a paste made with flour and hot water. He knew all the processes of papermaking and would use them to fill the holes and tears in paper. He could split India paper till it looked almost like a spider web. He was far along in years, sweet, jolly, modest, with a plain quiet pride in the mysteries of his craft that were a part of him." It is agreed among those who knew Mr.

Cross that if God used any element of paper in the making of him that would have been all right with him.

Albert J. Beveridge, in preparations for writing his biography of Lincoln, made extensive use of the Barrett Collection. "For several months he worked, with two stenographers, day and night going full blast, in an old-time Prairie Avenue mansion," says Barrett. "At one time he said that his plans were to complete the first two volumes of his biography and then in 1928 to run for President. His main recreation in such evenings as he took off from his work was wild melodrama. I would be out there working with him and we would jointly try to locate the most exciting blood-and-thunder play going that week. We would go home, and more than once it happened the phone would ring at two or three in the morning and here would be Beveridge asking some question or making such a statement as 'I've got a new point about Herndon'—then he would tell it and ask what I thought of it. Beveridge worked hard, he was at it day and night. He worked himself to death on his Lincoln book."

Then there was Henry Horner, eighteen years Judge of the Cook County Probate Court, Horner at one time in Chicago having a law partnership with Frank Hamlin, son of Hannibal Hamlin of Maine, Vice-President of the United States during four years of the Lincoln Administration. When Horner died in his eighth year of devoted toil as Governor of Illinois his will made reference to his Lincoln Collection of "approximately 6,000 books, pamphlets, broadsides and other memorabilia," his "many happy hours" in the assembling of it, and his being surrounded by it in his home "an unfailing joy and encouragement." In bequeathing it to the Illinois State Historical Library he wrote of being influenced in this "partly by my respect and affection for Oliver R. Barrett, Lloyd Lewis and Irving Dilliard, the trustees of the Library whom it has been my privilege to appoint, and the Librarian, Paul M. Angle, scholars and men of unselfish public service."

Horner and Barrett went over their Lincoln materials together, advised each other on wanted items, once staying up till daybreak over their mutual enthusiasms as collectors and lawyers. They joined in appraisal of the William E. Barton Collection for the Lincoln Library of the University of Chicago.

Horner could tell of the probating of the will of Mrs. Julius Rosenwald. At one point Mr. Rosenwald's attorney advised his client of procedure that he believed could probably save to the estate a sum of $100,000. And Horner heard Rosenwald say, "Oh, let it go—I'm ashamed to have so much money."

This was in a period during which Rosenwald had been published as paying the highest Federal income tax in the Chicago area. Horner could tell of a night in 1933 when kidnapping for ransom, "the snatch racket," was going strong among gangsters who were losers by prohibition repeal. And shortly after ten o'clock on this winter night of a below-zero weather, Horner's neighbor and friend Julius Rosenwald called at the Horner apartment in Madison Park. Rosenwald seemed to Horner to belong to the Lincoln Collection because Rosenwald had been born in Springfield, Illinois, in a house on the same street as the Lincoln home. They visited an hour and when Rosenwald was leaving Horner tried to insist he must send for a policeman or a guard or companion to see safely home the little harmless-looking man whose fortune ran above $100,000,000. Rosenwald insisted on going alone. "Can't I go with you?" asked Horner. "No," said Rosenwald, "I'll be all right." And Rosenwald went out into the blowing snow and the blowing air of Chicago's streets where anything could happen.

Horner worried. It was a load on his mind. He could see the morning headlines, "Julius Rosenwald kidnapped," and how he would never forgive himself. The present writer was there and saw this little scene. It was the same night he saw the future Governor of Illinois in the Lincoln room shift a collapsible desk into a bed, lay sheets and blankets on a mattress, fit slips on pillows and then command his vagabond guest, "Now hit the hay, boy, you need sleep to write your books." After which Horner phoned the Rosenwald home, heard good news, and said, "Now I can sleep tonight."

Weaving in and out of the corners and byways of the Barrett Collection, her fingers nearly always finding the item called for, has been Linnea Klefbohm. Between hours of routine law-office typing, across twenty-three years she has familiarized herself with files, boxes, chests, closets, envelopes manila and fibroid, a variety of containers, bundles, bindles, and packages beyond description. Amid what to outsiders would be a jungle Miss Klefbohm, known to the office girls as "Kleffie," can find her way smiling and confident. Barrett rates her an indispensable coadjutor.

The son of a rabbi of Appleton, Wisconsin, Ehrich Weiss, went far and made himself famous under the name Houdini. When Harry Houdini the magician and mystifier died, there were suits, with his attorney Barrett in defense, for damage claims of more than a million dollars, suits brought by spiritualist mediums. In theater performances, in newspaper and billboard announcements, Houdini had said that the work of these mediums claiming to summon departed spirits from another world was a bunco game, hocus-pocus, shenanigans, charlatanry, and they were defrauding good and innocent people of money that wasn't hay. One witness examined by Barrett declared that Houdini's slanders and libels had reached departed spirits who were staying away from Chicago and could no longer be summoned to that city. The aforesaid spirits could still be had in Detroit or Fort Wayne or Omaha, but not in Chicago. "We can no longer make a livelihood," it was testified. "Houdini's falsifications have reached our prospective patrons and the money no longer comes in." The million-dollar damage claims had to be dropped because the law holds a dead man doesn't and can't pay damages for slander or libel.

Houdini's heir, his widow Beatrice, wrote Barrett of her sorrow at losing a partner with whom she had traveled the world over for thirty-two years, seeing him handcuffed, buried alive, thrown into rivers in a coffin, locked in escape-proof prison cells, roped and manacled all the ways there are, and always making his escape so that in the vernacular a smooth get-away was known as "doing a Houdini." Beatrice knew of the many times Houdini had taken Barrett with him to the dark-room séances of mediums, Houdini using his devices to catch the frauds at their tricks. Beatrice wrote: "I must write you about my beloved, I just cannot rest, he was so proud of his friendship with you, and I know you truly mourn with me. I am a mere shadow, weigh scarcely eighty-five pounds, have been confined to my bed six weeks now, long before my sweetheart went away, yet I live and he in his glorious strength died. His brilliant clear mind never left him for a moment." Later she mentioned "a sheet of music he wanted you to have." It came along to Barrett, who on seeing what it was in his hands clutched it the tighter—Stephen Foster's song "Maggie by My Side" in Foster's handwriting, catalogued "very scarce."

There was Alexander ("Al") Hannah, manager and owner of the Brevoort Hotel and other properties, a son of Alexander Hannah of Hannah and Hogg, whose saloon under Sam T. Jack's burlesque theater at one time was reputed the largest west of the Alleghenies. Al's home was near that of Barrett in the suburban town Kenilworth. They were cronies, pooled their efforts in collecting, and with results. Hannah was Scotch and Catholic, his wife Norwegian; they had eight children. Hannah had a luminous kindly smile and loved people.

Barrett had wakened Hannah's interest in collecting, but failed at making a collector of a law partner, Jesse J. Ricks, who later became chairman of the board of the Union Carbide and Carbon Company. When Ricks moved to New York and a farm on Long Island, the two men wrote long letters to each other, often about birds. They were lawyers but nevertheless ornithologists, and as such naturally had their disputes about the habits of warblers, creepers, and thrushes.

A letter came to Barrett from the son of Robert Latham, the man who retained Lincoln in 1853 to survey and lay out the town of Lincoln, Logan County, Illinois, Lincoln being attorney for the promoters of the new town. He was a farmer, W. W. Latham, and had in 1926, as he wrote, "lost my entire corn crop of 1200 to 1400 bushels by floods this last October." He mentioned having a manuscript in Lincoln's handwriting that for the first time, under financial stress, he was anxious to dispose of. In a reply to Latham's letter, Barrett indicated a method used by him and other collectors, writing, "If you would be willing to part with the manuscript that you have, I would be glad to have you send it to me C.O.D. by express, with the privilege of examination, making the charges the amount for which you would be willing to part with the manuscript. The copy will then be opened and shown to me and if satisfactory I will pay them and they will pay the money to you. If not, they will return the manuscript. They are responsible for it until it comes back to you or until the amount which you have specified is paid you."

Later Latham called at Barrett's office. The manuscript proved to be a note of several pages in Lincoln's handwriting on "Sectionalism." Barrett recognized it as having come from Mrs. Grimsley's carpetbag, Latham saying that Mrs. Grimsley had given it to his father. Barrett told Latham that he could pay $5000 for the manuscript, but the chances were that a better price could be had at a New York auction. In a letter to Latham, Barrett wrote the following:

I think it is probably one of the longest Lincoln manuscripts in existence and it is very doubtful if so fine a manuscript of Lincoln will ever appear on the market.

You may be very much surprised at the price it would bring. There is quite a difference between a collector buying a manuscript direct from a dealer or an individual and buying it at public auction.

Auctions in New York at the American Art Association are held in a room somewhat resembling a theater, and the wealthy collectors from all over the United States are there, either in person or by representative, to bid upon the important items, and when millionaires begin bidding against each other for Lincoln items, they seem to get rather careless with their money.

I enclose a clipping from the Boston Transcript of May 4th, showing that two pages of a Lincoln speech which were copied by him *in pencil* brought $5000. Of course, that speech was more interesting than yours, but it was not the original manuscript and was merely copied in pencil, while yours is very fine and is the original.

Mr. Arthur Swann of the American Art Association said he expected to be in Chicago in a couple of weeks. He has charge of the sales of manuscripts for the American Art Association and if you think you would like to come to Chicago and talk the matter over with him, you might either write them, or I can write, to ascertain the exact date of his arrival, and then you could meet him in my office.

The upshot of the matter was that Latham sent the manuscript to New York for auction, bidding was lively and even breathless, and in the end the eminent New York and Philadelphia collector and dealer, also a Doctor of Letters, A. W. Rosenbach, walked away with the manuscript for making the highest bid of $18,000.

As against the occasions when death interposed between Barrett's getting what he sought there were times when life interfered, life once in the form of a living young woman. At the home of Jesse W. Weik in Greencastle, Indiana, amid many boxes, trunks, chests, and bundles, the coauthor with William H. Herndon of a famous biography of Lincoln showed Barrett his collection. Suddenly in the processional of items came a paper that had Barrett a little groggy. "It was a letter of my father to Herndon," says Barrett, "and of his meeting Lincoln on the way to the duel with Shields. No offer of mine for this letter of my father seemed to interest Weik. He would sell it only in case I bought the whole collection. Finally I showed him a bank draft I had brought with me. I told him I would give him for my father's letter a blank check signed by me and that he might fill in the amount and I would not even take a peek at it until he had cashed it at the bank. That letter of my father to Herndon stayed in the Weik collection until his death."

It was earlier that they had practically agreed on a sale and purchase of the whole collection. Then Weik began to have moments of pause. His talk ran about his granddaughter. She was a slim, swift-moving girl, gliding quietly in and out of the rooms, Weik's eyes following her as one to be cherished. She was making herself useful getting the dinner, and that her sweet bloom and frailty needed his care and protection was plainly in the thought of Jesse Weik.

"His eyes kept on following her," says Barrett. "It seemed that almost in a moment his desire to sell dried up. He ended the hope I had when he said that she meant so much to him, that he hadn't a great deal more to leave her than the collection, that if he sold it now he couldn't know what might become of the money, but he could feel that he had done his duty by her if she could have it when he was gone."

2. "That Immortal Emblem"

A NEWLY found speech of Abraham Lincoln, apparently never published since it appeared in various obscure prints of generations ago, is here reproduced as of record in a campaign publication the *Rail Splitter,* Cincinnati, Ohio, Wednesday, October 10, 1860. Its heading reads: *"Extract from an Extempore-Speech of Mr. Lincoln 1858."* The exact date and the place of delivery of the speech are not given. His campaign was of course for election to the United States Senate. No newspaper is named as the source of the text. It could be that a reporter, perhaps one familiar with shorthand, took down the complete address of Lincoln for a newspaper which printed the address in full. In such a case the *Rail Splitter* chose what it regarded as a highly significant passage from the address. It is less probable that some listener to the address made a memorandum and later reconstructed the passage and gave it to the *Rail Splitter* for publication. The most likely theory is that Lincoln made the speech, not prepared but impromptu or "extempore," and its first newspaper publication received little or no reprint or comment in other journals.

Naturally we cannot say with certainty that we have here a speech as Lincoln gave it and these are his exact words. Neither can we certify it by saying it sounds like Lincoln in some of his rare impassioned moments. Nevertheless we can say that whether Lincoln or someone else should have composed these sentences and delivered these announcements of the principles of human equality, they would demand our attention, they would call for study and discussion.

We have here one of the great American psalms. If there should be compiled an American Testament, this would belong. The occasions were frequent when Lincoln paid his respects and reverence to the Declaration of Independence, when too he spoke of the insignificance of individuals, including himself, in the presence of that document and its enunciation that "all men are created equal." In this speech, if or when it should be conclusively established as an accurate report of what he said, Lincoln surpassed himself in his other tributes to the Declaration of Independence and in his sinking of self before a great human cause. These "extempore" remarks, attributed to the man speaking offhand, straight from the heart and blood before some crowd of Illinois voters, contain the dithyrambics of oratory at its highest, and the passion of a true poem.

EXTRACT FROM AN EXTEMPORE-SPEECH OF MR. LINCOLN 1858.

The Declaration of Independence was formed by the representatives of American liberty from thirteen States of the Confederacy—twelve of which were slave-holding communities. It is sufficient for our purpose that all of them greatly deplored the evil and that they passed a provision in the Constitution which they supposed would gradually remove the disease by cutting off its source. This was the abolition of the slave trade. So general was the conviction—the public determination—to abolish the African slave trade, that the provision which I have referred to as being placed in the Constitution, declared that it should not be abolished prior to the year 1808. A constitutional provision was necessary to prevent the people through Congress, from putting a stop to the traffic immediately at the close of the war. Now, if slavery had been a good thing, would the Fathers of the Republic have taken a step calculated to diminish its beneficent influences among themselves, and snatch the boon wholly from their posterity? These communities, by their representatives in old Independence Hall, said to the whole world of men: "We hold these truths to be self evident: that all men are created equal, that they are endowed by their Creator with certain inalienable rights; that among these are life, liberty, and the pursuit of happiness."—This was their lofty, and wise, and noble understanding of the justice of the Creator to His creatures. [Applause] Yes, gentlemen, to *all* His creatures, to the whole great family of man. In their enlightened belief, nothing stamped with the Divine image and likeness was sent into the world to be trodden on and degraded, and imbruted by its fellows.—They grasped not only the whole race of man then living, but they reached forward and seized upon the fartherest posterity. They erected a beacon to guide their children and their children's children, and the countless myriads who should inhabit the earth in other ages. Wise statesmen as they were, they knew the tendency of posterity to breed tyrants; and so they established these great

ELIZABETHTOWN KY., Oct 2d, 1860.

Dr. J. B. MCKEENAN, Cincinnati.

DEAR SIR:—I send you, to-day, by Adams' express, a set of canes, cut off the birth-place of Abraham Lincoln, in Lark en county, formerly this county, (Hardin) I cut them myself last summer to send to some of my Republican friends in the free States You can certainly recommend them as coming from off of his birth-place, as I cut them my-self. They were sent to me at Louisville, but got mis-placed, and I have just recovered them.

The long-plumb stick was cut from the very place in the house where the bed stood when he was born. The house has been removed.

I don't know that it would be of any ad vantage to write any political news from here We COULD GET A LARGE VOTE HERE IF WE voted by ballot, or we had any show.

Although I was raised here I see I have lost a good deal of my custom in my business; but I can not sell my vote and active principles for a few copper cents. God speed "Honest Old Abe's election, which I consider certain

I would be pleased to hear from you and documents. I wish you to present my friend, W. S. M. Barret, of the firm of Tylor & Bar ret, willow and woodenware merchants of your city, one of the canes for me with my respects. Respectfully,

R. WINTERSMITH,
Elector for the Fifth Congres-sional District of Kentucky

LETTER FROM A "POOR WHITE" OF THE SOUTH.

[The following is a genuine letter from an overseer on a Southern plantation, and is worthy of attention as an evidence of a grow ing feeling among the poor whites of the South that their interests and rights are sacrificed to the interests of the small but powerful class who hold slaves. We, of course, withhold the name of the writer for his own sake.

—*Ed. Tribune.*

To the Editor of the N. Y. Tribune.

Sir: I am a plain, practical farmer, who has been raised here in the South, and who has never seen a Free State; but, notwithstanding, I feel, and a great class of our people here feel toward you of the North as brothers. I am certain that if people here would take a second thought, and study and reflect upon the dread ful consequences of Disunion, they would re coil with abhorrence from political agitator and their doctrines.

These agitators would make the Northern people believe that the South is united to a man. There could not be a greater mistake. The people here are divided into two classes—

EXTRACT FROM AN EXTEMPORE SPEECH OF MR. LINCOLN 1858.

The Declaration of Independence was formed by the representatives of American liberty from thirteen States of the Confederacy—twelve of which were slave-holding communities. It is sufficient for our purpose that all of them greatly deplored the evil and that they passed a provision in the Constitution which they supposed would gradually remove the disease by cutting off its source. This was the aboli tion of the slave trade. So general was the conviction—the public determination—to abol ish the African slave trade, that the provision which I have referred to as being placed in the Constitution, declared that it should not be abolished prior to the year 1808. A con stitutional provision was necessary to prevent the people through Congress, from putting a stop to the traffic immediately at the close of the war. Now, if slavery had been a good thing, would the Fathers of the Republic have taken a step calculated to diminish its benefi cent influences among themselves, and snatch the boon wholly from their posterity ? These communities, by their representatives in old Independence Hall, said to the whole world of men: "We hold these truths to be self evi dent: that all men are created equal, that they are endowed by their Creator with certain in alienable rights; that among these are life, liberty, and the pursuit of happiness."—This was their lofty, and wise, and noble under -standing of the justice of the Creator to His creatures. [Applause] Yes, gentlemen, to all His creatures, to the whole great family of men. In their enlightened belief, nothing stamped with the Divine image was ever sent into the world to be trodden on and degraded, and imbruted by its fellows.—They grasped not only the whole race of man then living, but they reached forward and seized upon the farthest posterity. They erected a beacon to guide their children and their chil dren's children, and the countless myriads who should inhabit the earth in other ages. Wise statesmen as they were, they knew the tendency of posterity to breed tyrants; and so they established these great self-evident truths, that when in the distant future, some man, some faction, some interest, should set up the doctrine that none but rich men, or none but white men, or none but Anglo Saxons, were entitled to life, liberty, and the pursuit of happiness, their posterity might look up again to the Declaration of Independence, and take courage to renew the battle which their fathers began—to that truth, and justice, and mercy, and all the humane and Christian virtues might not be extinguished from the land: so that no man hereafter would dare to limit and circumscribe the great principles on which the temple of liberty was being built. [Loud cheers.]

Now, my countrymen, if you have been taught doctrines which conflict with the great landmarks of the Declaration of Independence; if you have listened to suggestions which would take from its grandeur, and mutilate the symmetry of its proportions; if you have been inclined to believe that all men are not

---

Reproduction from *The Rail Splitter*, Cincinnati, Ohio, October 10, 1860. (*Continued on opposite page*)

the rich and the poor—who are as distinct and separate as the North Pole is from the South Pole. It is only when election days are on hand, that the aristocracy ever countenance the poor man; and then they do it to get his vote. But poor men have changed of late years toward the aristocracy. They have found out that voting for the slave interest does not give them clothing, meat and bread, and lands to cultivate; no such thing. They begin to see that for every negro brought into the country, one white man has to make roots not only in farming, but in every branch of business.

Can you not see, my countrymen, that where a man owns his one, two, three, or four thousand acres of land, and negroes to cultivate it, that the poor white man of the middle class has no chance, because he has no land and can get none either for love or money; while the rich man can make, with his negroes, three to four hundred dollars to the hand? The negro mechanics, here in Montgomery, have monopolized the trade; and the slave holders want to dissolve the Union, and open the Slave-trade at the South, to drive all the poor white people out.

Within four miles of Montgomery, the capital of Alabama, and two miles from William L. Yancey's plantation, James Porter and others in Montgomery, have smuggled African negroes (twenty five in number) upon their plantations within the last month, and have them at work in sight of the Capitol; and this is known to all the Government officers about Montgomery. These negroes can not speak English. Where they came from I have never asked, for it is enough for me to know that they have been brought here in violation of the laws of the land, and nothing is said against it.

William L. Yancey will preach to the people, and tell them that the laws for the recovery of fugitive slaves ought to be enforced, but when it comes to enforcing the Slave trade laws, he does not open his mouth. Here he is speaking night and day for Breckinridge, and perhaps will be one of his cabinet if elected. Can you, in the face of these facts, have any confidence in the man or his party?

I have been for fourteen years an overseer in this State, on some of its largest plantations, and I think my opinion is entitled to some respect, from my long experience and daily intercourse with the people. I demand for them that truth, equality, justice, and the Constitution shall prevail.

Yours, for a free country.

MONTGOMERY COUNTY, Ala. Aug. 4, 1860.

created equal in those inalienable rights enumerated by our charter of liberty: let me entreat you to come back. Return to the fountain whose waters spring close by the blood of the revolution. Think nothing of me—take no thought for the political fate of any man whomsoever—but come back to the truths that are in the Declaration of Independence. You may do anything with me you choose, if you will but heed these principles. You may not only defeat me for the Senate, but you may take me and put me to death. While pretending no indifference to earthly honors, I *do claim* to be actuated in this contest by something higher than an anxiety to office. I charge you to drop every paltry and insignificant thought for any man's success. It is nothing; I am nothing; Judge Douglas is nothing. *But do not destroy that immortal emblem of Humanity—the Declaration of Independence.*

self-evident truths, that when in the distant future, some man, some faction, some interest, should set up the doctrine that none but rich men, or none but white men, or none but Anglo Saxons, were entitled to life, liberty, and the pursuit of ha[p]piness, their posterity might look up again to the Declaration of Independence, and take courage to renew the battle which their fathers began—so that truth, and justice, and mercy, and all the humane and Christian virtues might not be extinguished from the land: so that no man hereafter would dare to limit and circumscribe the great principles on which the temple of liberty was being built. [Loud cheers.]

Now, my countrymen, if you have been taught doctrines which conflict with the great landmarks of the Declaration of Independence, if you have listened to suggestions which would take from its grandeur, and mutilate the symmetry of its proportions; if you have been inclined to believe that all men are *not* created equal in those inalienable rights enumerated by our charter of liberty; let me entreat you to come back. Return to the fountain whose waters spring close by the blood of the revolution. Think nothing of me—take no thought for the political fate of any man whomsoever—but come back to the truths that are in the Declaration of Independence. You may do anything with me you choose, if you will but heed these principles. You may not only defeat me for the Senate, but you may take me and put me to death. While pretending no indifference to earthly honors, I *do claim* to be actuated in this contest by something higher than an anxiety to office. I charge you to drop every paltry and insignificant thought for any man's success. It is nothing; I am nothing; Judge Douglas is nothing. *But do not destroy that immortal emblem of Humanity—the Declaration of Independence.*

Momentous in tone, neither widely published then nor since, is a memorandum here written by Lincoln July 1, 1854. He was rehearsing himself on what he might present to the public. Also he was trying to clarify a tangled issue in his own mind by the use of inexorable logic. This sheet of handwriting is, one might say, tremulous and shadowy with tumults of democratic passion recollected in tranquillity. It could well be included in grade-school readers and in textbooks on human affairs used in schools and colleges in this country and in the various other countries that are members of the organization named the United Nations. The full text of it, at several times printed incorrectly, is here given in complete fidelity to the original manuscript, which is also presented.

[Memorandum in Lincoln's handwriting]

> If A. can prove, however conclusively, that
> he may, of right, enslave B— why may not—
> B. snatch the same argument, and prove
> equally, that he may enslave A.?—
> You say A. is white, and B. is black—
> It is color, then; the lighter, having the right
> to enslave the darker? Take care— By this
> rule, you are to be slave to the first
> man you meet, with a fairer skin than—
> ~~your own—~~
> You do not mean color exactly? You
> mean the whites are intellectually the superi:
> or of the blacks, and, therefore have the
> right to enslave them? Take care again— By
> this rule, you are to be slave to the first
> man you meet, with an intellect superior
> to your own—
> But, say you, it is a question of interest;
> and, if you can make it your interest,
> you have the right to enslave another—
> Very well— And if he can make it his
> interest, he has the right to enslave you—

Memorandum in Lincoln's handwriting—text follows below. Lincoln, and others whose letters are printed herein, often used a short dash to end a sentence. These are printed here as periods.

If A. can prove, however conclusively, that he may, of right, enslave B. why may not B. snatch the same argument, and prove equally, that he may enslave A.?—

You say A. is white, and B. is black. It is *color*, then; the lighter, having the right to enslave the darker? Take care. By this rule, you are to be slave to the first man you meet, with a fairer skin than ~~yourself.~~ your own

You do not mean *color* exactly? You mean the whites are *intellectually* the superiors of the blacks; and therefore have the right to enslave them? Take care again. By this rule, you are to be slave to the first man you meet, with an intellect superior to your own.

But, say you, it is a question of *interest;* and, if you can make it your *interest,* you have the right to enslave another. Very well. And if he can make it his interest, he has the right to enslave you.

We present a biography of Lincoln written in a comic vein. Supplied by the American News Company, those not able to get it on railroad trains could send 5 cents by mail to the office of the *Comic Monthly,* 109 Nassau Street, New York, who announced it as a "Burlesque Campaign Life" and

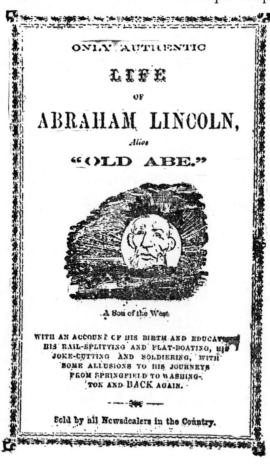

assured readers it was "Sold by all Newsdealers in the Country." Naturally there can be argument as to where to laugh here, or whether to laugh at all. There will be deadpan duffers who may say this belittles the Emancipator; still others will go so far as to say that if a copy of it came into the hands of Lincoln, he would read parts of it aloud to others and laugh the loudest of all. The humor is akin to that of Lincoln himself in his more hilarious moods with select company, such as when the man from Sangamon County, Illinois, asked him how it feels to be President and got the answer: "Well, I'm like the man they rode out of town on a rail. He said if it wasn't for the honor of the thing he'd just as soon walk." The style of this miniature biography is related to that of the three leading comics during the Lincoln administration, Artemus Ward, Petroleum Vesuvius Nasby, and Orpheus C. Kerr, whose pieces Lincoln often read aloud to others even at Cabinet meetings. A word of appreciation could be said for what the publishers call the "funny pictures." They are pictures and they are funny.

The title page reads: "Only authentic Life of Abraham Lincoln, alias 'Old Abe.' A Son of the West. With an account of his birth . . . and BACK again."

THE LIFE OF ABRAHAM LINCOLN

It is now four years and some months since all doubts were dispelled concerning the birth of the subject of this biography.

No one now doubts that he was born.

Further, it is believed that he is the son of Old Lincoln, by his wife, Mrs. Lincoln. A better geneology [sic] could not be desired.

Little Abraham, as his political friends called him at that time, first saw the light in Hardin county, Kentucky.

He was six feet two inches in height, and though his grandfather had been

HARDIN COUNTY, KENTUCKY.

scalped by the Indians, felt pretty comfortable.

It is said that Hardin county still remains where it was. Little Abraham, however, has moved.

At the age of seven, Mr. Lincoln, who had already become widely known about his father's farm, went to school. Here he began to develope the characteristics which have since been instrumental in the direction of our Government and the conduct of the War. He speedily learned to read and write, to chew tobacco, to cure the spasms in horses, to play the guitar, and to do sums in addition.

This was in 1703.

THE SOARING EAGLE, NOT REPLYING.

Considering his education complete, he now migrated to Indiana, where he built him an eyrie home upon the cloud-capped brow of a mountain crag and shouted at morn to the soaring eagle.

The soaring eagle did not reply.

On his way to Indiana, however, his flatboat got upset by a tropic hurricane, and he lost seven barrels of whiskey and a new saw-buck.

Here in the solitude of Nature, Abraham began to feel a yearning for wisdom, and was shocked one day by meeting a free nigger who knew more than he himself. This gave him a love of liberty and a horror of slavery. From that sentiment, so early inspired, resulted the famous Emancipation Proclamation.

Haunted by a fierce desire for more knowledge, then, Abraham once more attended school. He had a retentive memory and a buckskin suit.

For six months he labored, early and late, at his books, and at the end of that time was rewarded by the glorious consciousness that he knew everything.

CAPTAIN LINCOLN, ON DECK.

LINCOLN SPLITTING RAILS, IN SANGAMON.

He then left school and gave himself gladly up to a longing he had hitherto been unable to gratify; a maritime taste, and desire for nautical adventure.

He became captain of a long, low, rakish-looking flatboat, manned with a hardy, rollicking crew, and set sail, one fine morning, upon the flashing brine, for New Orleans. Nothing happened to him, and he returned.

Weary of the transient pleasures of a sailor's life, Abraham removed to a rose-embowered cot in Illinois, where he dwelt peacefully beside the silver Sangamon. His sole pursuit, at this time, was the splitting of rails.

His honesty became conspicuous at about the same period.

The dread alarm of bloody conflict now resounded through Illinois. The Black Hawk war broke out, and the simple peasants of the forest sprang to arms. Was this a time for Lincoln to remain inert and tranquil? Not much.

The ghastly battle-field now saw his towering form stalk, gloomy, magnificent and tremendous, through the thick vapors of the cannon's mouth. At least such would have been the case, had it not been for the Indians who resolutely refused to come near Abraham's regiment.

It was in camp, at Beardstown, where he remained during the entire struggle, that Abraham acquired the marvelous ability of telling little stories, for which he is now so deservedly known.

LINCOLN TELLING LITTLE STORIES, IN CAMP.

In 1776, the Indian war being about played out, this great good man was unanimously defeated as a candidate for the Legislature. His constituents loved him too much to let him leave them. To divert himself he set up a post-office in New Salem.

Shortly after this, came the turning-point of his existence.

He once more entered the political arena, was twice elected to the Legislature, fell into evil company, and became a lawyer!

How many poor wretches, alas! have dated back their fall, and the triumph of the fiend over them, to the time when they began to associate with bad companions!

From this moment, Abraham's course was rapid. First a Presidential Elector, he passed to the condition of Congressman, and was subsequently nominated for the Senate, but defeated.

About this time, he was married. He married Mrs. Lincoln.

In 1853 it was determined to have a Governor of Illinois, and Abraham wrote several letters in which he said "I am just the man you want." The Republican party was thus induced to support him, which was done in luxurious style, until the choice came before the people, a vulgar, ignorant set, who said they would rather have Judge Douglas. The Judge was therefore made Governor. This is the reason why Illinois has never been able to prosper.

Abraham now returned to splitting rails and telling little stories.

The length of the former, and the breadth of the latter attracted the attention of the world, and people began to ask themselves, "If so, why so?" and, "If not so, why so?" The result was that whispers circulated.

It was now determined that Mr. James Buchanan had been long enough in office, and that he was getting soiled, so the nation prepared to put on a clean President.

LINCOLN SPEAKING AT COOPER INSTITUTE.

Abraham, though quite as modest as he was honest, thought this a good chance to make twenty-five thousand a year, so he went to New York and advocated his claims to the position, in a speech at Cooper Institute, charging two shillings admission fee. The Republicans admired his cheek, and nominated him at the Chicago Convention of 1860. He accepted, in a letter, in which he said he almost wished they had chosen a statesman instead.

The whole country has wished so, since.

In due time, Abraham was elected. There were two other candidates, and more people voted against Lincoln than voted for him. He was therefore made President.

His trip from Illinois to Washington was a great spree. The country-folk crowded copiously about the railroad stations all along the route, and the new lawyer told them a little story every-

LINCOLN WRITING HIS LETTER OF ACCEPTANCE.

where he stopped. At Baltimore they proposed to tell him a little story in turn, but he gave them the slip and went through that city at night, disguised

LINCOLN PASSING BALTIMORE.

in a long cloak and Scotch cap, long ago become historical.

Baltimore is the home of the canvas-back duck, the terrapin, the Blood-tub and the Plug-ugly. It is called the Monumental City, and its inhabitants wanted to give Abraham a monument there. As has been said, however, he arrived safely in Washington without that mark of appreciation.

Most of the readers of this biography have probably heard of the Rebellion. It has formed the subject of several newspaper articles. It is situated in the South, and its back-bone is much broken. It arose when Abraham was inagurated [sic], and claimed that ceremony as its papa. Maybe it was so, and maybe it wasn't; but if anybody asks you, tell him you don't know.

The State of Virginia sent three commissioners to ask the President what he was going to do about it.

He said, "Go 'way."

They went.

He then called for 75,000 troops, and requested the Rebels to stop their nonsense. Meanwhile he stopped their ports.

The insurrection fed well on this sort of food, and assumed dangerous proportions.

The industry of the South having gone to grief, all the men were at leisure to join the army, and as there was no more commerce, privateering became a profitable trade.

Seeing which, Abraham issued a proclamation recommending the gradual Emancipation of the niggers.

This showed Mr. Greeley, Mr. Chase, Mr. Wilson, Mr. Sumner, and others, that his back was weak on the question of Slavery, and they went at him. Meanwhile, remembering his martial life in the Black Hawk war, and his maritial [sic] experience on the bounding flatboat, he assumed command of the Army and Navy of the United states [sic].

LINCOLN ASSUMING COMMAND OF THE ARMY AND NAVY.

Getting mixed on the nigger question, he scolded General Fremont for emancipating the slaves of Missouri Rebels, and, shortly after, emancipating those of loyalists in the District of Columbia, paying however, a small price for them. The result was that all the old used-up slaves within two hundred miles were brought on to Washington and sold to the Government for emancipation purposes.

Abraham's cabinet was rather a curious affair at this time. His Secretary of State was Mr. Seward, a well known Albany politician and a sort of whitewashed Democrat. His Secretary of War was a Pennsylvania demagogue, Mr. Cameron. His Secretary of the Navy was an old gentleman from the backwoods, Mr. Welles, who had never smelled tar. His Secretary of the Treasury was Mr. Chase, who had never handled money before in his

A GOOD GOVERNMENT BARGAIN.

life. The other post—that of the Post-office—was filled by Mr. Blair, who made the usual changes for the worse in the arrangement of that department, and who was very fatal to country post-masters.

These gentlemen went on beautifully as might have been expected. Their time was chiefly devoted to the frustration of each other's designs, and their success in that line was really remarkable.

Hence what is called the conduct—meaning the misconduct—of the war.

Mr. Cameron was soon caught in suspicious connection with the contract-business and was discharged from the Cabinet. Mr. Stanton, a Philadelphia lawyer, took his place, with General Halleck as a sort of military backbone, but the country was so disgusted with this change from the frying-pan to the fire, that Abraham feared to remove even Welles the sleepy, or Chase the muddle-head.

LINCOLN AND HIS CABINET.

The fratricidal struggle, then, looked very queer. Mismanagement and division of councils wearied out the people's patriotism, wasted their money and demoralised our Army in Virginia.

SECRETARY SEWARD AND HIS LITTLE BELL.

So, to add to the rare and strange estimation in which Abraham was coming to be held, he ordered a conscription of Three Hundred Thousand men, and issued a proclamation for the Emancipation of all slaves in Rebellious States.

The effect may be easier imagined than described.

At about this time, Secretary Seward came in possession of a Little Bell, which had a very sweet sound to his ear.

Whenever he rang it, somebody was sent to jail, on good charges, bad charges or indifferent charges, and somebody therefore objected, naturally enough. To do away with such objections, then, the Secretary prevailed upon Abraham to suspend the writ of *habeas corpus,* so that men might be sent to jail without any charges whatever.

The President good-naturedly acquiesced and ordered that the writ of *habeas corpus* must not be observed, but that, by way of offset, the Sabbath must.

CONSCRIPTS IN THE FIELD.

This won him great popularity among those who liked to go to church and those who liked to go to jail.

Three Hundred Thousand more conscripts were then called out, and the Rebellion continued to flourish, though the conscripts were sent to the field.

Let it not be thought that Abraham did not make preparations, all this time, for the reception of peaceful overtures from the Rebels. He sent a corn-doctor to Richmond; confiscated the property of the enemy; sent a half-crazy philosopher from Colorado after the corn-doctor; a Methodist parson turned colonel and a sensation magazine-writer after the Colorado lunatic; called for Five Hundred Thousand more conscripts, and wrote a letter "to whom it may concern," offering to make

LINCOLN OUT WALKING.

peace if the Rebels would give up their theories, their property, their lives, and do just as he wanted them to forever after.

What more could be desired?

The ingrates have not accepted the terms of this letter, so far as heard from, and Abraham's season of rulership promises to expire before the Rebellion.

Thus much for the history of a truly great and good man, brought down to the present time.

This biography can not chronicle the close of Abraham's long and useful life. Perhaps it is to be regretted.

Some particulars, however, of his personal appearance, habits, etc., may not be unacceptable, for it is not likely that any such person will ever again occupy the Presidential chair.

Mr. Lincoln stands six feet twelve in his socks, which he changes once every ten days. His anatomy is composed mostly of bones, and when walking he resembles the offspring of a happy marriage between a derrick and a windmill.

When speaking he reminds one of the old signal-telegraph that used to stand on Staten Island. His head is shaped something like a ruta-bago, and his complexion is that of a Saratoga trunk. His hands and feet are plenty large enough, and in society he has the air of having too many of them. The glove-makers have not yet had time to construct gloves that will fit him.

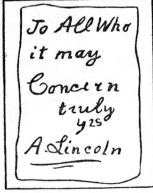

FAC-SIMILE OF LINCOLN'S HANDWRITING.

In his habits he is by no means foppish, though he brushes his hair sometimes, and is said to wash. He swears fluently. A strict temperance man himself, he does not object to another man's being pretty drunk, especially when he is about to make a bargain with him. He is fond of fried liver and onions, and is a member of the church. He can hardly be called handsome, though he is certainly much better looking since he had the small-pox. As a public speaker he differs considerably from Daniel Webster and Artemus Ward. He is hospitable, bilious, and writes a good hand. Mrs. Lincoln thinks well of him. He is 107 years old.

Such is Abraham Lincoln. Take him at his best he is much better than those think him who underrate his virtues. For his friends, who like his administration, he would make a better candidate for re-election than some man they do not like so well. With others, it is different. There are several editions of his life published, but the foregoing is the best. He himself says so. The writer agrees with him. So does he.

This is all.

THE END.

3. Saved from Flame and Time

THERE was a schoolteacher in Chicago having an interest in an inheritance case. The suit was lost, but in the course of the action she heard about the opposing counsel, Oliver R. Barrett, being even more interested in Lincoln letters than he was in law practice. After the trial she telephoned Barrett, inviting him to come to her home and see some letters Lincoln had given her father. In company with his fellow collector, Alexander Hannah, Barrett called on her.

Her story was simple. Her father was a cabinetmaker whose shop was directly under Mr. Lincoln's law office. Into her father's shop one morning of February 1861 had come Mr. Lincoln with a sheaf of papers in one hand, saying he was going to put them in the stove. Her father had said to Mr. Lincoln, "Why not let me have them?" And Lincoln had done so. Into the cabinetmaker's hands went letters of friendly and anxious men giving counsel or sending good wishes and prayers, letters warning of assassination by gunshot or poison, letters of ridicule and belittlement and wild curses—inquiries from a gun inventor and a desperate beggar, and the long letter of a horse thief who wished to turn informer and share a reward with Lincoln.

This series might be termed the Hot Stove Letters. While the letters didn't go into a hot stove and perish by fire, they nevertheless do articulate the anxieties and tensions of many American citizens who in that winter gathered around the stove of a country store, a livery stable, the shop of a harnessmaker or a cabinetmaker.

These findings set Barrett on a quest. He was asking whether it could be that Lincoln's old house desk was still around. If so, how could it be located? If found, would there be anything in it? He began in Springfield among the houses roundabout the old Lincoln home. "I canvassed that whole

45

neighborhood just like you would looking for witnesses in a lawsuit. I went from house to house knocking and asking if they knew anything about Lincoln or an old desk he had. I came finally to the house where the woman in the doorway was saying, 'Why, yes, sure enough' she had in the house the old desk of Mr. Lincoln himself. I can see her face now but I didn't tax my memory with her name."

She asked him into the house, led him to the desk. There in each of two pigeonholes was a bundle of letters addressed to Lincoln, postmarked late 1860 or early 1861. She had never read the letters, had never untied the threads and strings that bound them. At an auction sale of the Lincoln household effects she had bought the desk, had regarded the letters with something of reverence and a feeling they should be kept. She was willing to let Barrett have the letters, but refused to part with a diary that had been kept by her daughter reporting early days in Springfield, including parties where she saw and talked with the Lincolns. And whereas the Hot Stove Letters mostly wanted to kill Lincoln, the Old Desk Letters wanted to help him or show their faith in him.

The climate of opinion, the winds of doctrine, the hopes and faiths of men and women, their hates and deep scorn, their trust in him or their abiding and unchangeable contempt—these are registered in letters coming to Lincoln in January and February of 1861, on paper that came so near being thrust into a hot stove and turned to black ashes, on paper that lay dusty and forgotten in an old desk of light-brown wood, perhaps cherry. The tone of those seeking strange favors from him, the accents of those ready to die with him or for him—or again those who would be pleased to kill him or see him killed—they are set forth here in their own words, the Republican Party man or the seasoned Abolitionist, each with a heart prepared for war against slavery, the Douglas Democrat and the Roman Catholic adherent who preferred war rather than lose the Union, the early Northern Copperheads who anonymously made Lincoln a member of the Ugly Club, the anxious Southern Unionist and the forsworn Southern loyalist. These Old Desk and Hot Stove Letters follow:

THE OLD DESK LETTERS

Peoria Feb 3 1861

To Abraham Lincoln

When I read over from time to time your views as to the policy our Government should pursue in reference to slavery, I say God bless Old

Abe. Coming generations will bless you and say a prouder inheritance could not be left to your children. I write this because Kellogg proposed resolutions looking to the amendment of the Constitution perpetuating the Slave Power. Lincoln dont fear to stand straight up to the line of duty of conscience; To Back down will disgrace and demoralize the party and set back the sun of freedom. Better die right here. I will die with you if necessary, but the cause is ruined if we take counsel of our fears. I shall not trouble you much. My heart is in the cause and you are its representative. Hold the banner aloft. it will at last triumph. No offensive movement is required. You have been fairly elected. When inaugurated, it will be time enough to concede. But Abe be President untramelled or die with your fame unclouded.   Old Abe   Good bye   H. Grove

Cin.   Jany 30. 1861

Hon. A. Lincoln
Springfield, Ill.
Dʳ Sir.

The object of this is not office,—but to communicate information. Our country is in peril & all should do what can be done, to avoid the danger. Correct information is more necessary than aught else—for half—more than half, our trouble proceeds from error.

The undersigned has been for 20 years in the habit of visiting the States of Georgia, Mississippi & Louisiana. Since 1846 I have had professional business before the Legislature of Louisiana. I have a daughter married & living in New Orleans—I have many relatives in Mississippi & Georgia. These social and business relations have caused me to mingle much with people of the South of all classes, and thus have been enabled to judge of their true sentiments.

Citisens of the north are apt to believe and generally do believe *they* are the only aggrieved people: that those of the South are acting contrary to their true convictions. If our public men or our people adopt measures in this belief, they will commit a great wrong. The press of the North & the press of the South. Speakers of the North & speakers of the South, charge on *each other* precisely the same offences—designs of aggression—breaches of the constitution—violations of good faith & such like.

Citisens of the South, as a general thing have far fewer opportunities for correct information than those of the North have. Here all is free—free speech—free press—free people. All classes of speakers are heard, with all shades of opinions: all classes of reading is within the reach of all. In the

South this is not so.—Within a few years with the progress of embittered feeling, the opportunities for correct information are less & less. The Northern papers circulate generally, very limitedly.—Last year, in New Orleans, only the N.York Herald & Journal of Commerce & such Kindred prints could be procured. The present fact communicated, of 700 bags of mail matter undistributed there designates a purpose to *with*-hold the northern press from circulating and is only an index of what I know has been. In the South, no Seward—nor any northern Statesman is heard. The people, reading their local press & confiding in the same—finding charges of the gravest impropriety on the Republican party, believe the same. The people, hearing uncontradicted these political speakers charge republicans with every impropriety believe the same. The institutions of the South are of that peculiar character as to make citisens credulous & uneasy.

In the South Republicanism is Abolitionism. Abolitionism is every thing abominable. The Doctrine of Wendal Phillip is believed to be the doctrine of Republicans. Southern people *generally* are sincere in *this* belief, and they necessarily act on the same. They are right in so doing. Without undeception—in this full faith, is not there due to them—as brethren erring through ignorance *many* efforts—much concession? Should we not *prove* them in error & undeceive them?

The argument of Benjamin on Secession, is & has been, heard by me for a long time in the south. The great mass of people believe it *legal—constitutional*. If by any *trial*, the case could be adjudicated, they would have faith in such adjudication, & act on it.

For over two years the violent have, in New Orleans, & the South been having the upper hand. Business men, not mingling more, there than in the north, in political meetings, have kept back. For a year they have been intimidated. Property—life—social relations—were jeoparded by any advocacy of measures or views contrary to those of the violent. Carolina is largely represented, & the Carolina feeling has been the active feeling. The policy of the U.S. has intimidated. There has been—is now, no certainty that the Government would protect the citisens of the South in their property or their citisenship. They have been doubtful of the *law*. Hence, near one half—of Southern voters are passive; are afraid. Does the Government not owe them a measure of protection within our own limits, greater their [sic] would be done, if the same rights were violated in France? If the Government did protect or show its purpose the passive would be active. Whilst on the one hand many—very many of the active in the South are so under *error* as above stated—others are passive from the same. Energy and at the same time *effort* to undecieve, would do great good. The South deserves that effort, & in kindness for their errors.

Intercourse alone will enable any one correctly to appreciate the heart of the affairs in the South. I have thought few would take this trouble and hence write you on the impulse. If any have,—no harm will be done.

I have been a citisen here since 1832, and long connected with the Cin. [cinnati] Gazette.—I refer to this simply to designate that I am your friend.

Crafts I Wright.

Judge Wright (I. P. Wright) sends his best respects.

P.[S.] Would it not better subserve public good, to reach Washington in these times of excitement, without parade or display.

Nolinville Tenn. Jan. 23 1860

Hon. Abraham Lincoln
　　Springfield Ill.—

Dear and respected Sir [1] Through a sense of duty to yourself as well as in some way to avert the danger that threatens my native state and south as well as the whole country, I take my pen in hand to write you a few lines, believing you and your position as well as future policy is greatly and designedly misrepresented by designing politicians to accomplish their own treasonable designs. our election for delegates to a state convention takes place in a short time. we will then elect either Union or Disunion delegates. you are aware of the results in our late elections in our sister states. the people of my state are desirous, overwhelmingly so, of remaining loyal to the flag and standard of their country true to the principle of our immortal Jackson and loved Polk; but the emissaries of treason are on the alert, occupying high places. their utmost efforts will be made to precipitate our immediate sesession. the voice of Tennessee will be felt in all the states yet to act. will you be so kind as to transmit to me by return mail your intended policy relative to our institutions in the states and territories? I will secure their thorough circulation among all classes throughout the state. you have the power now to avert the dire calamity that threatens the country, to save Tennessee to the Union. will you do it? I believe you will. write fully and explicitly, and I repeat you will hear a voice from Tennessee that will do your heart good, that will be felt in the border states, nay, in the gulf

---

[1] In the body of this original letter the writer gets along with never a period or a comma. He hates and shuns punctuation. The editor has inserted punctuation in the above for reader convenience. Sentences beginning without a capital are left.

states, that will consign treason and trators [sic] to that oblivion and contempt they so much merit. hoping to hear from you by next mail I am, honered and respected Sir

Yours truly
And sincerely

W. N. Barnes

P.S. My address is Nolinsville Tenn. I again insist on an immediate answer. I will have no more than time to give any answer from you the circulation it should have. Sen Seward Speach had quite a sanitary effect. the public mind is on the verge of reaction politicians (secessions) will prevent if possible   W. N. B.—

Monuk, Jany 23rd 1861

To Ab. Lincoln Pres Elect of U.S.

Dear Sir Excuse me for this Epistle as I am a stranger to You and also a humble and retired Citizen of the Northern part of Iowa, Winnesheik County. It apears from reports from Washington that difficulty is about to take place between the Southern and the General Government In consequence of the Slave Question. our Republican friends should be aware of the fact particularly the Members of Congress, that the electors of the U.S. has Virtually said No More Slave Territory and in order that the South be appeased Amendment to the Constitution must take place for the further Extension of the wicked institution. God forbid that any alteration Should take place for that purpose. As matters now stand there is but one fact about the Matter, that is if the Constitution remains as it is it will be so kept Sacred by the Republican party, and it also rests on the Republicans whether the Union be preserved or not And from the sentiments of the Republicans it appears there should be no giving or yielding of the least Magnitude. The difficulty has to be met at some day And for My part I see no grounds they may not as well be Settled now as at a future day. If the South desire war let them have it to their entire satisfaction. Compromises are not to be relied upon therefore of no use. The great difficulty is there has been too much yielding heretofore And is probably the ground work from which our presently difficulty has originated from. as the saying is give the little finger shortly the whole hand is required. And refusal brings on a difficulty between the parties [and] is not the present trouble if rightly viewed in the same relation to the finger and hand. I do not wish you to think that in writing my object is to have any influence in Your future conduct for I

presume Your knowledge of our National Matters has long before this settled in Your mind and in what manner our National matters will be conducted as far as you have power to controll them. My object is more to
give the sentiments of the Republicans in Northern Iowa [—] the Constitution first, 2ⁿᵈ the Republican principles given at Chicago is the only
doctrine that will preserve the Union and the Republican party. If properly
manag[ed] all will in time be well.   Respectfully Yours
Drop me a line if you have time   Daniel D Webster
to Monuk, P.O. Winnesheik County Iowa

    There has a question arose in our vicinity that draws out various opinions,
the Democrats taking one side, the Republicans the other. It occurred to
my mind to write You on the subject—"Is the Slave in the Slave States
assessed and Taxed as personal property or not [?"] If you will drop me a
line on the subject I suppose You are posted on the question living as you
do in a State adjoining Slave States and also from Legal knowledge.
                                                        Yours
                                                        Daniel D. Webster

                                                Dont wan an office

Dr Sir
    Although an humble citizen I feel a deep interest in the maintainance of
the union of states and the enforcement of the Laws. Equally, honourably,
and with equal Justice to all—
    I have gloried in your Election to the chief Magistracy of this nation in
view of maintainance and perpetuation of our glorious union, and in this
the most criticle period of hir history you will I trust allow me to sugest
a firm and decided stand against all compromises, while Treason holds its
sway, and trators assume to rule
    Treason stalks abroad from our present chief Magistrate, from Cabinet
officers, from Members of our Legislation Halls, from our army and naval
officers, as well as in our daily midst. In view of all this with serious appre-
hentions that our National Capital may at any moment be seized and con-
trolled by a mob, and while compromising appears to some to be the only
salvation for us, Would it not be well for you to repair to Washington at
an early day, and by so doing strengthen the hands of the weak by your
council, bring back the wavering, and generally to advise for the maintainance of this beloved Nation inviolate by a firm and decided Stand on your

part to maintain the Constitution as it is, and the Enforcement of the Laws without regard to cost

This does appear to me to be the only course to pursue in view of the maintainance of Nationality either at home or abroad—

Hoping you will give no countinance to compromising with trators, rebels, or Mobs. But on the contrary, to pursue the course of our A. Jackson in 1832 & 33, by giving all to understand that you will be the President of the whole of the of the 34 United States, compelling the observing of the Constitution and the Enforcement of the Laws.

This and this alone will will [sic] maintain our Nationality

Very Truly Thine

Silas Merrick

To A. Lincoln
   President Elect
   Of U.S. of America
         New Brighton Penn^a
         Jany 31/61

New Orleans, Jan 25th 1861

Hon^l Abraham Lincoln
         Dr Sir.

I will offer no apology for addressing you upon the extraordinary attitude, which the North & the South occupy towards each other. You are the president elect of the U.S. and on the 4th of March next, will be the President of the Northern portion, while the South, will have formed a confederation of the Seceding States, & will have taken the necessary measures for being recognised as such, by all those states with which it is to their interest to maintain amicable commercial relations. What a spectacle for the contemplation of the statesman and the philanthropist! The decree has gone forth, and will not return, until its mission has been performed. The spectacle of a great nation, torn into fragments & indulging in bitter vituperation, or perhaps in an exterminating war, is not a picture to be contemplated with stolid indifference—especially when we reflect, that the primary increment, had its origin in a mere abstraction, which should never have found its way to the hall of Congress.

The North complains that Slavery is an evil, which should be abolished. This is a mere abstract opinion, which it may be proper to indulge. So far as their civil rights are involved, but I doubt the feeling, or even the propriety of carrying their sympathy into those states, where it existed and was recognized at the adoption of the Constitution. It seems to me, that the anxiety about slaves, has grown out of a morbid philanthropy whose indulgence is contrary, both in principle & practice to the teachings of the Constitution or the dictates of humanity. The condition of the slave has not been ameliorated by the interference of northern fanatics, nor, on examination, do I find that the character of the negro is improved by his being transferred to a free state, even though, as in some of them, he has been elevated to an equality with his white bretheren. Then why press the question, to such a fatal issue? Why drive out of the old Union, States whose commerce and production, have built up the manufactures of the Country, on the one hand, and added so largely to the wealth of those western States, whose surplus of grain, pork, &c. have always found a ready & profitable market in the Slave States? Policy above, would, in my opinion, point out a different course—and, unless Something is done, and that quickly, the two Sections will never unite again. I am not certain that a Union could now be formed, as more might be demanded on the one side, than would be conceded on the other. But an effort in the right direction should be made, and those who possess the power, should not be slow to act. The case is one of emergency, and should be promptly met, in the spirit of mutual concession. If the North has any complaints to make of wrongs received at the hands of the South, let them be stated. But at the same time our claims for a redress of grievances must not be overlooked or disregarded.

I am of the opinion that, a Convention clothed with full authority, composed of delegates from all the states, should be called, and that this convention should dispose of the question of Slavery, then and forever. So as to take its discussion from the halls of Legislation, and leave it in the hands of those who deem it an institution, necessary to their interests, & promotive of the happiness of the Slave.

By meddling with this question, the North will lose, in the next ten years, more than the value of all the Slaves in the South. They may, today, be ignorant of this fact, but it is nevertheless a truth which will come home to them before the Time expires, to which I have referred.

You, as president, can do much in the adjustment of pending difficulties, and I have confidence in your patriotism & wisdom; & believe that you will do all you can to arrest the horrors of a civil war, which may grow out of a separation of the two Sections. I am not certain that the south will ever again unite with the north; but of this I am confident, that no measures of coercion will or can be successful. Upon this point there is a perfect Union. But whether the sections are or can not united, they may adopt such treaty stipulations as will be mutually beneficial, in a commercial point of view, while it will prevent any aggressions, on either side, which, if indulged in, might lead to open hostility. As an old Clay Whig (for my friend Corwin writes me that you are of this faith.) imitate the example of one who could yield a great & long cherished principle, for the sake of the Union. Whatever may be your opinions in regard to Slavery, make these subservient to the Spirit of patriotism. I have written freely & hastily, but without intending any offence. My great desire is to see harmony and good fellowship restored.

Yrs very truly.

Jno. W. Watkins

St. Louis Jan 31st/61

Honored Sir

You Will Excuse me for Tampering With your valuable time In this critical juncture of our Affairs Well Knowing That you are bored to Death by Correspondents. being an humble member of the Republic Party From the Time of Its birth and an ardent Supporter Of your claims for the high office To which you have Been Elected, you Will Please Excuse me for broaching To you Some things that may have Escaped your attention. Being very Sensitive of the Position In Which our Party Has been Placed by the Enemies of our country, I thought It Would be Well To call to your attention Honored Sir To the Catholic Element In our Politics Particularly Of the Irish Portion. And Sir Whatever you can Do to Make Them Freinds of your Administration Will Redound To the Interests of the Party For all Time I Refer you In this connection Honored Sir. To the Distinguished Catholic Writer Orestes A Brownson of N.y. Who I Believe From the Reports Made a Speech In your Behalf In New jersey In the Last Canvass. And also To Archbishop Purcell of cinn Who Is Strong For the Union. And Speaking of this matter Sir I Believe that Archbishop Hughes of N.y. Is a Strong Freind of Wm H Seward. by Refering To the Democrat of the 24 Inst you Will There Find a Portion of a Speech Of Thos Debrey McGee, member of Parliament Canada, In opposition To Slavery Delivered To his countrymen Which Was Well Received. The Gentleman himself I Have not allways Endorsed. My object In addressing you Honored Sir Is Plain In this time of our countrys Trial I Would not be one To Withhold any thing from you That Would Assist you To Carry out the Laws. Taking Every Thing Together and Also Reflecting That the Catholic & Irish People are Grateful, you Would Do Well To Consider The Claims of Some of there best men at this Time. Honored Sir I am no Irishman but I Plead for them Knowing That In them you Would have a Tower of Strenght. For myself I ask nothing being To[o] obscure. the Style of My Letter Is Evidence Enough of that Fact, but I am An American and a Catholic and a True Lover of my Country and I am anxous to See our First Republican President Do What Is Right for himself and his Party In the Future. I Would State That With The Prominent Members of our Party and Most Especially Our Noble Leader F P Blair, I am very well acquainted. Having Lived Here for the Last 17 years I ought To be. Having Stood Shoulder To Shoulder With Them at the Polls. With The contents of this Letter Nobody Is acquainted But yourself and the Writer

Wishing you a Long Life and

Excuse the Impertenence   Success In your Administration
And also my   I Remain With The
Name this Time   Highest Regard yours Truly

Thames

City of Fall River, Mass. January 28. 1861.

Dear Sir,

Though personally a stranger, I have felt an irrepressible impulse to write to you in relation to the affairs of our country.

It is not the fortune of every one to be placed in a position, where the weal or woe of his country for generations, may depend upon the influences of his individual action. Such apparently, in the wisdom of Providence, is your position.

The Preamble to the Constitution, among other things, declared, that it was formed to "Secure the blessings of liberty to ourselves and our posterity." Much has been said by the Secessionists about "the guarantees of slavery." May not the people hope, that in your administration, they will be secure in the Guarantees of Liberty? For myself, having for the last twelve years, thrown none but a Republican vote, I love and respect the Constitution as it is; but not as the Secessionists or others propose to change it.—and I fervently trust that you may find such to be the sentiment of the great body of the people.

Knowing from personal observations that not only the Republicans, but every other class of the people in this Commonwealth, will support the Constitution as it is, with their heart's blood if need be—and not knowing who else might communicate the facts, I have ventured to suggest them as I believe they exist.

The Republicans, and I may add the members of other parties also, seem to have an abiding faith, from the prudence of your course, that they may rely with unwavering confidence upon the integrity of your character and the sincerity of your principles to reform the administration of our government and to protect the Constitution as it is. The people here want no compromise with Slavery beyond what has already been made, and they see no reason to yield their deliberate judgment to idle or ambitious fears, made into threats to dissolve the Union for none but an imaginary cause.

Trusting you will not regard, as an intrusion, communications from an earnest Republican or from one of your constituents, I have the pleasure to be,

Respectfully, your obt. servant,

Louis Lapham

Hon. A. Lincoln
Springfield, Ill.

West Hartford, Ct. Jan. 28, 1861.

To the Hon Abraham Lincoln.
Dear Sir,

We are strangers, but God made us boath and we are traveling to Eternity to give acount to God, for the deeds don in the body, whether good or bad. I am a privet citizen (a farmer) you are the President elect of the U.S. of America. I hope you will be a good one. I hope you will look to God (and not man) for direction, and do what He shows you to be right without respect of persons. if you do so God will bless you, but if you do not, God will leave you to be a disgrace to the nation, and to the world, as He has Buchanan.

I am *only* a Bible abolitionest—See Isah LVIII Chap. 6 V. and Matth. XXII Chap. 37,38,39,40, Vs, no Constitution can stand against that—Gods word will be fulfilled.

you and I know that Slavery is a curse to this nation, and ought to be abolished, therefore all lawful means ought to be used to that effect.

We have one of the most miserable administrations that ever disgraced the earth, a poor weak pusillanimous if not conniveing president, with a cabinet if not now, it has been full of trators, while a part of Congress, like whipt pupies, are crawling to Slavry. Shame, Shame! Why don't this admi[ni]stration sustain the honor of this nation by protecting its property, its citizens, and execute its laws instead of tampering with trators.

Their is no Union of freedom and Slavery, one or the other must recede and disappear. then why compromise with Slavery. this nation will always have trouble while Slavery exists in it. then why not use all lawful means to bring Slavery to an end.

No doubt their is deep laid plots to prevent your inauguration, dont trust the Slave power (even the most conservative) for protection, if you do they will deceive you. Under God, have people of the free States for Council men, and soldiers, have plenty at Washington the quicker the better. Above all look to God through Jesus Christ for Grace and protection, is the wish of your friend—

With much Respect,

Willard Gladding.

Isaiah 58:6:

Is not this the fast that I have chosen? to loose the bands of wickedness, to undo the heavy burdens, and to let the oppressed go free, and that ye break every yoke?

Matthew, 22:37-40:

Jesus said unto him, Thou shalt love the Lord thy God with all thy heart, and with all thy soul, and with all thy mind. This is the great and first commandment. And a second is like unto it, Thou shalt love thy neighbour as thyself. On these two commandments hang all the law and the prophets.

Dunnington   Ten   Jan 21st 1861

Mr. Lincoln

Our Glorious Union is about to close. Let the world stand still and her sons and daughters hold their breath for the peace which cost our fathers blood will take wings and fly to heaven never to return to be trampled under foot by men who would sell their birth right for a mess of potage. The Lord has seen fit to show me in a dream the only way there is to save this Union. You are the only man on earth who can save this union? Will you do it? Have you the nerve the honor the love of your country in short have you the soul of a man? You will have more glory in this one act than you would have if you were president the rest of your life. Why did the lord in old times choose a female to fill so many important stations it was a female who saved moses and mary saved the life of our Lord & savior I have the honor of showing you how you can save your childrens homes to save the constitution and the Union you may have the honor I will with- hold my name from you and from the world. The con[s]ciousness to know I have done my duty is reward enough for me

This is your duty to Call on Mr. Stephen. A. Douglas, to take your place as president of these United States he must accept the offer for he is the peoples choice and they have confidence in him. all will go right never fear. Mr. Douglas must pay you one half the money he gets for being president or more if you wish it. He is a man of honor and will save his country without a dollar, no insult to you. I know this money would be yours if we had peace. If we have war at this time we will also have famine it will be all we can do to till our ground & save our people from famine we must not have war if we do your days are numbered. My father was shot in Jacksons war he was a Colonel at Taladego we have the bullet that was taken from his right arm. You must also appoint a day of prayer The young ladies & gentle of every county must march under a pure white linnen flag to & from church this must be done in evry county in the Union If this union is once broken up no power on earth could bind it together again if you spurn this little sheet woe to the world for who can say when war shal seace.

All this has been brought about by or on acount of the negrows who fare better than your poor white people.

Not four months ago at a tavern in one of your large Citys a beautiful young girl was on her knees rubbing the floor and a fine dressed rusty [?] negro man stood over her cursing her for not being faster. Was it right? no God made them black and strong to indure hardships and why do you place them over the weakly white. It is Gods will that you change put your negrows in a servants place and your whites over them if you would be hapy I am your friend

[Marginal notes as follows:]
(You must also send a pure white satin flag with ~~twenty~~ [sic] Thirty Two golden Stars on it in the name of the ladies of the united Stats to South Carolina to implore her to come back She as an undutiful child must first be pursuaided back. in haste a friend no one shal know of this if you listen to the warning. I have eleven children have taught school twenty years

(direct your letter to a lady Dunnington Tennessee.   I bare the name of my state Ten   if you or yours are ever in trouble call on me a freind in need is a friend

Under date of February 1, 1861, the most famous of American penmen, originator of a system of penmanship that had his name, Platt Rogers Spencer, a militant Abolitionist, sent a specimen of his elaborately shaded flourishes and the sentiment, "The Pen is mighty and so are our Bayonets."

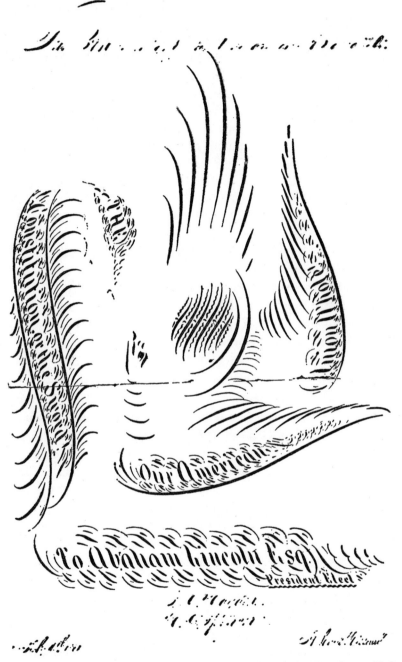

The famous penman, Spencer, writes to Lincoln. (*Original reduced one-third*)

Waterville   Jan 25 1861

Hon. A. Lincoln.

Dear sir. you will excuse me (a stranger) for writing you at this time, when your time is evidently, ubsorbed with, the momentous questions of the day. yes, sir, questions that, are of vast importance to all of us, and, in which, *all should* feel a deep interest. and, I am happy to inform you, we, of Minnesota are interested in. the great secession movement is, the theme on, every mans Tongue. it has driven away all party feudes and it is now, Union, or, no Union. We, Republicans, are all for the *Union, now and, for Ever* and a large majority of Democrats are on our side. We all feel that you have a critical, and important position to fill. just now, every one is en-quiring, "what will Lincoln do with them Southern traitors, and the re-sponce is, hang them. you will see by this that, we are for the Union, and in case their is a neceasity, Minnesota will be ready to assist you in maintaining, *to the last,* this glorious Confederacy of States, this free govern-ment, that cost our dear forefathers so much blood and treasure, and one that has been of so vast importance to us under it. we have grown prosperous and great, and we should not allow it to be torn asunder by a few disap-pointed demagogues. but sir I took up my pen to make a sad question in view of the great danger you will be in—(when you enter upon your presidential duties) of being assassinated it would be well that you be well guarded, you are hated with a perfect hatred, by, the miserable Traitors of the south and would take your life in an unguarded moment. indeed some of them have already threatened to stab you to the heart, before you should rule over them. in New Orleans there was a reward offered of $55,000 to any one that would take your life indeed we have fallen upon evil times and we shall all look to you for deliverance but to do so. your life must be preserved. our hope is in you. we are confident that you are the man for the times, if your life is spared, God grant that it my be.

—it has been sudgested here by many that you employ one or more persons, as a *body guard* and I think it would be a wise yea, a ne[ce]ssary pre-causion, against personell danger you may think this of no moment. but sir, how many valuable lives have been saved by the timely interferance of a friend now such a body guard, could, serve under the title of a servent, waiter, porter or any other you might apply to him to be always ready in times of danger armed and, equipped as you should direct. if you think such a precaution expedient, and want that I (as the one, or one of them) should serve you in that dangerous position, let me know at your earliest convenience. if you wish references, I can give you sufficient to establish my Republicnism, abilities, integrity, character, &c. addess the undersigned at Waterville, Leseuer Co, Minnesota

>I am most respectfully
>your obedient servent—
>John D. Hunt

January 25th 1861

Washington   Washington County   Penna

Mr Lincoln I take the liberty of sending a few lines to you with my respects to you and, your familys welfare The time has arrived that every good Citisen should look out for himself It is a duty incumbent on us You sir are on the eve of being placed in a very important situation before the American people as President of the Federal States Now sir what i wish to say that a great many of your friends are fearful you will not receive fair play with respect to your Occupiing the Presidentiat Chair during your term of office Now Sir we the people have not had a Republican officer to occupy that post for several years General Harrison livd but a Short time after he was Installd in office General Taylor livd but a short time after he took his seat A great many wise heads beleive he was not fairly dealt with after his arrival at Washington City When he passd through our town he was a hearty robust man for his age with a florid complexion

Now Sir be careful at the Kings table what meats and drink you take there might be poison in the cup Your life and health are precious Sir I hope you will form a Cabinet around you that will be an ornament to you and your country of men Fearing God and hating Covetousness excuse the liberty i have taken it is for your wefare [sic]—

I am Sir with sentiments of respect

>your Humble Servant   David Wylie

February 1st 1861.

Jerseyville Jersey County Illinois

Hon, Abraham Lincoln ⎱
Springfield Illinois   ⎰   Dear Sir,

A few days since I received a letter from a friend and relative of mine, who resides in Sumner County, Tennessee. I will take the priveledge of transcribing a portion of it for your perusal. "Our people seem to have lost all love for the Union. Some change in the policy of your section must soon occur, or you and I will soon be under different governments. There are no party distinctions in our resentments towards the North. We do not intend to live under Mr Lincoln except upon such condition as we will propose. By the way if you will promise not to tell Old Abe, as you are a cousin of mine I will whisper into your ears a family secret viz. That a project is on foot to prevent Old Abes inaugeration at Washington. I am for it. The Constitution from frequent violations has become null and void. I dont think any man has any right hencefourth to characterize the acts of another as unconstitutional, will you get out of humor If I do attempt to keep Old Abe upon his own soil? I hope not, the North Elected him, and I say with most southern men that he should stay North, and not come among those who he hates, and who hate him"

I have no comments to make but fear that there is a Treasonable plot forming in some of the southern States to prevent your inaugeration and overthrow the government. I send you this as your friend—trusting that God will bring the wrath of man to praise Him. and that he will give you wisdom—and Guide, direct, and protect you at all times.

Truly your friend

John C. Barr

Christley Run Jan 24th 1861. Alleghany Co. Va.

Dear Sir. Although you are an Entire Stranger to me I feel interested for your welfare, and the success of your Administration. I take this Liberty to address a few lines to you, By way of Caution when you go to the City of Washington, as I suppose you are apprised of the Bad feeling Existing against you in the Southern States. I think not on account of you being an abolitionist But on account of the loss of Money, Place, and Power, and as the Democrat motto is, Rule, or Ruin. it seams as they have lost the Power to Rule, they are Determined to Ruin. I mean the Leaders or would be Leaters. I think you should be well guarded when you go to Washington. Neither eat nor Drink with Pretended friends which are our worst enemies. I feel well satisfied that Harrison and Taylor were Poisoned By Pretended Friends. you being a stranger I hardley know how to address myself to you my apology is that I have well grounded fears that your life may be taken. if you Desire any refference to me as to my Charachter if you are acquainted with Allen Persinger, who lives in Schuyler County Illinois, refer to him. I must Close By saying I have the Honor of being your Sincear Strange Friend.

Achilles Dew

To Abraham Lincoln.

if you can get time Drop me a few lines and oblige your friend Direct to the Mountain House Craig Co, Va.

Cincinnati Jan 24/61

Hon A. Lincoln
        My Dr Sir
    I venture none of your friends inclined to congratulate you, and our country, and thank the God of the whole earth more than I did on your election, yet I never gave utterance to the feelings of my full heart in a line to you lest I should add to the weight of your numerous ever perplexing cares.
    I now beg your indulgence while I submit a few words for your consideration. I have no opinion to express, no suggestion to make about *men* or *measures*. I rest perfectly easy and well satisfied that your department of the government will be administered with prudence & skill, as well as firmness and efficiency according to well matured and *fixed principals*. And if I can have any influence at the court of heaven you and your constitutional advisers will be guided from above and divinely assisted in your difficult and important duties.
    What I now desire to say is, that, in these times of *political traders*, stock jobbers, and panic makers, as well as numerous desperados and traitors both north and south I fear your precious and valuable life *is in danger*. And it may be possible that many in *secret associations* have bound themselves by an oath, as in the case of St Paul, to take your life
    The midnight or noonday assassin may lie in wait for you. There may be corrupt men who would be willing to destroy many lives to reach your plate with poison. "WATCH" I hope the Lord will make you immortal until the 5th of March 1865 as he did George Washington until *his* work was done.

I am dear sir with much respect and sincere esteem your *friend*

John F. Wright

Hon A. Lincoln
Springfield Ill

Mr. L. may recognize my name as the same person who wrote him last septr and to whom he kindly replied

Pittsfield Ill. Feb 2ᵈ 1861

Mr. A. Lincon   I have known you by reputation for the last 15 years therefore think it my Indispensible duty of informeing you of three moste notorious villians that lives in Kansas they are collegued to gather in viliany and i can safely informe you that just so Shure as you trust them in power they are bound to deceive one is Mark W. Dellyhay and the other is Sias L. Nores and the other is winchel of wyandot in kasas Territory Delyhay followed me to leavenworth in 1858 i wos taken Sick thare and could not tend to business for some four weeks in this time Dellyhay informed me that a friend of his had a note calling for 1000 Dollars on mister winchel that wos just as good as the goald that he could get for Eight hundred Dollars and have the money Collected again in four weeks and he would collectit for me by Suing winchel the first term of Cort Cort came around he Informed me that winchel had got the suit put off and that his friend Novis had got a virginia State bond that wos worth ninety Eight cents to the dollar and that i should traid for that he could send to Newyork an get the returns for that in two weeks and i would Better traid for that so i haveing Confidence in him as he was my agent I traided for the bond and behold when i came to get the bond Examened it wos not worth any thing alall the bond was not avirginia State bond a tall which he recommend to me i sued them for fraud and they Rascallyed me out of it intirely I would advise you to Write to Doctor J. D. S. Haslet of Saint louis and he wil informe you of what villiany he practised on him His office South west corner fifth and Market streete Saint Louis Entrance on fifth Streete I can further informe you that he Rascaled his own father enlaw out of 500 Dollars and he made a bold attempt to wrong my wifes Little orphan Son out of what Money he had   Yours truly

Joseph Harshman

PS I refer you to OM Hatch
        M Hay [?] or
Lyman Scott of Leavenworth   I under stood that he Raskeled
Haselet out of 1500 Dollars

Dayton Ohio Feb 5th /61.

Hon. Abraham, Lincoln,
> Sir,

A constitutional majority of the american people has elected you to the high office of President of the United States.

Permit me, therefore, a woman, who could not contribute by my vote, to express my approbation of that election, by asking you to accept the accompanying garment [a shawl? a pair of socks?] made with my own hands.

If agreeable to you, it would please me much, if you would wear it on the occation of your Inauguration.

May Wisdom and Justice Signalize your administration; and may you, in the providence of God, be instrumental in placing upon the true and enduring foundation, of the constitution, the peace, prosperity and happiness of this great people; and in perpetuating the Union and glory of these States.

> I am Very Respectfully,
> Your Obt Servant,
> Mrs. Margaret M. Ackerman

THE HOT STOVE LETTERS

Fillmore La November 25th 1860

Old Abe Lincoln

God damn your god damned old Hellfired god damned soul to hell   god damn you and goddam your god damned family's god damned hellfired god damned soul to hell and god damnation god damn them and god damn your god damn friends to hell god damn their god damned souls to damnation god damn them and god dam their god damn families to eternal god damnation god damn souls to hell god damn them and God Almighty God damn Old Hamlin to[o] to hell God damn his God damned soul all over everywhere double damn his God damned soul to hell

Now you God damned old Abolition son of a bitch God damn you I want you to send me God damn you about one dozen good offices Good God Almighty God damn your God damned soul and three or four pretty Gals God damn you

And by so doing God damn you you

> Will Oblige

> Pete Muggins

Fillmore Ia Nov 25th 1860
Old Abe Lincoln
God damn your
god damned old Hellfire god damned
soul to hell god damn you and god dam
your god damned familys god damned
hellfired god damned soul to hell and
goddamnation god damn them and goddamn your goddamn frinds to hell goddam
thir god damned souls to damnation goddam
them and god dam thier god damn families
to eternal goddamnation god damn souls
to hell god damn them and God Almighty
God damn Old Hamlin to to hell god damn
his God damned soul God all over every wher
double damn his god damned soul to hell
Now you God damned old abolition
son of a bitch God damn you I want you
to send me God damn you about one
dozen good offices Good God Almighty
God damn your God damned Soul and
three or four pritty Gals God damn you
and by so doing God damn you you
will Olige
Pete Muggins

Pete Muggins tries for a malediction

Deformed Sir, The Ugly Club, in full meeting, have elected you an Honorary Member of the Hard-Favored Fraternity.—Prince Harry was lean, Flastaff was fat, Thersites was hunchbacked, and Slawkenbergus was renowned for the eminent miscalculation which Nature had made in the length of his nose; but it remained for you to unite all species of deformity, and stand forth the Prince of Ugly Fellows. In the bonds of Ugliness— Hinchaway Beeswax, President. Eagle-Eyed Carbuncle, Secretary of the Ugly Club.

Abraham Lincoln Esq
Sir

You will be shot on the 4th of March 1861 by a Louisiana Creole we are decided and our aim is sure.

A young creole.

BEWARE

Washington. D.C.
November 24. 1860

Dear Sir.

Caeser had his Brutus! Charles the First his Cromwell And the President may profit by their example.

From one of a sworn Band of 10 who have resolved to shoot you from the south side of the Avenue in the inaugural procession—on the 4th March 1861.

Vindex.

Sir,

This is to inform you that there is a club of 100 young men in this place who have sworn to murder you.

Jos Bradley
Jos Roints
Mike O'Brien

New Albany Ind. Jan/29/61

Hon. Abraham Lincoln
   Springfield Ills.
     Dear Sir

Read immediately, Sixth Chapter, Second Volume, Macaulay's History of England, character of King James—

Very truly
your
humble svt.
J. D. Cromwell

Washington. D.C.
November 24. 1860.

Dear Sir.

Cæsar had his Brutus! Charles the First his Cromwell! And the President may profit by their example!

From one of a sworn Band of 10 who have resolved to shoot you from the south side of the Avenue – in the inaugural procession – on the 4th March 1861.

Vindex.

Anonymous prediction of the day of death

Confession of motive to murder?

Hopkinton, Jan 29. 1861.

Sir,

Please excuse me for troubling you, but to be short, I want to know if a machine that will fire four or five hundred balls in a minute would be *worth* any thing, if it *is*, I *have it*.

Will you please give me your opinion.

Gilman C. Morgan
Hopkinton
New Hampshire.

A. Lincoln.

Grand Meadow Jan. 26/61

Mr. A. Lincoln

Dear Sir permit me to introduce myself to you in this letter I am a man that has had the misfortune to mortgage my house & cannot Rase the money to pay for it the mortgage & interest amounts to Seventy Six Dollars

Now if you will give me that amount of money you will Be well paid it will save my home the mortg was for the Entrance Monies if you send me $76 God noes you will get it Back agane as soon as I can Earn it if you send it to me you are trusting a stranger But you will never loose anything by it. answer my letter wheather you send the money or not

Youres truley

Asahel Green

Asahel Green

Grand Meadow

Mower Co.

Minnesata

Rockford Ills

Jan, 29/61

To Mr.

  Abraham Lincoln, Esq.

    Dr. Sir,

I take the Liberty to adress A few lines to you. perhaps you May be surprised at my doing so. but I trust that if your patience will allow you to peruse my somewhat lenghty letter, that you will forgive my presumpsion. My name is Josiah Bowles, and I live three miles west of Rockford Winebago, Co Ills. Well I have been in this country ten years, and the most part of that time I have been Engaged in Horse Stealing and Robbery and Counterfeiting. Now do not start and throw this paper into the fire, but hear me out. Now sir perhaps you are aware that there has been an Organnised band of such characters in this state for the Last ten or fiveteen years. well I am a member of that Band I was sent to Alton Penetentury for one year. in the year 1852, I staid my time out and Lost my Citizenship. Now sir I just have been reading the History of your life, and believeing you to be a man that will do as you agree to, and also haveing the power, I wish to make the following proposition to you. On the 29, of Last March at Ottumwa, Iowa, Mapelo co, One Lunt Mc Combe Murdered Laura Harvey, and George Lawrence, who left this place (Rockford) on the 16 of last March, in Company with said Lunt Mc Combe. well, the Govenerr of Iow[a], Mr. Kirkwood, has offered $500.00 dollars, and the Citizens of Ottumwa $500.00, and the county of Winebago the like sum, makeing fiveteen hundred dollars $1500.00 reward. Now Sir I am willing to inform you where he can be found, and also to give you such information as will enable you to Break up the whole gang, and also to get the persons (if not got) who Robbed the bank of S. S. Phelps and co. at Oquaka Ills, on the 2 of Jan last of $10,000, ten thousand dollars, providing you will endeavour to get my Cittizenship restored, and allow me to have one half of the reward, for I have come to the conclusion that sooner or later if I do not quit this life I will get catched again, and I think that if I can get on the right side of the law again I can keep so My situation, at the present time is not very Agreeable I assure you

For on one side I am hunted by the law, on the other watched by my comrads. Now if you think curious that I do not go to C. A. Bradley, or Pinke[r]ton of Chicago (who are Detectivs) or to the Sheriff of this county, and make them this offer, I can give you my reasons for not doing so I am afraid to trust them for, I doubt their veracity and truth very much, and they have not the power to get my Cittizenship restored, Now Mr. Lincoln if you will send some man up here to me, who is an Officer, and send me a paper written by yourself that if I do as I have agreed too, that you will help me as I have hereinbefore mentioned and give me one half of the mony received by you as rewards, for these men you will find that, though I am what I am, I can keep my word, with them that keep it with me. if you conclude to to [sic] do this you can send a man to Rockford, then come three miles west to One Riley Halls, and within Sight of his house, on farther west, about 40 rods, there is a little red house on the south side of the road, well stop there and inquire for Joe and the folks will tell you where I am, do not ask any questions, of the folks, only inquire where Joe is, (do not let any person see this letter except your (friends) do not let Bradley of Chicago see it. I have to write this with a lead pencil, in an Old Stable if you do not take the matter up, please drop me a line So that I will know that you have got this. Direct your letter to James Logan, Rockford Winebago co Ills, if you Send send quick, or write quick Yours, Respectfully,

Josiah, Bowles

THE BONFIRE LETTERS

One winter morning in early 1861 there was a little bonfire going on in the alley back of the Lincoln house in Springfield, Illinois. A woman stood by watching the fire. She was Mrs. Abraham Lincoln. From a house opposite came a woman, on a fast walk, saying as she came into the alley, "Good morning, Mrs. Lincoln. What are you doing here?"

"Just burning some old letters we don't want to take to Washington."

"Why can't you let me have some of them?"

"Well, I guess you're welcome to them."

Then out of the black ashes the woman's fingers managed to scrape five letters that the flames hadn't touched. She spoke her thanks to Mrs. Lincoln and took the five letters home.

Somewhat like this the story was often told, here and there in Springfield. More than seventy-five years after, there were men who wondered what might be in the letters and whether the letters still existed. In the course of time they learned that it was a man and not a woman who had plucked the letters from the alley bonfire. They located the man's granddaughter in Jacksonville, Illinois—Mrs. Laura Jane Hopper. Alexander Hannah, boon companion and fellow collector with Barrett, asked if it could be true that some letters had been saved out of an alley bonfire started by Mrs. Lincoln. This was so, Mrs. Hopper assured Hannah. And she still had the letters, had kept them through a rather long term of years. In the end they passed to Barrett and Hannah, who divided them.

Two of the letters that Mary Todd Lincoln in housecleaning hurry and worry, in preparation for Executive Mansion occupancy in Washington, came so near destroying carry intimate domestic exchanges between Lincoln and his wife. From Mrs. Hopper later came a letter to Barrett saying, "My grandfather Jared P. Irwin lived just across the street from Mr. Lincoln. They were neighbors and friends. When the family broke up the house some letters were thrown out to be burned. My grandfather picked these up as a souvenir. My mother kept them for years and then bequeathed them to me."

The letters give somewhat the tones and voices of the Lincoln marriage at its best, periods of connubial serenity. They give support to the impression that whatever there might have been of bliss or strife in the Lincoln household, there were, at times, amicable discourse and even plain domestic happiness.

Washington, April 16, 1848.

Dear Mary:

In this troublesome world we are never quite satisfied. When you were here, I thought you hindered me some in attending to business; but now, having nothing but business—no variety—it has grown exceedingly tasteless to me. I hate to sit down and direct documents, and I hate to stay in this old room by myself. You know I told you in last Sunday's letter, I was going to make a little speech during the week; but the week has passed away without my getting a chance to do so; and now my interest in the subject has passed away too. Your second and third letters have been received since I wrote before. Dear Eddy thinks father is "gone tapila." Has any further discovery been made as to the breaking into your grandmother's house? If I were she, I would not remain there alone. You mention that your Uncle John Parker is likely to be at Lexington. Don't forget to present him my very kindest regards.

I went yesterday to hunt the little plaid stockings as you wished; but found that McKnight has quit business and Allen had not a single pair of the description you give and only one plaid pair of any sort that I thought would fit "Eddy's dear little feet." I have a notion to make another trial to-morrow morning. If I could get them, I have an excellent chance of sending them. Mr. Warrich Tunstall, of St. Louis is here. He is to leave early this week and to go by Lexington. He says he knows you and will call to see you; and he voluntarily asked if I had not some package to send to you.

I wish you to enjoy yourself in every possible way, but is there no danger of wounding the feelings of your good father by being so openly intimate with the Wickliffe family?

Mrs. Broome has not removed yet; but she thinks of doing so to-morrow. All the house—or rather, all with whom you were on decided good terms—send their love to you. The others say nothing.

Very soon after you went away I got what I think a very pretty set of shirt-bosom studs—modest little ones, jet set in gold, only costing 50 cents a piece or $1.50 for the whole.

Suppose you do not prefix the "Hon." to the address on your letters to me any more. I like the letters very much but I would rather they should not have that upon them. It is not necessary, as I suppose you have thought, to have them come free.

Are you entirely free from headache? That is good—good considering it is the first spring you have been free from it since we were acquainted. I am afraid you will get so well, and fat, and young, as to be wanting to marry again. Tell Louisa I want her to watch you a little for me. Get weighed and write me how much you weigh.

I did not get rid of the impression of that foolish dream about dear Bobby till I got your letter written the same day. What did he and Eddy think of the little letters father sent them? Dont let the blessed fellows forget father.

A day or two ago Mr. Strong, here in Congress, said to me that Matilda would visit here within two or three weeks. Suppose you write her a letter, and enclose it in one of mine, and if she comes I will deliver it to her, and if she does not, I will send it to her.

Most affectionately

A. Lincoln.

Lexington May—48—

My Dear Husband—

You will think indeed, that *old age*, has set *its seal*, upon my humble self, that in few or none of my letters, I can remember the day of the month, I must confess it as one of my peculiarities; I feel wearied & tired enough to know, that this is *Saturday night*, our *babie's* are asleep, and as Aunt Maria B. is coming in for me tomorrow ~~night~~, morning, I think the chances will be rather dull that I should answer your last letter tomorrow— I have just received a letter from Frances W. it related in an *especial* manner to THE BOX, I had desired her to send, she thinks with you (as good persons generally agree) that it would cost more than it would come to, and it might be lost on the road, I rather expect she has examined the specified articles, and thinks as *Levi* says, they are *hard bargains*— But it takes so many changes to do children, particularly in summer, that I thought it might save me a few stitches— I think I will write her a few lines this evening, directing her not to send them— She says Willie is just recovering from another spell of sickness, Mary or none of them were well— Springfield she reports as dull as usual— Uncle S—— was to to leave there on yesterday for Ky— Our little Eddy, has recovered from his little spell of sickness— Dear boy, I must tell you a little story about him— Boby in his wanderings to day, came across in a yard, a little kitten, *your bobby*, he says he asked a man for it, he brought it triumphantly to the house, as soon as Eddy, spied it—his *tenderness*, broke forth, he made them bring it *water*, fed it with bread himself, with his *own dear hands*, he was a delighted little creature over it, in the midst of his happiness Ma came in, she you must know dislikes the whole cat race, I thought in a very unfeeling manner, she ordered the servant near, to throw it out, which of *course*, was done, Ed—screaming & protesting loudly against the proceeding, *she* never appeared to mind his screams, which were long & loud, I assure you— Tis unusual for her *now a days*, to do any thing quite so striking, she is very obliging & accommodating, but if she thought any of us, were on her hands again, I believe she would be *worse* than ever— In the next moment she appeared in a good humor, I know she did not intend to offend me— By the way, she has just sent me up a glass of ice cream, for which this warm evening, I am duly grateful— The country is so delightful I am going to spend two or three weeks out there, it will doubtless benefit the children— Grandma has received a letter from Uncle James Parker of Miss saying he & his family would be up by the (county?) fifth of June, would remain here some little time & go on to Philadelphia to take their oldest daughter there to school, I believe it would be a good chance for me to pack up & accompany them— You know I am so fond of *sight-seeing*, & I did not get to New York or Boston, or travel the lake route— But perhaps, dear husband, like the *irresisti*be *Col Mc*, cannot do without his wife next winter, and must needs take her with him again— I expect you would cry aloud against it— How much, I wish instead of writing, we were together this evening, I feel very sad away from you— Ma & myself rode out to Mr. Bell's splendid place this afternoon, to return a call, the house and grounds are magnificent, Frances M would *have died* over their rare exotics— It is growing late, these summer eves are short, I expect my long *scrawls*, for truly such they are, weary you greatly, if you come on, in July or August *I* will take you to the springs— Patty Webbs', school in S— closes the first of July, I expect Mr. Webb, will come on for her, I must go down about that time & carry on quite a flirtation, you know *me*, always had a p*enchan*t that way— ~~With love,~~ I must bid you good night— Do not fear the children, have forgotten you, I was only *juesting*— Even E. eyes brighten at the mention of your name— My love to all— Truly yours,

M L—

THE CARPETBAG PAPERS

There were manuscripts Lincoln didn't care to burn or give away. These he put into a carpetbag that he turned over to Elizabeth Todd Grimsley. She remembered how distinctly he said to her, in effect, that this "literary bureau," as he termed it, was put in her charge and custody and if he should not return to Springfield for it, then she might dispose of the manuscripts as she thought best. This was in early 1861 and "Cousin Lizzie," as Lincoln called her, thought he spoke a little absent-mindedly, as though he had plenty else on his mind. The carpetbag held what of his writings he wished to preserve and he did not care to be encumbered with in Washington.

After the death of President Lincoln, Mrs. Grimsley would occasionally mention to friends the carpetbag of manuscripts, the "literary bureau" of writings. She would hear a request or a hint from one who would prize very dearly a paper that held handwriting of Lincoln. At least five times Mrs. Grimsley handed over a Lincoln manuscript to another person. Then came the sorry day when she still had the carpetbag but it was empty of Lincoln writings. There was no puzzle or mystery as to what had happened to the precious paper contents of the carpetbag. It was too utterly clear and simple. In good conscience and doing her best to keep the house clear of trash, working fast to "clean up and get things straightened," the naïve housemaid reported that she had taken these scrambled papers in this old carpet sack as rubbish that ought to be burned and out of the way—so she burned them.

Years later Barrett in a series of interviews managed to trace down and locate five of these carpetbag manuscripts. These include two fragments of memoranda on slavery, one on the Constitution, the nine sheets on which Lincoln wrote his lecture on "Discoveries and Inventions" delivered in 1859 in various places and on February 22, 1860, before the Springfield Library Association. Parts of the lecture read:

. . . Now, it was the destined work of Adam's race to develope, by discoveries, inventions, and improvements, the hidden treasures of this mine. But Adam had nothing to turn his attention to the work. If he should do anything in the way of invention, he had first to invent the art of invention —the *instance*, at least, if not the *habit* of observation and reflection. As might be expected he seems not to have been a very observing man at first; for it appears he went about naked a considerable length of time, before he even noticed that obvious fact. But when he did observe it, the observation was not lost upon him; for it immediately led to the first of all inventions, of which we have any direct account—*the fig-leaf apron.*

We have all heard of young America. He is the most current youth of the age. Some think him conceited and arrogant; but has he not reason to entertain a rather extensive opinion of himself? Is he not the inventor and owner of the present, and sole hope of the future? Men and things, everywhere, are ministering unto him. Look at his apparel, and you shall see cotton fabrics from from Manchester and Lowell; flax linen from Ireland; wool cloth from Spain; silk from France; furs from the arctic region; with a buffalo-robe from the Rocky Mountains, as a general outsider. At his table, besides plain bread and meat made at home, are sugar from Louisiana, coffee and fruits from the tropics, salt from Turk's Island, fish from Newfound-

mind.—But Adams had nothing to turn his attention to the work.—If he should do anything in the way of invention, he had first to invent the art of invention—the instance at least if not the habit of observation and reflection.—As might be expected he seems not to have been a very observing man at first; for it appears he went about naked a considerable length of time before he even noticed that obvious fact.—But when he did observe it, the observation was not lost upon him; for it immediately led to the first of all inventions, of which we have any direct account— the fig-leaf apron.—

Fragment from Lincoln's written lecture on Discoveries and Inventions

land, tea from China, and spices from the Indies. The whale of the Pacific furnishes his candle-light, he has a diamond ring from Brazil, a gold watch from California, and a Spanish cigar from Havana. He not only has a present supply of these, and much more; but thousands of hands are engaged in producing fresh supplies, and other thousands in bringing them to him. The iron horse is panting and impatient to carry him everywhere in no time; and the lightening stands ready harnessed to take and bring his tidings in a trifle less than no time. He owns a large part of the world, by right of possessing it, and also the rest by way of wanting it, and INTENDING to have it. As Plato had for the immortality of the soul, so Young America has "a pleasing hope, a fond desire—a longing after" territory. He has a great passion—a perfect rage—for the *"new"*; particularly new men for office, and the new earth mentioned in the *revelations*, in which, being no more sea, there must be about three times as much land as in the present. He is a great friend of humanity; and his desire for land is not selfish, but merely an impulse to extend the area of freedom. He is very anxious to fight for the liberation of enslaved nations and colonies, provided, always, they *have* land, and have *not* any liking for his interference. As to those who have no land, and would be glad of help from any quarter, he considers *they* can afford to wait a few hundred years longer. In knowledge he is particularly rich. He knows all that can possibly be known; inclines to believe in spiritual rappings, and is the unquestioned inventor on "*Manifest Destiny*." His horror is for all that is old, particularly "Old Fogy"; and if there be anything old which he can endure, it is only old whiskey and old tobacco. . . .

. . . speech alone, valuable as it ever has been and is, has not advanced the condition of the world much. This is abundantly evident when we look at the degraded condition of all those tribes of human creatures who have no considerable additional means of communicating thoughts. Writing, the art of communicating thoughts to the mind through the eye is the great invention of the world. Great is the astonishing range of analysis and combination which necessarily underlies the most crude and general conception of it—great, very great, in enabling us to converse with the dead, the absent, and the unborn, at all distances of time and space; and great not only in its direct benefits, but greatest help to all other inventions. Suppose the art, with all conceptions of it, were this day lost to the world, how long, think you, would it be before Young America could get up the letter A with any adequate notion of using it to advantage? The precise period at which writing was invented is not known, but it certainly was as early as the time of Moses; from which we may safely infer that its inventors were very old fogies.

Webster, at the time of writing his dictionary speaks of the English Language as then consisting of seventy or eighty thousand words. If so, the language in which the five books of Moses were written must at that time, now thirty-three or -four hundred years ago, have consisted of at least one quarter as many, or twenty thousand. When we remember that words are sounds merely, we shall conclude that the idea of representing those sounds by marks, so that whoever should at any time after see the marks would understand what sounds they meant, was a bold and ingenious conception, not likely to occur to one man in a million in the run of a thousand years. And when it did occur, a distinct mark for each word, giving twenty thousand different marks first to be learned, and afterwards remembered, and would present such a difficulty as would lead to the conclusion that the whole thing was impracticable. But the necessity still would exist; and we may readily suppose that the idea was conceived, and lost, and re-produced, and dropped, and taken up again and again, until at last the thought of dividing sounds into parts, and making a mark, not to represent a whole sound, but only a part of one, and then of combining those marks, not very many in number, upon principles of permutation, so as to represent any and all of the whole twenty thousand words, and even any additional number, was somehow conceived and pushed into practice. This was the invention of phoenetic [sic] writing, as distinguished from the clumsy picture writing of some of the nations. That it was difficult of conception and execution is apparent, as well by the foregoing reflection, as by the fact that so many tribes of men have come down from Adam's time to our own without having possessed it. Its utility may be conceived by the re-flection that to it we owe everything which distinguishes us from savages. Take it from us, and the Bible, all history, all science, all government, all commerce, and nearly all social intercourse go with it. . . .

And yet for the three thousand years during which printing remained un-discovered after writing was in use, it was only a small portion of the people who could write, or read writing; and consequently the field of invention, though much extended, still continued very limited. At length printing came. It gave ten thousand copies of any written matter quite as cheaply as ten were given before; and consequently a thousand minds were brought into the field where there was but one before. This was a great gain—and history shows a great change corresponding to it—in point of time.

I will venture to consider it the true termination of that period called "the dark ages." Discoveries, inventions, and improvements followed rapidly, and have been increasing their rapidity ever since. The effects could not come all at once. It required time to bring them out; and they are still coming. The *capacity* to read could not be multiplied as fast as the *means* of reading. Spelling-books just began to go into the hands of the children, but the teachers were not very numerous or very competent, so that it is safe to infer they did not advance so speedily as they do nowadays. It is very probable—almost certain—that the great mass of men, at that time, were utterly unconscious that their *condition* or their *minds* were capable of improvement. They not only looked upon the educated few as superior beings, but they supposed themselves to be naturally incapable of rising to equality. To emancipate the mind from this false underestimate of itself is the great task which printing came into the world to perform. It is difficult for us *now* and *here* to conceive how strong this slavery of the mind was, and how long it did of necessity take to break its shackles, and to get a habit of freedom of thought established. . . .

Lincoln rated his effort at a lecture as rather poor. We have here a letter of April 7, 1860, declining a lecture engagement, and "I am not a professional lecturer—have never got up but one lecture; and that, I think, rather a poor one. Besides, what time I can spare from my own business this season, I shall be compelled to give to politics."

Among the items that got away as gift or loan before the carpetbag contents were burned was a fragment on slavery:

FRAGMENT ON SLAVERY [1854?]

. . . The ant, who has toiled and dragged a crumb to his nest, will furiously defend the fruit of his labor, against whatever robber assails him. So plain, that the most dumb and stupid slave that ever toiled for a master, does constantly *know* that he is wronged. So plain that no one, high or low, ever does mistake it, except in a plainly *selfish* way; for although volume upon volume is written to prove slavery a very good thing, we never hear of the man who wishes to take the good of it, by being a *slave himself*.

Most governments have been based, practically, on the denial of the equal rights of men, as I have, in part, stated them; ours began by *affirming* those rights. *They* said, some men are too *ignorant*, and *vicious*, to share in government. Possibly so, said we; and, by your system, you would always keep them ignorant and vicious. We proposed to give *all* a chance; and we expected the weak to grow stronger, the ignorant, wiser; and all better, and happier together.

We made the experiment; and the fruit is before us. Look at it—think of it. Look at it in its aggregate grandeur, of extent of country, and numbers of population—of ship, and steamboat, and railroad.

One manuscript stood out over all other of the carpetbag findings—two sheets on which Lincoln wrote what he was to say in 1858 in his speech in Springfield, Illinois, closing the stormy campaign of that year for United States Senator. Election day was November 2, and on October 30 William H. Herndon wrote from Springfield to Theodore Parker in Boston that in a little while Mr. Lincoln would open on the square, close to the State House, on the great vital and dominant issues of the day and age.

A railroad train of nine cars had arrived from Jacksonville and intermediate

Lizzie Gilmer, Postmistress, Pittsfield, Illinois

Martha Short Marsh in later years

Reverend George J. Barrett, father of Oliver R. Barrett

Ellen Watson Barrett, mother of Oliver R. Barrett

Ax handle with jackknife signature, A. Lincoln, dated New Salem, 1834

Rail fence and log cabin of Lincoln family, Goose Nest Prairie, near Charleston, Illinois. Here Barrett located letters and papers of family and kin. Young Lincoln helped his father build cabin

No Exercise Multiplication

There were 40 men concerned in paying
a sum of money and each man paid 12 7¼
how much was paid in all———

```
  12 7¼
    40
40)50840
  12 7¼
```

If 1 foot contain 12 inches I demand how ^many there
are in 126 feet———

```
        126
         12
        252
        126
   12)1512
       126
```

# of Compound Division

Q What is compound Division

A When several numbers of Divers Denomination
are given to be divided by 1 common divisor this called
Compound Division———

```
   £  S  D
2)18--12--6½
  24--6--3¾
        2
  18--12--6½
```

```
   Cb  0½  dr
5)46--12--10
  9--5--113
        5
  46  12--10
```

Abraham Lincoln His Book

Walking along this sidewalk, Lincoln turned in to building at end of block and walked up to the second floor to the law office of Lincoln and Herndon. Original photograph of west side of square, Springfield, Illinois, 1858

Yours truly,
A. Lincoln.

The small cartes de visite signed by Lincoln are scarce, but the large photograph autographed by Lincoln is almost nonexistent. Of the latter, Barrett has never seen an advertisement of one offered for sale and across the years has acquired only two

"A rare item" in collectors' lingo. One of the two instances in the Barrett Collection where Lincoln authenticated a photograph as a likeness of himself

Charles F. Gunther, candy man and collector

Dennis F. Hanks on exhibition as the man who "learnt Abe Lincoln how to read and write"

The aged Dennis F. Hanks, cousin of Abraham Lincoln

points to the south, while from McLean and Logan counties to the north came another train of thirty-two cars bringing some four thousand passengers, two locomotives, flags and bunting, singing and yelling, cheers for Lincoln, jeers for the opposition. Thousands of wagons, buggies, gigs, saddled horses, delegations flying banners and streamers, had poured into Springfield. At twelve o'clock noon a crowd of ten thousand had swarmed in and around State House Square, so the *Springfield Journal* estimated. Two days later, having had Saturday night and Sunday in which to get and to write a report of at least a part of Lincoln's speech, the *Springfield Journal* gave its readers no sentence, phrase, or word of what Lincoln said. The reporter raved over the size of the outpouring, as a sign of victory on election day three days later, which victory fizzled.

As Barrett lived with the manuscript of this unreported speech he meditated with regret that what Lincoln said one October day in his home town closing a long and fierce campaign should have been ignored and lost. It deserved national attention and discussion, presenting a Lincoln possessed of more patience and magnanimity than was generally understood, and particularly in the South. There came from Barrett his one book, published by the University of Chicago Press in 1924, titled *Lincoln's Last Speech in Springfield in the Campaign of 1858*. In his introduction Barrett wrote, "It is of interest that the speech delivered by Abraham Lincoln on that day should be now first published, after the lapse of more than sixty-five years." Amid records of other related periods in the book is a long reprint from the *Springfield Journal* of November 1, 1858, reporting everything of importance in the day except Mr. Lincoln's speech. A lifetime student of Lincoln utterance, Roy P. Basler, hears new tones in this occasion, "an avowal of faith and resignation, phrased with lyric calm and cadenced beauty of expression which Lincoln had never before equaled, and would afterward excel only in the three or four passages that are graven in the mind of humanity more permanently than in the granite of all monuments to his greatness." A sober appeal, in an hour of hair-trigger tension, the speech reads:

My friends, to-day closes the discussions of this canvass. The planting and the culture are over; and there remains but the preparation, and the harvest. I stand here surrounded by friends—some *political, all personal* friends, I trust. May I be indulged, in this closing scene, to say a few words of myself. I have borne a laborious, and, in some respects to myself, a painful part in the contest. Through all, I have neither assailed, nor wrestled with any part of the constitution. The legal right of the Southern people to re-claim their fugitives I have constantly admitted. The legal right of Con-

their institution

gress to interfere with ~~slavery~~ in the states, I have constantly denied. In resisting the spread of slavery to new territory, and with that, what appears to me to be a tendency to subvert the first principle of free government itself my whole effort has consisted. To the best of my judgment I have labored *for*, and not *against* the Union. As I have not felt, so I have not expressed any harsh sentiment towards our Southern brethren. I have con-stantly declared, as I really believed, the only difference between them and us, is the difference of circumstances.

I have meant to assail the motives of no party, or individual; and if I have, in any instance (of which I am not conscious) departed from my purpose, I regret it.

I have said that in some respects the contest has been painful to me. Myself, and those with whom I act have been constantly accused of a purpose to destroy the Union; and bespattered with every imaginable [sic] odious epithet; and some who were friends, as it were but yesterday have made themselves most active in this. I have cultivated patience, and made no attempt at a retort.

Lincoln writes of personal motives in speech closing 1858 senatorial campaign. (*Slightly reduced from original*)

Ambition has been ascribed to me. God knows how sincerely I prayed from the first that this field of ambition might not be opened. I claim no insensibility to political honors; but today could the Missouri restriction be restored, and the whole slavery question replaced on the old ground of "toleration by *necessity* where it exists, with unyielding hostility to the spread of it,["] on principle, I would, in consideration, gladly agree, that Judge Douglas should never be *out*, and I never *in*, an office, so long as we both or either, live.

Before the word "both" Lincoln wrote the word "be." Presumably at first he meant to write "so long as we be both, or either, *alive*." Then, not crossing out the word "be," he got rid of it by the way it reads.

The *Louisville Courier-Journal* in comment on the speech after its publication in Barrett's book found its authorship unmistakable and said:

Lincolnian in every sentence this little address is likely to take rank with the two inaugurals and the letter to Mrs. Bixby.

Like the first inaugural and the letter to Mrs. Bixby, the Springfield utterance frequently employs the first personal pronoun, and employs it with the fine sense of humility with which the "I" is invested in so many of Lincoln's letters and addresses. Like all his great utterances, this one is steeped in human sympathy. Fair, generous, soundly reasoned, it is all-logical one moment, all poetical the next. . . .

One touch. "Through all I have neither assailed nor wrestled with any part of the Constitution," would identify this speech as Lincoln's. Another sentence— "As I have not felt, so I have not expressed any harsh sentiment toward our Southern brethren"—followed as it is by "I have constantly declared, as I really believed, the only difference between them and us is the difference of circumstances," is a natural forerunner of his "We are friends, we must not be enemies" in the first inaugural, and forerunner, also, of the "With malice toward none and with charity for all," of his second inaugural. Withal, Lincoln's passion for the Union is interwoven in the warp and woof of this Springfield speech—a passion that subordinated all else in his life.

"The legal right of the South to reclaim their fugitives I have always admitted," may shock some persons nowadays who do not know Lincoln as they think they do. Into his "To the best of my judgment I have labored for and not against the Union," is poured the one overwhelming passion to which Lincoln's life was consecrated. . . .

Lincolnian in every line, the Springfield address will be treasured by everyone who loves the nation Lincoln lived for and died for.

The *Louisville Courier-Journal* was not yet through. Another day and it came back to Lincoln's Springfield speech of October 30, 1858, under the heading "The Reporters Missed It." The sense of history, the flair for a great event, the instinct for contemporary record of a fine performance in its very hour and moment—where was it? With dignity and ironic humor the *Courier-Journal* recited an affair of neglected eloquence.

This speech marks the peak of Lincoln's argument in favor of the Union and opens the way for the high achievement of his later life in his unwearied effort to keep the nation whole, to destroy the institution of slavery and to maintain the liberal, in contra-distinction from the strict, interpretation of the Constitution. With its delivery, Lincoln the partisan becomes Lincoln the patriot, Lincoln the dialectician becomes Lincoln the statesman.

As already indicated by *The Courier-Journal*, the Springfield speech significantly harks back to the "house-divided-against-itself" speech made earlier in the Senatorial campaign of 1858, and points forward to the second inaugural address wherein Lincoln's tolerance and generosity were revealed in his "With malice toward none, with charity for all" pronouncement. It is thus that the Springfield address becomes the keystone in the arch of Lincoln's public utterances.

In view of the rare qualities of this short speech of Lincoln's, it is interesting to note how little attention was paid to it in the issue of the *Springfield Journal* of November 1, two days after the address was made. The *Journal's* account of the meeting takes up almost six columns of the little newspaper.

"At 2 o'clock," begins paragraph nine of this report, "the vast multitude being congregated around the stand, Mr. Lincoln began his speech." Then comes this masterpiece in the art of reporting a political meeting:

> We have neither time nor room to give even a sketch of his remarks today. Suffice it to say, the speech was one of his very best efforts, distinguished for its clearness and force, and for the satisfactory manner in which he exposed the roorbacks and misrepresentations of the enemy. The conclusion of this speech was one of the most eloquent appeals ever made to the American people. It was received with spontaneous bursts of enthusiasm unequalled by anything whatever before enacted in this city. . . . Mr. L. was followed by the Hon. Richard Yates of Morgan, who held the vast multitude enchained by his eloquence until near 6 o'clock, when the crowds dispersed to obtain some refreshment and prepare for the evening. . . . A very large meeting assembled in the rotunda of the Court House after supper . . . and adjourned with nine rousing cheers for Lincoln and the cause.

Six columns of labored description, stilted narrative and commonplace characterization and not one word of a speech that was made not for an age, but for all time!

Evidently, "Mr. L." had failed at Springfield almost as dismally as he was to fail five years later at Gettysburg, to engage the services of what nowadays would be called "a competent press agent." Enthusiastic reporters at Springfield were so moved by "the unpropitious weather," the "incoming crowds," "the beautiful display," "the amusing and pungent mottoes which abounded on all sides," "the gaily decorated stores and public buildings," "banners flying and flags flying," "marching and counter-marching through the streets" and many another spectacular feature, that forty-eight hours after the speech was heard they had "neither time nor room to give even a sketch of his remarks." These enthusiastic newspaper reporters at Springfield failed thereafter to find time or room for the reproduction of one of the greatest of speeches.

4. Lincoln Kith and Kin

Fire-Logs

Nancy Hanks dreams by the fire;
Dreams and the logs sputter,
And the yellow tongues climb,
Red lines lick their way in flickers.
Oh, sputter, logs.
         Oh, dream, Nancy.
Time now for a beautiful child.
Time now for a tall man to come.

Cornhuskers   Carl Sandburg
page 46.[1]

IN THE recently opened Robert T. Lincoln papers in the Library of Congress was a letter to Abraham Lincoln from his cousin Dennis Hanks, who had written to him in late May of 1849 of the sickness of his father Thomas Lincoln . . . "anxious to see you before He dies & I am told that His Cries for you for the last few days are truly Heart-Rendering. . . . He Craves to See you all the time . . . his only Child that is of his own flush & blood." Lincoln's anxiety and care for his father and his stepbrother are seen in a letter, of January 12, 1851, here in the Barrett

[1] From *Cornhuskers*, copyright Henry Holt and Company, 1918.

Collection, to John D. Johnston, then living with his mother and stepfather on the Goose Nest Prairie farm near Charleston, Illinois:

. . . You already know I desire that neither Father nor Mother shall be in want of any comfort either in health or sickness while they live; and I feel sure you have not failed to use my name, if necessary, to procure a doctor, or any thing else for Father in his sickness. My business is such that I could hardly leave home now, if it was not, as it is, that my own wife is sick abed. (It is a case of baby-sickness, and I suppose is not danger-ous.) I sincerely hope Father may yet recover his health, but at all events, tell him to remember to call upon, and confide in, our great, and good, and merciful Maker, who will not turn away from him in any extremity. He notes the fall of a sparrow, and numbers the hairs of our heads; and He will not forget the dying man who puts his trust in Him. Say to him that if we could meet now, it is doubtful whether it would not be more painful than pleasant; but that if it be his lot to go now, he will soon have a joyous meeting with many loved ones gone before; and where the rest of us, through the help of God, hope ere long to join them.

Lincoln writes to a stepbrother giving a message for his father. (*Reduced from original*)

This John D. Johnston, to whom Lincoln wrote so somberly, arrived at a curious reputation. He was a son of Sarah Bush Lincoln by her first hus-band. When she married Thomas Lincoln, Abraham Lincoln's father, she took the stepson as one of her own and there was between them a lasting depth of affection and understanding good to see. The two stepbrothers were about the same age and a law colleague, Henry C. Whitney, who had traveled much with Lincoln on the Eighth Circuit wrote of hearing Lincoln say as to himself and John D. Johnston that "they were raised together— slept together—and loved each other like brothers." Evidence runs that Thomas Lincoln seemed in early days to think more of his stepson John D. Johnston than he did of his own son. Neighbors said that Thomas liked the stepson for a fishing and hunting companion while Abe, as he said, was still "fooling himself with eddication." Neighbors did quote the father as saying of Abe and his books, "I tried to stop it but he's got that fool idea in his head and it can't be got out."

Ida Tarbell quoted a Mr. Booner, "When the Lincolns were getting ready to leave Indiana, Abraham and his stepbrother, John D. Johnston, came over to our house to swap a horse for a yoke of oxen. John did all of the talking. If anyone had been asked that day which would make the greatest success in life I think the answer would have been John Johnston."

Sorry and yet lovely, pointed and significant, were the words from Sarah Bush Lincoln after son and stepson were dead and she was asked about them. Her words: "I had a son, John, who was raised with Abe. Both were good boys; but I must say, both being now dead, that Abe was the best boy I ever saw, or ever expect to see." And from a clipping pasted in a scrapbook that Barrett had, with other contents, from an old trunk in the log cabin where Sarah Bush Lincoln lived with kinfolk, we read:

John D. Johnston is remembered by the early settlers of Coles County, Ill., as a foppishly dressed young constable, who made his nice clothes conspicuous in the vicinity of the abandoned town site of Richmond, three miles southwest of Mattoon. John Cunningham, one of the older residents of Coles County, says of him: "He was the Beau Brummel of Goose Nest Prairie, and would sport the best clothes to be had, regardless of whether they were ever paid or not. His relationship with Lincoln was that of a stepbrother, his mother having been the second wife of Thos. Lincoln, Abe's father, and the term shiftless fitted him in respect to his having no particular occupation. He was always prepared to make a pleasing address, and was smart for a young man of those days, but without other education than that acquired by contact with others. Some persons thought him a brighter man than the immortal Lincoln. Had Johnston lived in this age, he would have filled the niche of the dude to perfection."

Early in November 1851 Lincoln had been in Charleston, Illinois, among kinfolk. The news may have come to him that his stepbrother John D. Johnston was not only preparing for a fool sale of a farm but was also getting ready for his second wife, a girl of sixteen, so ran rumor and suspicion. Lincoln wrote a letter of rebuke, telling off the stepbrother for lazy, squirming, and crawling ways. A famous epistle, it has been widely and often reprinted. In these many reprints, however, it has most often happened that the closing lines have been omitted. These lines actually constitute a separate letter (see page 91). They have been described as the only known letter that Lincoln wrote to his cherished Sarah Bush Lincoln. He signed it "Sincerely your Son" after word had come to him from Augustus H. Chapman, whose wife was a daughter of Lincoln's cousin, Dennis Hanks, that Sarah Bush Lincoln would be welcome at their home.

Shelbyville, Nov. 4, 1851.

Dear Brother:

When I came into Charleston day before yesterday, I learned that you are anxious to sell the land where you live and move to Missouri. I have been thinking of this ever since, and cannot but think such a notion is utterly foolish. What can you do in Missouri better than here? Is the land any richer? Can you there, any more than here, raise corn and wheat and oats without work? Will anybody there, any more than here, do your work for you? If you intend to go to work, there is no better place than right where you are; if you do not intend to go to work, you cannot get along anywhere. Squirming and crawling about from place to place can do no good. You have raised no crop this year; and what you really want is to sell the land, get the money, and spend it. Part with the land you have, and, my life upon it, you will never after own a spot big enough to bury you in. Half you will get for the land you will spend in moving to Missouri, and the other half you will eat, drink, and wear out, and no foot of land will be bought. Now, I feel it is my duty to have no hand in such a piece of foolery. I feel that it is so even on your own account, and particularly on mother's account. The eastern forty acres I intend to keep for mother while she lives; if you will not cultivate it, it will rent for enough to support her—at least, it will rent for something. Her dower in the other two forties she can let you have, and no thanks to me. Now, do not misunderstand this letter; I do not write it in any unkindness. I write it in order, if possible, to get you to *face* the truth, which truth is, you are destitute because you have *idled* away all your time. Your thousand pretences for not getting along better are all nonsense, they deceive nobody but yourself. *Go to work* is the only cure for your case.

A word for Mother:

Chapman tells me he wants you to go and live with him. If I were you I would try it awhile If you get tired of it (as I think you will not) you can return to your own home. Chapman feels very kindly to you; and I have no doubt he will make your situation very pleasant.

Sincerely your Son

A. Lincoln.

On Barrett's first visit to the farm of Lincoln's father near Charleston, Illinois, and to the homes of Lincoln kinfolk in that neighborhood, he was told of the previous visits of William H. Herndon and others and learned that Herndon had secured all of the letters that had been written by Lincoln to the home folks. There was, however, an old trunk which it seemed that previous visitors had paid slight attention to or not seen at all. In this trunk the family papers had been kept and there were carefully preserved documents and letters dated from December 1813, legal papers signed by Thomas Lincoln and Sarah Bush Lincoln, in every instance Thomas signing his name in full and Sarah signing with her mark X. Included were papers of the Hall family who had moved with the Lincolns from Indiana to Goose Nest Prairie. Among these was a small-sized invitation, probably out of Indiana days, addressed to Squire Hall, which reads:

M^{ss} H. Watkins J Rose— managers	Present this Complement to Squire hall and Lady to attend a ball held at Jasper littles on the 19 of this instant p m

Here too were many letters of all the kinfolk, including Dennis Hanks and his children, some members of Sarah Bush's family, not forgetting letters, and an account book of John D. Johnston mostly concerning whisky sales. And the family had still retained the letters received from Herndon, the earliest being one of September 1865.

John D. Johnston, usually sporting fine clothes, for a short term was village constable. That was the height of his eminence. He married the young girl Nancy Williams. That he was going to marry her he kept hid from his stepbrother and the kin. If he had had his way he would have sold the ground away from under his mother's rocking chair. With Nancy Williams he heads for Taney County, Arkansas. And after a few months down in it is any improvement. I wish it in ernest, if possible, to get you to face the truth — which truth is, you are so careless because you have <u>idled</u> away <u>all</u> you time — Your thousand pretences for not getting along better, are all nonsense — they deceive nobody but yourself — <u>Go to work</u> is the only cure for your case —

A word for Mother:

Chapman tells me he wants you to go to and live with him — If I was you I would try it awhile — If you get tired of it (as I think you will not) you can re-turn to your own home — Chapman feels very kindly to you; and I have no doubt he will make your situation very pleasant —

Sincerely your son

A. Lincoln .

Arkansas is he a man of affairs? Are things up and coming and booming with him? He lets the folks back home know that they are. Has he got two double houses, a pretty start of young apple trees, peach trees, twenty-five improved acres, plus one hundred sixty acres of river bottom he is going to clear? He has. How did he get this farm? Before leaving Goose Nest Prairie, Illinois, he got Nancy's father and mother to sell their place and let him have the money for a new start in a new country. Also besides farming we learn from his letter back home he has bought him a distillery and is about to commence making whisky. From account books in the Barrett Collection we may know that John D. Johnston had his whisky customers back in Coles County, Illinois, letting them have the strong water at 50 cents a gallon, appearing too in his own records as a liberal buyer of his own merchandise.

He has "Corne a pleanty to winter 100 head of Cattle" and of his "20 Akers of good Corne Som Lows it will make 50 bushels to the Aker." Having reported how fair and fine are his prospects in his new Canaan, he prepares the minds of the Illinois folks for any future adverse events. He reminds them of a bank debt they owe. He gives assurance "Nance is one of the best of Wives" yet piles enough woe into one sentence to explain coming failure. "My family is all Kinda puney withe ague & I my Self & by us all gitting Sick it has nocked us out of Coming this fall & a nother thing I am afraid to under Take the Trip with Nancy for She miss Carried a Coming heir, & She is now in the Same fix." It was like him to refer to a miscarried infant as "a Coming heir" to his unrealized and insubstantial estate.

So we are now permitted a gaze at a portrait of John D. Johnston, self-revelatory, no rumormongers creating a false reputation, no busybodies gabbing about him, not naked but as he himself wished to appear to the folks back home in his new role of Arkansas lord of the manor and manufacturer serving the wants of dauntless drinking men.

Taney County Augst 3 1852

Dear Brother & Sister

I Take my pen in Hand, after a Long Time, a grable to prommis, all thow I Should have writin Suner to you, you must excuse me for not wrighting Suner, for I haddent Seen Much of the Country before now, & Coudent Tell you how I Liked it un till now. I am well pleasd, with My Exchange of Country both in furtility of Soile, & range for Stock, & Health of Countrys, & Climat & advantages of Market at home. This is a grate Stock growing Country & it is eaqualey good for Wheet as the North part of Illinois & as good for Irish Potattos & a gradeal better for Corne & Tobaco I am Living on the bank of White River my hous is with in 80 yeards of the River I & the Childern had the pleasure of Seeing Somthing the rise of 80 flat Bootes goe Down & Steame Boot the Youghagany Caring 65 Tones up the river to Foresythe & Back agane with hur Collers flying.

I Bought a place on White River a bout 25 Miles from pap Bankes it Cost me, one hundred & Sixty Dollar. Ther is Two Doble houses & good Blue-grass Loots & a very purty Start of young Apple Trees a bout a hundred Some of them Bore this year & any quantaty of peach Trees, & about 25 Akers of improvement & a bout a hundred & Sixty Akers of good River Bottom yet to Clear, & Three good Springs My place has ben settled 40 years & it is a bout 30 miles South of ForeSythe Just in the edge of Arkensas. I have Corne a pleanty to winter 100 head of Cattle a Winter I have a bout 20 Akers of good Corne Som Lows it will make 50 bushels to the Aker, I find every thing as Cheap here as I do in Illinois Flower is from $1.50 to 2.00 per hundred, we all got here Safe & Sound the 1st Day of March & found all of Fathers famley well & Doing Tollarble well, Tell Nancy They all receaved us with all the Kindness of a Sun & Daughter & that his Mother has broke very fast, but She nocks a round nearley as Same as ever I Dont think his father has broke but Very Lyttle all thow They all had the Sore eyes narley all Summer, & in August they all tuck the Ague & Jim & Charles Marion has Lived with Old man all Summer James has but a Clame a bout 4 miles from me Charles Lived with me till he got Married a bout the Last of July he married a girle a bout 20 years old by the name of Eady Stallcup Dick is Living on White River a bout 4 miles a bove me a Doing very well He owens the Land your Father Lives on I expect in regard to the Bank Debt, My famley is all Kinda puney withe ague & I my Self & by us all gitting Sick it has nocked us out of Coming this fall & a nother thing I am a fraid to under Take the Trip with Nancy for She miss Carried a Coming heir & She is now in the Same fix I have bought me a Distilery & wont to Commence maken Liqur in about 3 wekes I recon you found a bead, I wish you would Come & bring Tom & See a bout your bank Debt, They have opened a Lead mines a bout 7 milles from me I live in a bout 5 miles of a Town Cold Debucke it has 2 good Stores in it I wont you to answer this as soon as you git this Direct your Letters to Marion County, Worth Post Office Arkensas. Nance is one of the best of Wives.

J. D. Johnston &
Nancy Johnston

Lincoln's scalawag stepbrother, John D. Johnston, writes of his prospects

Not hitherto published, reposing many years in an underground steel archive, is a letter crying its own woe of toil and land. The language runs in a vernacular familiar to the boyhood and youth of Abraham Lincoln, the everyday words of his early formative years. The handwriting is in the indubitable cramped style of Dennis F. Hanks. He is writing to a crippled, thieving, scheming jailbird son of John D. Johnston. Dennis in writing "I have Bin to See old Abe" means to report that when he visited the Executive Mansion in Washington he talked with the President who still held, as he once wrote to the boy's father, "that that forty acres was Left for your grand mother's suport." The implication seems to be that the grandson, like his father, was hoping for sale and profit from the forty acres, and Dennis declared he will "prosed" (proceed) in action to protect the grandmother's ownership. The grandson, though signing himself with the initials T. L. D., seems, among the kin, to be called John. The vehemence, the blunt colloquial, the mention of tears, herein, are to be seen in other writings of Dennis F. Hanks. He wrote the date "June the 8th '64" and the text of a letter as follows:

John I want you to cum and take grand Mother and Keep hir untile I See that your ant lives or Not. It Looks Very strange to me ~~that~~ to no that you have nomore Simpany for your ant than you have that has waited on you a Many a time and Matilda allso John She has worked hir Self Down just at Such Biziness But the time has cum that you all cant trot a Round and She doo the worke for all John you would not no hir My hart is grieved with teres in my Eyes But it dooes No good now the thing is Dun Now John I have Bin to See old Abe and Now I Say to you that that forty acres of Land was Left for your grand Mother's suport and if you Don't tend to it I will tend to it for you Shore I am treated very Rang a Bout it you think that it Can't Be Dun But I will show you a Bout it But if you will rather pay the Back [or Bank?] Rent Rather than keep hir you Must Do it Shore take your Choise a Bout it one or the other has to Be Dun Shore Not one of them that She has cooked for and waited on is any a Count to hir now So cum and take your grand Mother from here untile your ant Lives or Dies I have packed shit and piss as long as I Entend to Do it is not a fitting place for your grand Mother I Entend to doo as I Say a Bout it Shore take your Chies I want to here from you a Meaditly for I Shall prosed in time

D. F. Hanks

The cousin, Dennis F. Hanks, writes of household and family toils and miseries

The Matilda (Mathilda) to whom he refers was a daughter of Sarah Bush Lincoln by her first marriage, and so a sister of John D. Johnston. Lincoln in his letters occasionally referred to his stepsister.

If called on, Dennis could prove that he had seen his cousin in the Executive Mansion in Washington. At least he could show a keepsake he had from his boyhood playmate. He was in his old age, his feet and legs not so good any more, and thirty-five years had passed since that trip to Washington when Eleanor Atkinson interviewed him and gave this account of it:

A shrill cry, like that from a frightened child awakened by a bad dream, came from the chair in the sheltered corner.

"Whar's my watch? Whar's my watch?" Old Dennis was searching his pockets frantically, and tottering to a fall. Mrs. Dowling rushed to him and set him upright.

"Here, father, here's your watch! No-body's going to take it from you. Uncle Abe gave him that watch, and he gets to dreaming that someone is trying to rob him of it." She restored his cane and hat, and disappeared into the kitchen again.

"Come 'ere," he beckoned mysteriously. "If you won't tell nobody I'll show you something!" He pulled from a secret, inside pocket, a heavy, old-fashioned coin-silver watch, with a steel chain.

"Abe gimme that."

"When Abe left home": hoping to start the stream of memory to flowing, without a break in its continuity. He looked puzzled. Memory had leaped a gap of thirty-five years, to the next dramatic event in that simple life.

"I went down to Washington to see Abe, an' thar he was with a big watch an' a chain spread over his wescoat. I plagued him about bein' so fine, an' he sez: 'Denny, I bet you'd carry a watch if you had one, you old coon.' He went out and bought this fur me an' I've carried it ever sence. Ain't many folks ever gits to see it. Thar's a feller up in Chicago that's plumb crazy over Abe, an' he offered me five hundred dollars fur it." He stowed the precious relic away carefully.

"I went down to Washington to see Abe about a neighbor that'd got into trouble." [1]

Less than a year after his Arkansas letter, John D. Johnston as farmer and distiller went broke, "busted flatter than a pancake," came back to a Mattoon, Illinois, neighborhood and soon died. At a later time discussions raged in the newspapers, which clippings we have here, as to whether the man died a natural death or met his death in a brawl or by drowning. His fade-away realized his stepbrother's prediction ". . . Part with the land you have, and, my life upon it, you will never after own a spot big enough to bury you in." The date of his death in the controversy varies by five years. Of the end of his young wife Nancy we know no more than of the vanished blue supper smoke that wreathes spiraling from a prairie log cabin.

The John D. Johnstons, elder and son, were exceptions in the Lincoln-Johnston-Hall kin. They were grotesques, groping for numbers and getting the unlucky. They didn't belong. When the war came most of the boys went to the front and made good records. Some of them had fighting fiber mingled with a gentler quality, as witness the Hall boy writing from a bloody field to a brother, ". . . you had better let him kut what he ows you rather than to have another fus, try and keep frindly with him if you can for i dont want to hear of you and him a fighting." Among twoscore other letters here we find others of the kin likewise not so good at grammar yet being vivid enough when there is something worth telling.

The son of John D. Johnston, by his first wife, appears in a relentless and shadowed narrative we meet in Henry C. Whitney's *Life on the Circuit with Lincoln*:

A mass meeting was held at Urbana, our county seat to which Lincoln came as one of the speakers and as soon as he saw me, he said: "I want to see you all

[1] From *The Boyhood Life of Lincoln* by Eleanor Atkinson, pp. 45-47.

to yourself." When we had got beyond the hearing of others, he said: "There is a boy in your jail I want to see, and I don't want any one to know it, except us. I wish you would arrange with the jailer to go there, on the sly, after the meeting, and let us in." I then recollected this crippled boy, and Lincoln explained to me that when his father married his second wife, she had a boy of about his own age (John D. Johnston), that they were raised together—slept together—and loved each other like brothers. This crippled boy was a son of that foster-brother, and he was tending to the bad rapidly. "He is already under a charge of stealing a gun at Charleston," said Mr. Lincoln sadly; "I shall do what I can for him in these two cases, but that's the last. After that, if he wants to be a thief, I shan't help him any more." The jail was a rude log cabin structure, in which prisoners were put in through a trap-door in the second story—there being no other entrances. So Lincoln and I were secretly admitted into the small enclosure surrounding the jail; and as we approached the one foot square hole through which we could converse with the prisoner he heard us and set up a hypocritical wailing, and thrust out toward us a very dirty Bible, which Lincoln took and turned over the leaves mechanically. He then said: "Where was you going, Tom?" The boy attempted to reply, but his wailing made it incoherent, so Lincoln cut him short by saying: "Now you do just what they tell you—behave yourself—don't talk to any one, and when court comes, I will be here and see what I can do. Now stop crying and behave yourself": and with a few more words we left, Lincoln being very sad: in fact, I never saw him more so.

At the fall court, Amzi McWilliams, the Democratic prosecuting attorney, came to me and said that he had consulted Judge Davis and they had agreed that if the Greens would come into court and state that they did not desire to prosecute further, he would *nol. pros.* the case.

That same evening, Lincoln and others were to speak at a church in Champaign, near by where the watch was stolen: and at my suggestion, Lincoln and I left the meeting, while some one else was speaking, and made our way to the humble residence of these people. They were a venerable old couple, and we found them seated in their humble kitchen, greatly astonished at our visit.

I explained our visit, and introduced Lincoln, who stated his position and wishes in the matter in a homely, plain way and the good old couple assented and the next day came into court and formally expressed themselves quite willing to have the boy released.

Lincoln afterward told me that he had got him released from the Charleston larceny in a similar way.

Thus ran life for the crippled son of John D. Johnston. His intercessor, his worthy and excellent mouthpiece who sprang the jail doors for him, had moved from Illinois to the District of Columbia and farther yet, wherefore he was not on hand when in the year 1868 the same crippled boy was again in jail. From two letters of the young fellow we can see that he was not the kind of blowhard and showoff that his father was. He hopes his health will not last long "if I am to have truble all my life," and one pleading runs, "It seames that I am unluckey in this life." He has been in jail two months at the writing of the first letter and nearly six months when he wrote the second. He refers to his three lawyers "thinking I would give them a Deed for my title to that 40 Acres." This land presumably is the same forty acres which Lincoln warned John D. Johnston not to sell because they were meant for the support of the mother. Also it is presumably the same forty acres that Dennis Hanks warned the boy not to try to get and sell. A trace of his father's wily but futile ways, laying schemes for the fascination of scheming, runs through the youth's hope of selling his claim to the forty acres, so as to "beate the case."

Springfeild Ills Jan 29th 1868

Dear cosen I drop you a few lines to let you know of my sad situation I was a rested on the 29 of November for being with a crowde who got in to a row with a fellow who was verry near killed but he is a live and well but at the time he was wounded verry dangersley. I had no hand in it. but my freinds don the work. but they arested me with them and bound me over untill next aprile turm of coart in a bond of (800). Eight hundred Dollers and I could not give baile so I had to go to jaile. I have ben here 2 month to day and have to stay 2 months more and then I will be free for thare is no evidance a gainst me that will convicked me. I have rote to John Hall to find oute where my Brothers are stoping at. for I want to know where they are at. but John has treeted me with contemped he has not rote me a line and I have rote him 3 letters now Jane I want you to answer this as son as you git it. give my respects to libe and liza. tell them that they must excuse me for not riting to them for I have ben in a grate deale of truble ever sence I left them tell libe to let our buisness stand at preant untill I rite him or git one of my Brothers to come and see him. and I will make all rite with him. for I wont be in truble allways. but it seames that I am unluckey in this life. well it want last long for my health tells me I will not live long well I hope it wont if I am to have truble all my life. well I hant all the one that has truble so I am not a lone in the world. now Jane please rite as son as you git this for I am anexious to here from my Brothers and all of you. well Jane if all of the folks dont allready know of my situation please dont let them know it for it wont do them aney good. but some of them will be mighty glad but it wont do them aney good for I will come out all rite after while if I live long a nough well I am in as good health as could be expected.

rite son as you git this and Direct to me in care of O. H. Mcgraw Springfield Ills

yours as ever

T. L. D. Johnston

Springfield May 22 1868

John J. Hall

well John I drop you a note once more and ferever the last on this subject unless I here from you and you do something aboute it. in the first place my Baile is $600. and if I cant git Baile I can have my witness on hand when coart set in October next and beate my case easley but if not I will have to rely on ther Say So whether they will come or not, and if I don't give Baile my lawyers say they will see to it and cleare me if I will pay them for it. I have 3 verry good ones, Mr. Herindon Mr Hoblet and courneal Wythet are the ones who say they will Clear me and have worked this fare for me thinking I would give them a Deed for my title to that 40 Acres. they will take holt of it and clear me next fall if I will give them my claime now John if you will you can git that claime withoute it a costing you much if you was to go my Baile and I was to run off. you would not have to pay but $300. of it and it would be a year or 2 beffore they could make you pay it—but that is not my intentions for I can beate the case easley if I can git oute to tend to it and make money anough to pay my lawyers and my health is better then it ever was now if you dont think that title good to me go and ask some of the best lawyers aboute it Mr. Herindon says that Judge Daveis cannot give a deed to anyone else but John D. Johnstons Heirs. and I haveing a Deed from them makes my title good. Mr. Herindon has got a copey of the Bond from the record. now help me oute of this truble and I will give you a good title to it the minuet you sign my Bond and if you dont then it has to go to some one Else to help me out ove this truble for it will be foolish for me to lay here and suffer all summer while I can do otherwise if I git oute on Baile I am shure to have my witness thare and beate the case but if not I have got to pay some one to work for me and have ever thing ready when coart sets if you will sign my Bonds I will try and have them sent to Charleston and I will send the deed a long with them but if not then never blame me if you never git a good title to the land I am not shure that I can send the Bonds to Charleston but I will find oute by the tim you rite to me and do what will benifit you a gratedeel and me allso if you will look to your interest. I will look for a letter earley from you if you come to the conclusons to take me up at my offer or let it go in to some one else hands wich it will have to beffore I git oute of this truble.

I hope this will find you all well and dooing well rite and tell what you will do and what you want to so I will know how to Act I have not given any leane on that land yet but I have maide prommises and that is why they have worked for me.

I am ever as yours

T. L. D. Johnston

Box 291

From the fighting front of the long-drawn war two humble distant kins-men of the Commander in Chief at Washington wrote home folks their affection and the news of the day as they saw it.

Jan the 13 1863
Murfreesboro Tenn

dear brother i once more have the pleasure of riting you a few lines to let you see that i am well and i hope those few lines may find you in good health i have not got a letter from home for four weeks we are in camp now for the fust time in four weeks you must excuse me for not riting oftener i have not had a chance to rite John there was a big battle here but our Regiment was not in it we was after morgan at the time we march over the battlefield day before yesterday it was an awful looking place there was any amount of dead horses the men was mostly berried there was ten thousand kiled on our side they fought from nashville to murfeburo the distance is 30 miles the rebles fites to kill they drink whiskey and powder tey put six pounds of powder in a barrel of whiskey i dont think the war will be set-tled verry soon rite soon give my respects to all

your brother A L Hall

to J J Hall

give my love to mother and the rest i would like to see you all verry well *this come out of the State hous i was all over it it is a fine house* (handwritten facsimile)

On a separate sheet in his letter of January 13, 1863, Private A. L. Hall wrote, probably referring to the fine stationery on which he was writing: "This come out of the State hous in Nashville i was all over it it is a fine house"

Murfeesboro Tenn
Feb the 17th, 18

Dear brother I take my pen in [hand] to let you no that I am well at present and I hope when those few lines comes to hand they may find you in good health well John i received your letter that was mailed at Charleston feb the 9th and was glad to hear from you John i have just come in camp from scouting Col Monroe took 2 or 3 of his men and 20 cavelry and went out on a seven days scout and we had one little battle with about 300 rebels The fight lasted About fifteen minutes the bullets whistle pretty but we did not loose A man but kiled and wounded about fifty rebels there was six thousand about four miles from the fite wee had to double quick 8 miles and them after us we had to waid the river it was waist deep and as cold as ice thats nuthing to what we have to do we took eight prisoners and fifteen guns i got a pair of drawers that the rebels lost with the legs tide full of biscuits and chicking

i thought it eat mity well well John do the best you can till i come home try and get out of debt if you can if you can sell them mules you may do it i dont care what you do with any thing i have got well John i wish i could ben ther at bradys to a had sum fun John i would not have any more fuse with meril you had better let him kut what he ows you rather than to have another fus, try and keep frindly with him if you can for i dont want to hear of you and him a fighting i suppose we will draw money in a few days the pay master is here now I must bring my letter to a close by say ing i reman your brother until death

Alfred Hall
to John
J. Hall

There are many species of the illiterate and ungrammatical writers. There are those who get their say into a songlike cadence, who shadow forth inevitable scrawls in the timebeat of their conversational narrative voice. John T. Hanks, a son of Dennis F. Hanks, in the following letter was at times in the mood of Lincoln's favorite poem. Corrected freely, he reads: "Alas, those happy times as boys together are all over with us. Now it sometimes almost breaks my heart to think how time will change things. It appears to me but a short time ago when my old friends were in the bloom of life, but now they are sleeping in the grave and we, the surviving monuments, are left to tell the tale of those that are gone." The spelling might be improved but the sentiment can hardly be enriched toward the close of the letter: "give mi love to all inquring friendes ande take a grate portion your self." Who cares about the misspelling when he writes his cousin, "I am going to finde a wife some whear if I hav to cume back home fur one"?

the
October 25, 18.59
Roseburg Douglas Co Oregon
Mr. John D Hall   Charleston   Ills—

Dear Cosin   after a long time wayting to hear from you I have all moste came to th conclusion thate you have fur goten me or either you donte care fur one or Tow I some times sete down by mi self ande study a boute you thate you was once as near to me as mi owen Broth ate leaste I thoughte as much ove you and to think over the happey times thate yu hade when Boys to gethe bute alas those hapey times is all over with uss now ite some times all moste brakes mi harte to think how time will change thinges ite apears to me bute a shorte time a go when mi olde friendes wos in the bl! bloome of life bute now ar sleeaping in the grave ande we the surviving monumentes is lefte to tell the taile of those thate ar gon. John do you ever studey aboute those thinges. a meney a time has i laide in mi bede ande thoute ove home ande those dear friendes that I lefte be hind thate I shal neve see no more. John I think you hav treatede very mean ite has ben all moste sevin years senc I receivede a scrach of a pen from you then I was very promply to answer ite bute I hav hearde you once ande a while bute thate donte do me as much goode as to receive a lettor frome you I will stop ande tell you some newes ar you may think I am boring down on you tow harde in the firste plais I will say thate I am well and hartey and geting a long slow in the worlde I hav ben in origon a boute five monthes I lefte california laste Spring in compney with Lewis Hanks on a prospecte tower ande broute up in origon as fur as I hav seane of origon I like ite very well much beter than california fur I think ite is heather [healthier?] a cuntry I hav ben mining ever sence I lefte hav ben hear ande hav note travild a rounde much. John hear is the cuntry fur a man to live in I wish you was hear with me and I wode be satis fide to live hear all mi days I think you wode be pleased with the cuntry if you was hear as fur making money I think i will doe well this winter if nothing haping I expecte to mine this winter ande goode by digen fur golde I will try somthing else to make a living besides working so harde a goode living is all I wonte ande I think I can make thate I am going to finde a wife some whear if I hav to cume back home fur one. I expecte you hav one thate you call your owne by this time I hearde that Nancey ande Elisibeth was both mairrede I hope thay hav done well by doing so all so under stude thate your mother was singel thate her husbond was deade tell her she hade beter remain singel all the balence ove her days than to do as she has don. John I wode like to cum back ande cum down & take you on suprise I bleave thate you wodente kow me if you was to see me now I have changed considerible since I sow you I be gin to think thate I am geting olde I donte be gin to hav the same action thate I youste to hav when I was at home I hav a very long bearde ande ite is very heavey. when you receive this wonte you sende me your minatur so I can look at you when you gete ite taken go to charleston ande hav the beste looking gale thair is thair to sete with you ande send ite to me ande I will do the same hear tell her thate ite is mi wish fur you to doe so I received a lettor from father he give me hell fur coming to origon bute John donte you think [it] is fur me to doe the beste i can I hav to make a living fur mi self now ande I shoude think by this time thate I am olde a nuf to chose the plais ande way to make ite I no ite setes very harde on the olde folks to hav me a way from them I all ways indeverde to doe the beste can to be raised a poor boy thate you know I stayd with mi father till I was Twentey one in thate time I allways triede to obey him in ever thing now I think he oughte lete me chose fur mi self he has Tow boys at home your boy that you know I stayd with mi father till I was twenty one in that time I allways tried to obey him in ever thing now I think he ought let me chose far mi self he has two boys at home that is a nuff far him to take care one let a lone me John I want write to me and give me all this news that is going on give mi love to all inquiring friends and take a great portion your self so I will close for something write hoping to hear from you soon so good By old Boy.

Your Cosen

John. T Hawkes

To
John. D. Hooe

Gold hunter John T. Hanks sends news and love to Illinois kin thate is a nuff fur him to take care ove lete a lone me John I wonte write to me ande give me all the newes thate is going on give mi love to all inquring friendes ande take a grate portion your self so I will close fur somthing write hoping to hear from you sone so goode By olde Boy

Your Cosen

John . T. Hanks

To
John. D. Hall

When Abraham Lincoln's father died in a Goose Nest prairie log cabin near Charleston, Illinois, on January 17, 1851, the son was not at the bedside. Shortly after, however, he visited his stepmother, Sarah Bush Lincoln, joining in a reunion of kith and kin. And they gave the best of their information and belief to a record of the marriages, births, and deaths of the Lincoln family.

In Abraham Lincoln's handwriting this record went into the family Bible. Time passed, and a few years after the death of President Lincoln his cousin Dennis Hanks, leaving Charleston for a visit with his daughter, removed from the family Bible the record leaf written by Abraham Lincoln. In 1888 this documentary page came into the hands of Jesse Weik, the young Hoosier collaborating with William H. Herndon on a biography of Lincoln, Weik noting, "Dennis tore out and wore out the Bible record." Though creased and worn, it still serves students and biographers.

Not long ago Barrett finished a research that tells us what it was that Abraham Lincoln wrote in the five lines of the upper right-hand corner of this Bible leaf, a creased corner that got worn or torn off and lost.

On those five lines Lincoln wrote the birth dates of his father Thomas Lincoln and his mother Nancy Hanks and the date of their marriage. Having this data, we are able now to correct the mistaken dates now chiseled on gravestone and memorial tablets and to fill in the blanks where many chronicles are vague or incomplete. We have now the birth date of Lincoln's mother as the son himself wrote it in the family Bible. The missing five lines of the Bible leaf record as restored through the Barrett research read:

"Thos. Lincoln was born Jan. the 6th A.D. 1778 and was married June 12th 1806 to Nancy Hanks who was born Feb. 5th 1784.

Sarah Lincoln Daughter of Thos. and"

And how can we be sure these are the five lines torn or worn, lost and missing, from the Bible-leaf record that Lincoln wrote? By four separate and different pieces of evidence that are here:

1. John D. Johnston, a son of Sarah Bush Lincoln by her first marriage and a foster brother of Abraham Lincoln, was going to move to Arkansas. Johnston copied from the family Bible the entire record there made in Lincoln's handwriting. On a blank page of an account book Johnston entered the Bible-leaf record where it may be seen today, the outstanding item alongside a record of numerous sales of whisky at 50 cents a gallon.

2. John J. Hall, a cousin of Lincoln, and a grandson of Sarah Bush Lincoln living with her at the time that Lincoln wrote the family-Bible record, also made a copy of that record before Dennis Hanks removed it. Hall's copy was kept in the Lincoln cabin until 1891. Visitors to the cabin often saw this Hall copy of the Lincoln record. On at least three occasions John J. Hall's copy of the Lincoln record was given publication. *The History of Coles County*, published in Chicago in 1879, has this entry: "While in the old cabin where he [Thomas Lincoln] lived and died, we were shown the family record copied by Mr. Hall from a leaf of the family Bible. . . . It reads Thomas Lincoln was born Jan. 6, 1778, and was married June 12, 1806, to Nancy Hanks, who was born Feb. 5, 1784."

3. In a large scrapbook where plain handwriting tells us it was "made by Nancy A. Hall, great-granddaughter of Sarah Bush Lincoln, Goose Nest Prairie, near Charleston, Ill.," is a clipping of one of a series of newspaper articles titled "Half Century in Coles County," by John Cunningham, Chapter 11, "Pleasant Grove, The Lincoln Family." The writer tells of relic-hunters carrying off family records, though "Mr. John Hall has a copy, however, of a leaf from the Lincoln family Bible, which I give entire." Then follows the text with the birth dates identical with the record in the county history and the John D. Johnston account book.

4. There is still another newspaper clipping, this from the *St. Louis Globe-Democrat*, saying: "Mr. Hall retained nothing [of family relics] but a copy of the family record, the only genealogy kept by the Lincoln family, incomplete though it was, which is given in full below."

Newspaper clippings pasted in this Nancy Hall scrapbook report stories and sayings among the Lincolns. Short-spoken, humble, and reverent was the blessing young Abraham often heard at the table, if this account in one newspaper is correct:

"John Hall, a near relative of Abraham Lincoln's stepmother, says that Thomas Lincoln returned thanks at every meal, always using the same

Torn and worn leaf from Lincoln family Bible

words, 'Fit and prepare us for humble service, we beg for Christ's sake. Amen.' "

A yarn not yet included in any Lincoln biography is reported in this same scrapbook of Nancy Hall. The evidence seems to be that Thomas Lincoln was a worthy husband of Nancy Hanks, the mother of Abraham Lincoln who died when he was a child, and of Sally Bush, the beloved foster mother. But the only account we have from Thomas Lincoln in this regard is in this scrapbook. The newspaper clipping reads:

"One day when alone with her husband, Mrs. Lincoln said, 'Thomas, we have lived together a long time and you have never yet told me whom you like best, your first wife or me.' Thomas replied, 'Oh, now, Sarah, that reminds me of old John Hardin down in Kentucky who had a fine-looking pair of horses, and a neighbor coming in one day and looking at them said, 'John, which horse do you like best?' John said, 'I can't tell; one of them kicks and the other bites and I don't know which is wust.' It is plain to see where Abraham Lincoln got his talent for wit and apt illustrations."

We make an acquaintance with a nephew of Sarah Bush Lincoln, one R. Y. Bush, of Hawesville, Kentucky. He wrote of his visits with President Lincoln.

On December 3, 1864, he wrote to John F. Hall, in part:

Well John, Old Abe, as he is called, is again to be our President. I sincerely regret it indeed. I can see nothing but war, war, war, under his reign, and if ever a people were thoroughly scourged by war, the American people are certainly that people. Peace, with union or disunion would certainly be ten thousand times preferable to the people, even if the negro was continued in bondage to this desolating & heartrending strife.

Taxation, the large numbers of helpless widows & orphans, & the other untold calamities of this war will bear very heavily upon the people. All the small operators in farming or other business will suffer terribly in the end.

Since my return I have thought often of you all & really begin to think that I should like to visit you all again. I should be glad to see you & any of the family & relatives in Ky at any time. Cant you make us a visit this winter? How is George? Does he still drink cider?

On April 5, 1865, R. Y. Bush wrote to Hall at Farmington, Illinois, ending his letter:

I made a visit to Washington in the latter part of Winter & saw *Father Abraham*. I found him very busy, but very kind and agreeable. He seemed pleased to see me. Tell Aunt that they are working him very hard at Washington & if he had not been raised to *maul rails*, he could never stand the hard labor at the White house.

Give my most affectionate regards to Aunt, your Ma & all the family & relations generally.

                    Yours very truly

Write me immediately)   R. Y. Bush

Weaving amid the Johnston-Hanks-Hall kin was William H. Herndon, one of the three defense lawyers mentioned by the Johnston boy in jail.

On the hunt for material for his biography of Lincoln that was published decades later he wrote letters of inquiry.

Springfield Ills Sept. 28ᵗʰ 1865

Messr Johnson & Hall
My Dear Sirs.

I landed home some few days ago and have been busy ever since, or should have written to you long ago. I now give you my kindest and most sincere thanks for the kindness shown me, as well as the information you gave me. Please say this much for me to Miss Moore and grand Mother Lincoln. Give them my best love and my prayers. The word regards is too cold and I substitute the word love and send my love to them.

I wish to ask of you one favor and it is this—1st When did Mr. Hall marry Miss Johnson. What year and where?

2nd—Please give me the Exact words used by Mr Lincoln in his Copy book when he says he will be a good boy but God knows when. Please copy it exactly in a letter and send to me here.

3dly—What is the name of the little town you pass through in going from your house to Charleston.

If you know anything I did not get in reference to Mr Lincoln's life, please send it to me—please write it down in a letter and send to me here.

Your Friend
W. H. Herndon

Springfield Ills January 22ᵈ 1866

Friend Hall—

Will you have the kindness to Copy Mr Lincoln's bond to Johnson or your father, which I saw when I was down to see you. Copy every word—figure, and name *Carefully* from top to bottom, and send to me, if you *please*. Don't fail. I want it to defend Lincoln's memory.

Please write to me at any time you may think of any thing that is *good or bad* of Mr Lincoln, truthfully just as it happened and took place. Were any of you boys applicants for any office made to Mr Lincoln while he was President?

Hall—What is your honest opinion—Come *honest* opinion—in reference to Mr Lincoln's love for his kin and relatives generally. *Please*—friend—accomodate me

Your Friend,
W. H. Herndon

Springfield Ills Nov. 25th 1866

Mr Kline

My Dear Sir:

To-day, as per request, I send you my 4th lecture on Presdt. Lincoln. The first two were the attempted analysis of Mr L.'s. mind; the third was on *some facts* showing his Patriotism & Statesmanship; and the 4th one is an attempt to show the Modifications of his natural mind—the mind that God created uninfluenced by surroundings. Nature outside of man assists in making, modifying and developing it &c. The 5th lecture will be on his education—the process—means—methods—manner of education, and the development of his mind, &c. I will send you a copy if I deliver it—the first thing. I never publish any of the 3rd and the 1st & 2nd were *in part* stenographed and given to the world in the winter of 1865 & 6, part of which you possibly saw at the time. See Carpenters 6 mos in White House toward the end for part of the first one.

My four lectures somehow get a greater run than they are entitled to. The popularity is solely due I know to Mr Lincoln's fame &c

Yours Truly,

W. H. Herndon

Into the hands of Herndon in his researches came Lincoln letters. He presented one of these, the famous epistle to John D. Johnston, to one Chatterton, probably the Springfield jeweler whose store was below the Lincoln-Herndon law office, for Chatterton to give to a friend.

Springfield, Ills. May 1st 1875

Mr. Chatterton—

My dear Sir.

Enclosed find a letter from the great Pres^{dt}. Abm Lincoln to his step brother, Jno. D. Johnston, dated the 4th Novr. 1851. It was written from Shelbyville Ills to Johnston who lived near Charleston Ill. Mr. Lincoln wrote it while he was out on the Circuit attending to his professional business—going with the Court from County to County dispensing Justice or otherwise as the Case might be. This Johnston was the Son of Sarah Lincoln—the 2nd wife of Thomas Lincoln the father of Abm Lincoln. This letter "*puts me in mind*" of a thousand things—his wife—his domestic relations &c. but I shall not pen them for Strange Ears. You know much of them. I thought it proper to state the history of this letter and the exact relationship of Mr Lincoln & Jno. D. Johnston. Hand this as well as Mr Lincoln's letter to your friend.

Your Friend

W. H. Herndon

Herndon in writing to Gunther his thanks for candy sent to him by Gunther, recites the conditions under which he sells or gives away a Lincoln letter or relic:

Springfield Ills. Nov. 19th '86

Mr Gunther—
My Dear Sir:

On coming to the city this morning from my country farm I find your kind letter dated the 13th inst and for which I thank you. In the letter you inform me that you have sent me a package of candy in consideration of my *little* gift to you. I will accept the Candy, as I suppose it is in the til at the Express office, but do not offer me pay for any autograph—any Lincoln relic I may send you. I have never sold any such thing to any person, except to those who contemplated making money out of the relic. I have given away freely many precious things—Lincoln relics & have never charged those to whom I sent one cent, except as above

Your Friend

Thanks for the Candy.   W H Herndon

The note of pathos, the borderline of an outcry, so often there in what Herndon wrote, is there in a letter about his lectures. And in another letter he wishes it made clear that he never sought a Federal office from the President.

Messrs. Keys & Munson—

It was distinctly understood between Lincoln & myself that I wanted to hold no office under his administration, as I held the Bank Commissioners office under Govr Bissel who appointed me at the solicitation and request of Mr Lincoln.

Your Friend

W. H. Herndon

Messrs. Keys & Munson —

It was distinctly understood between Lincoln & myself that I wanted to hold no office under his administration, as I held the Bank Commissioners office under Govr. Bissell who appointed me at the solicitation and request of Mr Lincoln

Your friend

W. H. Herndon

Law partner Herndon makes clear he is no officeseeker

5. "Brothers in the Bond"

WHEN on a March day in 1837 the twenty-eight-year-old Abraham Lincoln rode a borrowed horse from New Salem to Springfield to begin practice as a newly licensed lawyer, his earthly possessions were in two saddlebags and he didn't know where he would stay in Springfield nor on what kind of bed he would sleep. He arranged with a carpenter to make him a single bedstead. Then at the general store of A. Y. Ellis & Company he asked the junior partner, Joshua Fry Speed, what he would have to pay for a mattress, blankets, sheets, a coverlid, and a pillow for a single bed. That would come to $17, Speed figured. Cheap enough, said Lincoln, but he didn't have the money and would have to ask credit until Christmas, when he would pay if he did well at the law, though of course he might never be able to pay.

Speed looked into Lincoln's face, caught in the eyes a sad look that melted him. Speed probably knew that Lincoln had failed as a storekeeper at New Salem and was sunk in a debt he only hoped to get paid sometime. Speed made an offer. It would keep Lincoln out of further debt and get him located. Speed offered to share with Lincoln his large room and double bed upstairs over the store. Lincoln moved in with his saddlebags. A friendship of these bedfellows began that ripened and deepened and lasted across Lincoln's lifetime. Lincoln had many friendships, with various and limited degrees of intimacy, but to no other man did he write so extended a series of long letters, the larger part of these having to do with love and marriage complications of the two men.

Fourteen of these letters written by Lincoln to Speed came into the Barrett Collection rather directly. J. S. Speed III, a kinsman and heir, wrote to Barrett saying he had had correspondence with New York dealers, but would prefer to have the group of letters go into a private collection, and if

Barrett wanted them he would sell them. Barrett wrote Speed to send along the letters and put a C.O.D. draft on them. A few days later a banker phoned Barrett to come see him. The banker was anxious, even somewhat alarmed. When Barrett arrived the banker said it seemed someone had stolen what was in the box and left nothing but some old Lincoln letters. "Just what I want," said Barrett. The banker explained, "Those are all hand-written, and a book is much easier to read. I just don't understand it." Barrett later reminisced, "I don't know whether he ever understood it, but I got the letters."

Lincoln was older than Joshua Fry Speed by four years and four months. Their backgrounds had contrast. Speed's father was Judge John Speed, a planter with large landholdings, seventy slaves on his elaborate "Farmington" homestead near Louisville, twelve living children—two by his first wife, ten by his second—at the time his son Joshua moved to Springfield, Illinois, to make his own way as a merchant. The migratory log-cabin Lincolns were in another class. Yet the two men hit it off, sleeping in the same bed four years, exchanging confidences and consolations. When in 1841 Speed, on the death of his father, moved to Kentucky, he met the black-eyed woman Fanny Henning whom he married early the next year of 1842, Lincoln taking his wife late in the same year. Eight of the letters here revolve about the loves and the marriages of the two men. Each made his committals to matrimony, pledged himself to a wedding, then each shrank from the final step. Lincoln's problem was the more tangled, but that of Speed gave him foreboding, alarm, and horror that brought philosophy, reasons, and advice from Lincoln.

Argument between the two men kept friendly, and when the war broke, Speed was one of the mainstays of President Lincoln in keeping Kentucky from seceding. Speed took an active hand in the secret movements for the raising of men, arms, and supplies for the Union cause. He made several trips to Washington during the war, gave his counsel when asked, de-murred to the Emancipation Proclamation, yet loyally took on assignments where he was of use to Lincoln in Kentucky affairs.

Speed could have had Cabinet appointment. On receiving the last of the series of letters given below he went to Chicago, and in Lincoln's room in the Tremont House, the two men alone, Speed had his first talk with the President-elect. Lincoln, stretched on a bed, had a question: "Speed, what are your pecuniary conditions? Are you rich or poor?" Speed gave his answer: "Mr. Lincoln, I think I know what you wish. I will speak candidly to you. My pecuniary conditions are good. I do not think you have any office within your gift I can afford to take." Thus Speed reported it later. He performed hard and dangerous tasks afterward given him by Lincoln, all rather quietly and shy of publicity. Speed had moved from his farm into Louisville, and with his wife's brother for a partner did a flourishing real-estate business, dying in 1882 at sixty-eight years of age, leaving an estate estimated at $600,000.

When Lincoln appointed James Speed to be United States Attorney General, he said he didn't know him as well as he did the brother Joshua, adding, "It is not strange, for I slept with Joshua for four years, and I suppose I ought to know." The letters to Joshua follow, the first being one that introduces Lincoln as a mystery-story writer.

Springfield, June 19th. 1841

Dear Speed:

We have had the highest state of excitement here for a week past that our community has ever witnessed; and although the public feeling is now somewhat allayed, the curious affair which aroused it is verry [sic] far from being even yet, cleared of mystery. It would take a quire of paper to give you anything like a full account of it, and I therefore only propose a brief outline. The chief personages in the drama, are Archibald Fisher, supposed to be murdered; and Archibald Trailor, Henry Trailor, and William Trailor, supposed to have murdered him. The three Trailors are brothers: the first, Arch., as you know, lives in town; the second, Henry, in Clary's Grove; and the third, Wm., in Warren County; and Fisher, the supposed murderee, being without a family had made his home with William. On Saturday evening, being the 29th May, Fisher and William came to Henry's in a one horse dearborn, and there stayed over sunday, and on monday all three came to Springfield, Henry on horseback, and joined Archibald at Myers', the Dutch carpenter. That evening at supper Fisher was missing, and so next morning. Some ineffectual search was made for him; and on tuesday, at 1 o'clock P.M., Wm. & Henry started home without him. In a day or so Henry and one or two of his Clary Grove neighbors came back and searched for him again, and advertised his disappearance in the paper. The knowledge of the matter thus far had not been general; and here it dropped entirely till about the 10th Inst., when Keys received a letter from the Post Master in Warren, stating that Wm. had arrived at home, and was telling a very mysterious and improbable story about the disappearance of Fisher, which induced the community there to suppose he had been disposed of unfairly. Keys made this letter public, which immediately set the whole town and adjoining county agog; and so it has continued until yesterday. The mass of the People commenced a systematic search for the dead body, while Wickersham was dispatched to arrest Henry Trailor at the Grove, and Jim Maxcy to Warren to arrest William. On Monday last Henry was brought in, and showed an evident inclination to insinuate that he knew Fisher to be dead, and that Arch. and Wm. had killed him. He said he guessed the body could be found in Spring Creek, between the Beardstown road and Hickoxes mill. Away the people swept like a herd of buffaloes, and cut down Hickoxes mill-dam *nolens volens,* to draw the water out of the pond; and then went up and down, and down and up the creek, fishing and raking, and ducking, and diving for two days, and after all no dead body found. In the mean time a sort of scuffling ground had been found in the brush in the angle, or point where the road leading into the woods past the brewery, and the one leading in past the brick-yard join. From the scuffle ground, was the sign of something about the size of a man having been dragged to the edge of the thicket, where it joined the track of some small wheeled carriage which was drawn by one horse, as shown by the horse tracks. The carriage-track led off towards Spring Creek. Near this drag-trail Dr. Merryman found *two hairs,* which, after a long scientific examination, he pronounced to be triangular human hairs, which term, he says, includes within it, the whiskers, the hair growing under the arms and on other parts of the body; and he judged that these two were of the whiskers, because the ends were cut, showing that they had flourished in the neighborhood of the razor's operation. On thursday last Jim Maxcy brought in William Trailor from Warren. On the same day Arch. was arrested and put in jail. Yesterday (friday) William was put upon his examining trial before May and Lavely. Archibald and Henry were both present. Lamborn prosecuted, and Logan, Baker, and your humble servant defended. A great many witnesses were introduced and examined; but I shall only mention those whose testimony seem to be the most important. The first of these was Capt. Ransdell. He swore that when William and Henry left Springfield for home on tuesday before mentioned, they did not take the direct route, which, you know, leads by the butcher shop, but that they followed the street North until they got opposite, or nearly opposite May's new house, after which he could not see them from where he stood; and it was afterward proven that in about an hour after they started, they came into the street by the butcher's shop from towards the brick-yard. Dr. Merryman and others swore to what is stated about the scuffle-ground, drag-trail, whiskers, and carriage-tracks. Henry was then introduced by the prosecution. He swore that when they started for home, they went out North, as Ransdell stated, and turned down West by the brick-yard into the woods, and there met Archibald; that they proceeded a small distance farther, where he was placed as a sentinel to watch for, and announce the approach of any one that might happen that way; that William and Arch. took the dearborn out of the road a small distance to the edge of the thicket, where they stopped, and he saw them lift the body of a man into it; that they then moved off with the carriage in the direction of Hickoxes mill, and he loitered about for something like an hour, when William returned with the carriage, but without Arch: and said they had put *him* in a safe place; that they went some how—he did not know exactly how, into the road close to the brewery and proceeded on to Clary's Grove. He also stated that sometime during the day William told him, that he and Arch. had killed Fisher the evening before; that the way they did it was by him (William) knocking him down with a club, and Arch. then choking him to death.

An old man from Warren, called Dr. Gilmore, was then introduced on the part of the defence. He swore that he had known Fisher for several years; that Fisher had resided at his house a long time at each of two different spells; once while he built a barn for him, and once while he was doctored for some chronic disease; that two or three years ago, Fisher had a serious hurt in his head by the bursting of a gun, since which he had been subject to continued bad health, and occasional aberrations of mind. He also stated that on last tuesday, being the same day that Maxcy arrested William Trailor, he (the Dr.) was from home in the early part of the day, and on his return, about 11 o'clock, found Fisher at his house, in bed, and apparently very unwell; that he asked him how he came from Springfield; that Fisher said he had come by Peoria, and also told several other places he had been at not in the direction of Peoria, which showed that he, at the time of speaking, did not know where he had been, or that he had been wandering about in a state of derangement. He further stated that in about two hours he received a note from one of William Trailor's friends, advising him of his arrest, and requesting him to go on to Springfield as a witness, to testify to the state of Fisher's health in former times; that he immediately set off, calling up two of his neighbors, as company, and, riding all evening and all night, overtook Maxcy and William at Lewiston in Fulton County; that Maxcy refusing to discharge Trailor upon his statement, his two neighbors returned and he came on to Springfield. Some question being made whether the doctor's story was not a fabrication, several acquaintances of his among whom was the same Post Master who wrote Keys, as before mentioned, were introduced as sort of compurgators, who all swore that they knew the doctor to be of good character for truth and veracity, and generally of good character in every way. Here the testimony ended and the Trailor's were discharged, Arch. and William expressing, both in word and manner, their entire confidence that Fisher would be found alive at the doctor's by Galloway, Mallory, and Myers, who a day before had been despatched for that purpose, while Henry still protested that no power on earth could ever show Fisher alive. Thus stands this curious affair now. When the doctor's story was first made public, it was amusing to scan and contemplate the countenances, and hear the remarks of those who had been actively engaged in the search for the dead body. Some looked quizzical, some melancholly [sic], and some furiously angry. Porter, who had been very active, swore he always knew the man was not dead, and that *he* had not stirred an inch to hunt for him; Langford, who had taken the lead in cutting down Hickoxes mill dam, and wanted to hang Hickox for objecting, looked most awfully wobegone [sic]: he seemed the *"wictim of hunrequited haffections,"* as represented in the comic almanic [sic] we used to laugh over: and Hart, the little dray-man that hauled Molly home once, said it was too *damned* bad, to have so much trouble, and no hanging after all.

I commenced this letter on yesterday, since which I received yours of the 13th. I stick to my promise to come to Louisville. Nothing new here except what I have written. I have not seen Sarah since my long trip, and I am going out there as soon as I mail this letter.

Yours forever,

Lincoln.

Nearly five years later, on April 15, 1846, an account of the Trailor case was published in the *Quincy* (Illinois) *Whig*, edited by Andrew Johnston, with whom Lincoln had exchanged letters about poetry and literary fancies. Indications are that Lincoln wrote this account. The *Sangamo Journal* reprinted it. Roy P. Basler has included it in *Abraham Lincoln: His Speeches and Writings*. Roger W. Barrett, now a practicing attorney and a son of Oliver R. Barrett, in a brochure titled *A Strange Affair* (1933), gave first publication to all known materials bearing on the Trailor case, which so haunted Lincoln as a true-life mystery story that he wrote of it and speculated about it for a long time after it was a closed incident.

There was about Dr. Gilmore, who testified he had seen the supposed murdered man, alive though feeble, ran the *Quincy Whig* narrative toward its close,

so much of the air and manner of truth, that his statement prevailed in the minds of the audience and the court, and the Trailors were discharged, although they attempted no explanation of the circumstances proven by other witnesses against them. On the next Monday, Myers arrived in Springfield, bringing with him the now famed Fisher, in full life and proper person . . . while it is readily conceived that a writer of novels could bring a story to a more perfect climax, it may well be doubted whether a stranger affair ever really occurred. Much of the matter remains in mystery to this day. The going into the woods with Fisher, and returning without him, by the Trailors, their going into the woods at the same place the next day, after they had professed to have given up the search; the signs of a struggle in the thicket, the buggy tracks at the edge of it; and the location of the thicket and the signs about it, corresponding precisely with Henry's story, are circumstances that have never been explained. William and Archibald have both died since—William in less than a year, and Archibald in about two years after the supposed murder. Henry is still living but never speaks of the subject.

Mention should be made that the *Illinois State Register* of June 22, 1841, three days after Lincoln wrote his letter to Speed about the Trailor case, reports that the citizens of Springfield hold a meeting and express to Archibald Trailor their apologies and regrets for believing that he was involved in the murder of Archibald Fisher.

A solution of the mystery was offered by one Dr. Alexander Shields, whose view is presented in *A Strange Affair*, as follows:

The result was that Archibald Trayler's [sic] usefulness was destroyed, and he wandered about like a person in a dream. About two years after, a messenger came for me at twelve o'clock at night, to see Trayler, who was very sick; when I saw him he was exhausted, and in a few hours departed this life. The plain, natural and just solution of this mysterious affair appears to be simply this. Wm. Trayler had a great fancy for Capt. Ransdell's niece, and she had a fancy for him, and the Capt. was intensely opposed to it. Trayler was determined to steal the girl, and she was willing to be stolen, and in order to be prepared for the theft, the three men went down into the timber to find if there were any byroads that would lead into the Beardstown road; then Fisher is sent home on foot, and arrangements made with the girl to meet him in the timber. When he departed from home he took that direction, and the girl being unable to escape the vigilance of the Captain and his spies, did not appear; after waiting a reasonable time, he then went to the Beardstown road on his way home.

Roger Barrett offered a solution of the mystery as follows:

The statement of Dr. Shields, instead of solving, seems only to cast the shadow of a new mystery. It is improbable that Henry Trailor would charge his brothers with an atrocious murder merely to avoid the mention of a girl in whom one of his brothers was interested.

The real mystery of the case is why Archibald and William Trailor would never reveal what occurred, nor the circumstances under which they parted from Fisher, nor tell why, after leaving the searching party on the following day ostensibly to go to their homes, they again returned to the thicket and remained there for an hour or so while Henry stood guard. In the silence of the three brothers, these questions have remained unanswered for almost a century and there is no voice that can "provoke the silent dust" to reveal their secret.

But, subject to information that may yet be discovered, and to any more plausible explanation which may be suggested, the following is offered as a solution which is consistent with all the facts and circumstances of the case as now known.

Lincoln, in his letter to Speed, relates that "Fisher had a serious hurt in his head by the bursting of a gun, since which he had been subject to continued bad health, and occasional aberrations of mind." Such an injury may cause mental aberration or epileptic fit, followed by catalepsy, leaving the sufferer in a state closely resembling, and occasionally mistaken for death.

Entering the thicket—either to meet the young lady or with a premonition of the impending attack—Fisher, seized with a fit, or mental aberration, may have struggled with the brothers, or, if he went in alone, may in falling, have sustained some visible mark of injury before the Trailors followed him into the thicket. The brothers, mistaking the unconscious or cataleptic state of Fisher for the sign of death, and fearing that because of the evidence of the struggle, or the possession of his money, they would be suspected of foul play, concealed the body in order to gain time to determine what course to pursue. Fisher may have turned his money over to them, or they may have taken it from his person to safeguard it.

Returning the following day and finding the body as they had left it, they apparently determined to dispose of it in the mill pond, so that when found it would be supposed that Fisher had accidentally drowned. Presumably the Trailors drove hastily away and Fisher, regaining consciousness through the effect of his sudden immersion, escaped drowning to wander in a daze over the prairies.

The Trailors must have been puzzled when the pond was drained and no body found, and bewildered when Fisher turned up alive. After their acquittal and vindication at the town meeting, it is not to be wondered that Archibald and William would never reveal their part in this strange affair.

(January 3, 1842)

My dear Speed:

Feeling, as you know I do, the deepest solicitude for the success of the enterprise you are engaged in, I adopt this as the last method I can invent to aid you, in case (which God forbid) you shall need any aid. I do not place what I am going to say on paper, because I can say it any better in that way than I could by word of mouth; but because, were I to say it orrally [sic], before we part, most likely you would forget it at the very time when it might do you some good. As I think it reasonable that you will feel very badly some time between this and the final consummation of your purpose, it is intended that you shall read this just at such a time.

Why I say it is reasonable that you will feel very badly yet, is because of *three special causes*, added to the *general one* which I shall mention.

The general cause is, that you are *naturally of a nervous temperament;* and this I say from what I have seen of you personally, and what you have told me concerning your mother at various times, and concerning your brother William at the time his wife died. The first special cause is, your *exposure to bad weather* on your journey, which my experience clearly proves to be very severe on defective nerves. The second is, *the absence of all business and conversation of friends*, which might divert your mind, and give it occasional rest from the *intensity* of thought, which will sometimes wear the sweetest idea threadbare and turn it to the bitterness of death.

The third is *the rapid and near approach of that crisis on which all your thoughts and feelings concentrate.*

If from all these causes you shall escape and go through triumphantly, without another "twinge of the soul," I shall be most happily, but most egregiously deceived.

If, on the contrary, you shall, as I expect you will at some time, be agonized and distressed, let me, who have some reason to speak with judgment on such a subject, beseech you to ascribe it to the causes I have mentioned; and not to some false and ruinous suggestion of the Devil.

"But," you will say, "do not your causes apply to every one engaged in a like undertaking?"

By no means. *The particular causes*, to a greater or less extent, perhaps do apply in all cases; but the *general one*,—nervous debility, which is the key and conductor of all the particular ones, and without which *they* would be utterly harmless, though it *does* pertain to you, *does not* pertain to one in a thousand. It is out of this, that the painful difference between you and the mass of the world springs.

I know what the painful point with you is, at all times when you are unhappy. It is an apprehension that you do not love her as you should. What nonsense!—How came you to court her? Was it because you thought she desired it, and that you had given her reason to expect it? If it was for that, why did not the same reason make you court Ann Todd, and at least twenty others of whom you can think, to whom it would apply with greater force than to *her?* Did you court her for her wealth? Why, you know she had none. But you say you reasoned yourself *into* it. What do you mean by that? Was it not, that you found yourself unable to reason your-self *out of it?* Did you not think, and partly form the purpose, of courting her the first time you ever saw or heard of her? What had reason to do with it, at that early stage? There was nothing *at that time* for reason to work upon. Whether she was moral, amiable, sensible, or even of good character, you did not, nor could then know; except, perhaps you might infer the last from the company you found her in.

All you then did or could know of her was her personal *appearance and deportment;* and these, if they impress at all, impress the *heart,* and not the head.

Say candidly, were not those heavenly *black eyes,* the whole basis of your early *reasoning* on the subject? After you and I had once been at her resi-dence, did you not go and take me all the way to Lexington and back, for no other purpose but to get to see her again, on our return, in that seeming to take a trip for that express object?

What earthly consideration would you take to find her scouting and despising you, and giving herself up to another? But of this you have no apprehension; and therefore you cannot bring it home to your feelings.

I shall be so anxious about you, that I want you to write every mail.

Your friend
Lincoln

Springfield, Ills. Feby. 3. 1842.

Dear Speed:

Your letter of the 25th Jany came to hand to-day. You well know that I do not feel my own sorrows much more keenly than I do yours, when I know of them; and yet I assure you I was not much hurt by what you wrote me of your excessively bad feeling at the time you wrote. Not that I am less capable of sympathising with you now than ever; not that I am less your friend than ever; but because I hope and believe, that your present anxiety and distress about *her* health and *her* life, must and will forever banish those horid [sic] doubts, which I know you sometimes felt, as to the truth of your affection for her. If they can be once and forever removed, (and I almost feel a presentiment that the Almighty has sent your present affliction expressly for that object) surely, nothing can come in their stead, to fill their immeasurable measure of misery. The death scenes of

painful

those we love, are surely ~~bad~~ enough; but these we are prepared to, and expect to see. They happen to all, and all know they must happen. Painful as they are, they are not an unlooked-for-sorrow. Should she, as you fear, be destined to an early grave, it is indeed a great consolation to know that she is so well prepared to meet it. Her religion, which you once disliked so much, I will venture you now prize most highly.

But I hope your mellancholly [sic] bodings as to her early death, are not well founded. I even hope, that ere this reaches you, she will have returned with improved and still improving health; and that you will have met her, and forgotten the sorrows of the past, in the enjoyment of the present.

I would say more if I could; but it seems I have said enough. It really appears to me that you yourself ought to rejoice, and not sorrow, at this indubitable evidence of your undying affection for her. Why Speed, if you did not love her, although you might not wish her death, you would most calmly be resigned to it. Perhaps this point is no longer a question with you, and my pertenacious [sic] dwelling upon it, is a rude intrusion upon your feelings. If so, you must pardon me. You know the Hell I have suffered on that point, and how tender I am upon it. You know I do not mean wrong.

I have been quite clear of hypo since you left—even better than I was along in the fall.

I have seen Sarah but once. She seemed verry [sic] cheerful, and so, I said nothing to her about what we spoke of.

Old uncle Billy Herndon is dead; and it is said this evening that uncle Ben Ferguson will not live. This I believe is all the news, and enough at that unless it were better.

Write me immediately on the receipt of this.

Your friend, as ever
Lincoln

[handwritten text] Ferguson will not live— This I believe is all the news, and enough at that unless it were better—

Write me immediately on the receipt of this,—

Your friend as ever
Lincoln

End of a letter to good friend Speed. (*Reduced from original*)

Springfield, Feby 25 1842—

Dear Speed:

Yours of the 16th. Inst., announcing that Miss Fanny and you are "no more twain, but one flesh," reached me this morning. I have no way of telling you how much happiness I wish you both; tho I believe you both can conceive it. I feel somewhat jealous of both of you now; you will be so exclusively concerned for one another, that I shall be forgotten entirely. My acquaintance with Miss Fanny (I call her this, lest you should think I am speaking of your mother) was too short for me to reasonably hope to long be remembered by her; and still, I am sure I shall not forget her soon. Try if you can not remind her of that debt she owes me; and be sure you do not interfere to prevent her paying it.

I regret to learn that you have resolved to not return to Illinois. I shall be very lonesome without you. How miserably things seem to be arranged in this world. If we have no friends, we have no pleasure; and if we have them, we are sure to lose them, and be doubly pained by the loss. I did hope she and you would make your home here; but I own I have no right to insist. You owe obligations to her, ten thousand times more sacred than any you can owe to others; and in that light, let them be respected and observed. It is natural that she should desire to remain with her relatives and friends. As to friends, however, she could not need them any where; she would have them in abundance here.

Give my kind rememberance [sic] to Mr. Williamson and his family, particularly Miss Elizabeth. Also to your Mother, brothers, and sisters. Ask little Eliza Davis if she will ride to town with me if I come there again. And finally, give Fanny a double reciprocation of all the love she sent me. Write me often, and believe me

Yours forever,

Lincoln.

P.S. Poor Eastham is gone at last. He died awhile before day this morning. They say he was very loth to die.

No clerk is appointed yet.   L.

Dear Speed: Springfield, Febr: 25—1842—

I received yours of the 12th. written the day you went down to William's place, some days since; but delayed answering it, till I should receive the promised one of the 16th., which came last night. I opened the latter, with intense anxiety and trepidation; so much, that although it turned out better than I expected, I have hardly yet, at the distance of ten hours, become calm.

I tell you, Speed, our *forebodings*, for which you and I are rather peculiar, are all the worst sort of nonsense. I fancied, from the time I received your letter of saturday, that the one of wednesday was never to come; and yet it *did* come, and what is more, it is perfectly clear, both from its *tone* and *handwriting*, that you were much *happier*, or, if you think the term preferable, less miserable, when you wrote *it* than when you wrote the last one before. You had so obviously improved, at the very time I so much feared, you would have grown worse. You say that "something indescribably horrible and alarming ["] still haunts you. You will not say that three months from now, I will venture. When your nerves once get steady now, the whole trouble will be over forever. Nor should you become impatient at their being even very slow in becoming steady. Again; you say you much fear that that Elysium of which you have dreamed so much is never to be realized. Well, if it shall not, I dare swear it will not be the fault of her who is now your wife. I now have no doubt that it is the peculiar misfortune of both you and me to dream dreams of Elysium far exceeding all that anything earthly can realize. Far short of your dreams as you may be, no woman could do more to realize them, than that same black eyed Fanny. If you could but contemplate her through my imagination, it would appear rediculous [sic] to you that any one should for a moment think of being unhappy with her. My old Father used to have a saying that "If you make a bad bargain, *hug* it all the tighter," and it occurs to me that if the bargain you have just closed can possibly be called a bad one, it is certainly the most *pleasant one* for applying that maxim to which my fancy can, by any effort, picture.

I write another letter, enclosing this, which you can show her if she desires it. I do this because she would think strangely perhaps, should you tell her that you received no letters from me; or, telling her you do, should refuse to let her see them.

I close this, entertaining the confident hope, that every successive letter I shall have from you, (which I hear [sic] pray may not be few, nor far between), may show you possessing a more steady hand and cheerful heart than the last preceding it.

As ever, your friend

Lincoln

Springfield, Oct. 5 1842—

Dear Speed:

You have heard of my duel with Shields, and I have now to inform you that the duelling business still rages in this city. Day before yesterday Shields challenged Butler, who accepted, and proposed fighting next morning at sunrising in Bob Allen's meadow, one hundred yards distance with rifles. To this, Whitesides [sic], Shields's second, said "No" because of the law. Thus ended, duel No. 2. Yesterday, Whitesides chose to consider himself insulted by Dr. Merryman, and so, sent him a kind of *quasi* challenge, inviting him to meet him at the planter's House in St. Louis on the next friday to settle their difficulty. Merryman made me his friend, and sent W. a note enquiring to know if he meant his note as a challenge, and if so, that he would, according to the law in such case made and provided, prescribe the terms of the meeting. W. returned for answer, that if M. would meet him at the Planter's House as desired, he would challenge him. M. replied in a note, that he denied W's right to dictate time and place; but that he M. would waive the question of *time*, and meet him at Louisiana Missouri. Upon my presenting this note to W. and stating, verbally, its contents, he declined receiving it, saying he had business in St. Louis, and it was as near as Louisiana. Merryman then directed me to notify Whitesides that he should publish the correspondence between them with such comments as he thought fit. This I did. Thus it stood at bed time last night. This morning Whitesides, by his friend Shields, is praying for a new-trial, on the ground that he was mistaken in Merrymans proposition to meet him at Louisiana Missouri, thinking it was the State of Louisiana. This Merryman hoots at, and is preparing his publication—while the town is in a ferment and a street fight somewhat anticipated.

But I began this letter not for what I have been writing, but to say something on that subject which you know to be of such infinite solicitude to me. The immense sufferings you endured from the first days of September to the middle of February you never tried to conceal from me, and I well understood. You have now been the husband of a lovely woman nearly eight months. That you are happier now than you ever were the day you married her I well know; for without, you would not be living. But I have your word for it too; and the returning elasticity of spirits which is manifested in your letters. But I want to ask a closer question. "Are you now in *feeling* as well as *judgement*, glad that you are married as you are?" From anybody but me this would be an impudent question not to be tolerated; but I know you will pardon it in me. Please answer it quickly as I feel impatient to know.

I have sent my love to Fanny so often I fear she is getting tired of it; however, I venture to tender it again.   Yours forever,

                                                                Lincoln

Springfield, Ills. Nov. 19. 1860

Dear Speed—

Yours of the 14th is received. I shall be at Chicago Thursday the 22nd Inst. and one or two succeeding days— could you not meet me there?

Mary thinks of going with me; and therefore I suggest that Mrs S. accompany you—

Please let this be private, as I prefer a very great crowd should not gather at Chicago—

Respects to Mrs S—

Your friend, as ever

A. Lincoln

The new President-elect asks an old Kentucky friend to meet him in Chicago

Springfield, Ills. Nov. 19. 1860

Dear Speed.

Yours of the 14ᵗʰ is received. I shall be at Chicago Thursday the 22ⁿᵈ Inst. and one or two succeeding days. Could you not meet me there?

Mary thinks of going with me; and therefore I suggest that Mrs. S. accompany you.

Please let this be private, as I prefer a very great crowd should not gather at Chicago.

Respects to Mrs. S—

Your friend, as ever

A. Lincoln

Here too in the Barrett collection we have a six-page manuscript of Speed's recollections of and comments on his lifelong friend.

6. Biographic Manuscript Serial

A CATALOGUE of the Barrett Lincoln Collection could begin with the forebears, ancestors, and early kinfolk of the Abraham Lincoln who made his way from birth in a dirt-floor, one-room Kentucky log cabin to residence in the Executive Mansion in Washington as the sixteenth President of the United States. Six of the documents are from the coastal area east of the mountains or in Berks County, Pennsylvania. These include an earlier Abraham Lincoln signing a receipt for service pay as a Sub-Lieutenant in a Revolutionary War unit of 1778, and another receipt for pay as a member of the Philadelphia Convention of 1790. There is an autograph document, signed, about the year 1730, wherein appears Mordecai Lincoln, one of the great-great-grandfathers of the sixteenth President of the United States. Another Abraham Lincoln, one of a line of Quakers in Berks County, Pennsylvania, signed a certificate of appraisement, November 2, 1774. A later Mordecai Lincoln, before whom appeared Andrew Johnson and Eliza McCardall with a marriage license, married them, and we may read in his signed certificate that "on the evening of the 17th of May, 1827, I sollomonised the bonds matramoney between the within named persons."

From lower Pennsylvania and down the Shenandoah Valley and through Cumberland Gap moved the Lincoln kin as land-seekers, the registration for a land entry of 11,875 acres in "Cantuckey adjoining Hananighah Lincoln entry" being in the handwriting of none other than Daniel Boone.

There is a mortgage and a deed of land transactions by the young Abraham Lincoln's father, Thomas Lincoln. Then emerge two specimens of the handwriting of the boy pupil Abraham Lincoln, including lines that begin, "Time, what an empty vapor tis!" and a leaf from an arithmetic, then known as a Sum Book, on which he wrote:

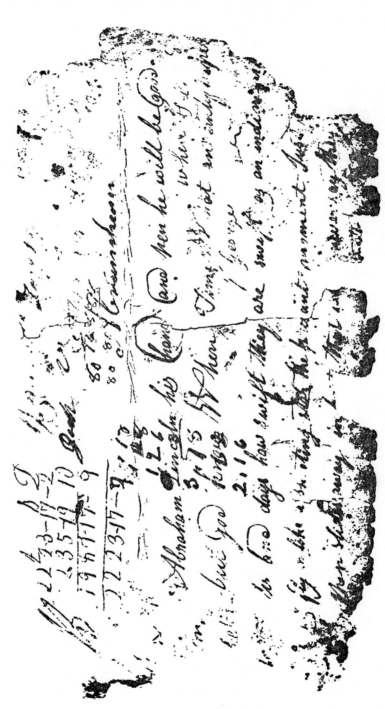

Page from Sum Book of the boy Abraham Lincoln—earliest specimen of his handwriting known to exist

Abraham Lincoln,
his hand and pen,
He will be good, but
god knows when.

One of the earliest textbooks borrowed and used by Lincoln as a boy is here, *The Kentucky Preceptor*, its preface saying, "Tales of love, or ro-

THE

KENTUCKY PRECEPTOR,

CONTAINING

A NUMBER OF USEFUL LESSONS

FOR READING AND SPEAKING.

COMPILED FOR THE USE OF SCHOOLS.

BY A TEACHER.

Delightful task ! to rear the tender thought,
To teach the young idea how to shoot,
To pour the fresh instruction o'er the mind,
To breathe the enlivening spirit, and to fix
The generous purpose in the glowing breast.
THOMPSON,

THIRD EDITION, REVISED, WITH CONSIDERABLE ADDITIONS.

COPY-RIGHT SECURED ACCORDING TO LAW.

LEXINGTON, (KY.)

PUBLISHED BY MACCOUN, TILFORD & CO.

1812.

Facsimile title page

mantic fiction, or anything which might tend to instil false notions into the minds of children have not gained admission." The eyes of the boy reader met such questions as "Who has the most right to complain, the Indian or the negro?"

There were essays on Magnanimity, Remorse of Conscience, Columbus, Demosthenes, On the Scriptures as a Rule of Life, the speech of Robert Emmet on why the English government should not hang an Irish patriot, stories of Indians, and the inaugural address of President Jefferson twenty-four years previous to that, Jefferson alluding to "the agonizing spasms of infuriated man, seeking through blood and slaughter his long-lost liberty" in the French Revolution.

Perhaps the mind of the young reader pondered this passage from the pen of Jefferson: "If there be any among us who would wish to dissolve this Union, or to change its Republican form, let them stand as monuments of the safety with which error of opinion may be tolerated where reason is left free to combat it. I know, indeed, that some honest men fear a republican government is not strong enough. . . . I believe this, on the contrary, the strongest government on earth."

Farmer Josiah Crawford near Gentryville, Indiana, a neighbor of the Lincoln family, wrote his name in the book as its owner. Many years later, when William H. Herndon visited the farmhouse, Crawford presented him with the book, Herndon writing in it a statement to that effect.

Autographs in pen and ink are common enough. Seldom do we meet a name carved by jackknife on an ax handle. A pioneer youth at New Salem, Illinois, it would seem, did put his name, the year, and his home village on an ax handle.

And there is in existence, for what derivations may be made from it, a stone from the New Salem neighborhood, "dug up" in 1890 near the Lincoln & Berry store, by the grandson of Bowling Green, according to affidavits. On the stone had been chiseled the legend:

A. Lincoln Ann Rutledge were betrothed here July 4 1833

We may glimpse Postmaster Lincoln franking a letter, "Free   A. Lincoln, P.M.   New Salem, Illinois, September 22."

Matthew S. Marsh, letter-writer extraordinary, chatty, pleasant, informative, telling his folks back East how affairs were coming along in New Salem in 1835: . . . "the Post Master Mr. Lincoln is very careless about leaving his office open & unlocked during the day—half the time I go in & get my

Legend chiseled on stone

papers etc. without any one being there as was the case yesterday. The letter was only marked 25 & even if he had been there & known it was double he would not [have] charged me any more—luckily he is a very clever fellow & a particular friend of mine."

Back East they had heard that Marsh was attentive to a "sucker girl." This has some truth in it, he admits.

Yes! her name is Martha Jane Short & lives in Morgan County on Indian Creek, the timber of which can be seen from her distant 13 miles acrost a Prairie in the S. West direction. She possesses more qualities which assimilate with my peculiar disposition & comes nearer to the standard of what I consider essential in a wife than any girl I have ever seen. In stature middling height & slim—Light brown hair, black eyes, which suppress half their fire until she speaks, then through their soft disguise will flash an expression more of pride than ire & of love than either—Her age 20. Such is all the description I can give of the girl who at present stands the highest in my estimation. How long she will continue to do so I cannot assure even myself as I have naturally a fickle disposition. But as I have told you all in a pre-

Postmaster Lincoln franks a letter

vious letter if you would come here to live I never will marry but devote all my attention to seeing you made happy. I have one objection to marrying in this state & that is, the women have such an everlasting number of children—twelve is the least number that can be counted on.

Bilious fever and ague were common and Marsh used quinine and bitters made of Indian turnip, bloodroot, and sarsaparilla. Land in that neighborhood is worth buying, as "every foot of it is susceptible of cultivation. No stones or broken land to obstruct the free course of the plow." A land rush is on. "Not less than 75,000 acres is entered monthly at the Springfield Land Office & Speculators are taking it up wherever they can find, some individuals have entered 20,000 acres in one day."

Of high winds, a tornado, prairie hens, wild turkeys, wrote Marsh, of two great wolves that passed thirty yards from him as he was putting up a fence: "I tried to scare them by taking off my hat and running towards them, but they would not quicken their gait."

Backwoods America? The hinterland? The uncouth frontiersman? Not much of it in Matthew Marsh's letter: . . . "if no better chance offers, I shall teach a private school on Indian Creek, Morgan County."

Two months later of this same year of 1835 it was that twenty-six-year-old Lincoln wrote to the Governor of Illinois asking a favor for a friend.

New Salem, Nov. 10th 1835

His Excellency Governor Duncan
Dear Sir

Understanding that Mr. Levi Davis of Vandalia, is an applicant for the office of Auditor of Public Accounts, I take the liberty to say to you, that his appointment to that office would be entirely satisfactory to me, and, I doubt not, to most others who are the friends of qualification and—merit.

Your Obt Servt
A. Lincoln.

Thomas Lincoln, the father of Abraham Lincoln, could write his name, and his signature appears here on one mortgage and on one deed to land. Thomas Lincoln's second wife, Sarah Bush Lincoln, like his first wife, Nancy Hanks Lincoln, could not write her name. She signed by mark one land deed and one receipt that are here. In the two following documents

New Salem. Nov. 10th 1835

His Excellency Governer Duncan
             Dear Sir
                        Understanding
that Mr Levi Davis of Vandalia,
is an applicant. for the office of Auditor
or of Public Accounts, I take the liberty
to say to you, that his appointment to
that office would be entirely satisfactory to me, and, I doubt not, to most
others who are the friends of quailifica-
tion and merit—

                    Your Obt Servt.
                        An Lincoln

FREE

His Excellency
Gov, Duncan

Jacksonville

Mo.

How the younger Lincoln asked office for a friend (*above*), and how he addressed the
envelope and had it franked (*below*)

we incidentally get acquainted with the earnest, spacious, and antique spelling of a frontier magistrate:

This indenture made and agreed upon this 3rd of may 1837th between Thomas Lincoln & Sarah Lincoln his wife of the County of Coles and State of Illinois of the one part & Alexander Mongumary of the County and State aforesaid of the other part witnesseth that the Said Thomas Lincoln & Sarah his wife for & inconsideration of the Sum of one hundred and forty Dollars Current money of the State of Ills to them in hand paid before the execution of these preasents by the Said Alexander Mongumary the receipt is hureby acknowledged have granted bargained & Sold and by these preasents do grant bargain Sell & confirm unto the Said Alexander Mongumary his heirs &C forever a Certain tract of Land in the County and State aforesaid known and designated as the North West quarter of the South West quarter of Section N⁰ 10 Township Eleven North of the base Line in range number Eight East of the third principal meridian containing Forty acres To have and to hold the Said tract or parcel of Land withol the appertainances there unto belonging to the only propper use benifit & behoof of him the Said Alexander Mongumary and his heirs forever and the Said Thomas Lincoln & Sarah his wife for their Selves and heirs do further covenant and agree to and with him the Said Alexander Mongumary his heirs &C that they will warrant and defend the aforesaid tract or parcel of Land with all the appertainance hereditaments and advantages thereunto belonging or in any wise appertaining from themselves and heirs and from Every other purson or pursons Whatsoever in Witness whereof the Said Thomas Lincoln & Sarah Lincoln his wife hath hereunto Subscribed there names and affixed there seales the day first Written

Signed Sealed and	Thomas Lincoln Seale
deliverd pursonly	her
attest	Sarah X Lincoln Seale
David Dryden J P	mark

Sate of Illinoise / that I hearby Certify,
/ Pesonally apeared
Coles County   / be fore mee
David Dryden an acting Justic of the peace in and for Said County Thomas Lincoln and Sarah his wife the subscribrs to the with in deed or instrement of writing and acknowledged the same to be thare act and deed

their selves and heirs to and with their Covenant and agree to and with them the said Alexander Montgomery his heirs &c that they will warrant and defend the aforesaid tract or parcel of Land with the appertainance hereditaments and advantages thereunto belonging on in any wise appertaining from them selves and heirs and from every other person or persons whatsoever in witness whereof the said Thomas Lincoln & Sarah Lincoln his wife hath hereunto subscribed there names and affixed there sealer the day first written

Signed sealed and delivered yourunly

Thomas [mark] Lincoln [Seal]

David Dye }

Sarah + Lincoln [Seal]
        mark

Lincoln's father signs his name, his step-mother by her mark in good faith and the said Sarah being Examined separate and apart from her husband Exknowledge that she did Signed the sam[e] Voluntarlary by and without fear of her husband and that she Relinqishis her right of dower into the same, and—I further certify that above named pe[r]sons are pe[r]sonally know[n] to me to be the Same whom names are hearunto attached given under my hand this 3 day of May in the year of our lord one thousand Eight hundred & thirty seven

David Dryden

J. P.

The young lawyer starting practice in Springfield, Illinois, was stepping out in society, more or less, if we judge by the invitation to a cotillion:

The pleasure of your Company is respectfully solicited at a Cotillion Party, to be given at the "American House," on to-morrow evening at 7 o'clock, P. M. December 16th, 1839.

N. H. RIDGELY,   J. F. SPEED,
J. A. M'CLERNAND,   J. SHIELDS,
R. ALLEN,   E. D. TAYLOR,
N. H. WASH,   E. H. MERRYMAN,
F. W. TODD,   N. E. WHITESIDE,
S. A. DOUGLASS,   H. EASTHAM,
W. S. PRENTICE,   J. R. DILLER,
B. W. EDWARDS,   A. LINCOLN,
                              Managers.

Society affair in Springfield

Possibly to gratify the curiosity of Mary Todd or perhaps to indicate to her his good political standing among the Sangamon County voters who elected him to the legislature, Lincoln painstakingly wrote on sheets of paper how the ballots had run for him in the various townships. Holding the sheets together is a long pink satin ribbon tied in a large fancy bow. The tabulation shows that in the Sangamon County 1832 election for state representative Lincoln stood eighth with 657 votes, in 1834 standing second with 1376 votes, in 1836 leading all others with 1716 votes. Also in the satin-ribbon-tied packet is a certificate of Lincoln's friend Noah W. Matheny that Lincoln under oath swore to the election figures as true and correct.

One could enumerate an extended series of letters, bills, declarations, related to the practice of the young lawyer and politician, Abraham Lincoln, across the ten-year period of 1837-1847. He and his partners took in almost any case that came along.

Many are the forms and ways in which a customer or client can be told he must pay cash or at least he ought to. Lincoln had his own way of letting a young lawyer know that a glimpse of a little of the wherewithal would be a help.

Springfield, Nov. 2 1842.

Jas. S. Irwin, Esq.

Owing to my absence, yours of the 22nd ult. was not received till this moment.

Judge Logan & myself are willing to attend to any business in the Supreme Court you may send us. As to fees, it is impossible to establish a rule that will apply in all, or even a great many cases. We believe we are never accused of being very unreasonable in this particular; and we would always be easily satisfied, provided we could see the money—but whatever fees we earn at a distance, if not paid *before*, we have noticed we never hear of after the work is done. We therefore, are growing a little sensitive on that point.

Yours &c

A. Lincoln

January of 1848 finds Congressman Lincoln in Washington writing the best advice he knows to the home postmaster at Springfield on what kind of reports and affidavits might help the postmaster toward a pay raise. He counsels "Friend Diller" in a tone of patience and humor rising above the weariness of office: "I am kept very busy here; and one thing that perplexes me more than most anything else, are the cases of Whigs calling on me to get them appointments to places in the army, from the President." Lincoln was a Whig and the President a Democrat, wherefore, "There are two great obstacles in the way which they do not seem to understand—first, the President has no such appointments to give—and secondly, if he had, he could hardly be expected to give them to Whigs, at the solicitation of a Whig member of Congress."

The famous letter of Lincoln of February 2, 1848, written from Washington to his law partner, William H. Herndon, is striking and memorable because of its shining affection for the little man who later became Vice-President of the Confederate States of America. It reads:

Washington. Feb. 2. 1848

Dear William:

I just take up my pen to say, that Mr Stephens of Georgia, a little slim, pale-faced, consumptive man, with a voice like Logan's, has just concluded the very best speech, of an hour's length, I ever hear[d]. My old, withered, dry eyes are full of tears yet. If he writes it out any thing like he delivered it, our people shall see a good many copies of it.

Yours truly

To W H Herndon   A.. Lincoln

Another letter to Herndon from Washington has the vocal tone of the laughing Lincoln:

Washington, July 11— 1848

Dear William:

Yours of the 3rd is this moment received; and I hardly need say, it gives unalloyed pleasure. I now almost regret writing the serious, long faced letter, I wrote yesterday; but let the past as nothing be. Go it while you're young! I write this in the confusion of the H.R, and with several other things to attend to. I will send you about eight different speeches this evening; and as to kissing a pretty girl, I know one very pretty one, but I guess she wont let me kiss her.

Yours forever
A Lincoln

Washington, Feb. 2. 1848

Dear William:

I just take up my pen to say, that Mr. Stephens of Georgia, a little slim, pale-faced, consumptive man, with a voice like Logan's, has just concluded the very best speech, of an hour's length, I ever heard. My old, withered, dry eyes, are full of tears yet. If he writes it out any thing like he delivered it, our people shall see a good many copies of it.

Yours truly
A. Lincoln

To W. H. Herndon

Facsimile letter of Congressman Lincoln to his law partner back home

Washington, July 11- 1848

Dear William:

Yours of the 3rd is this moment received; and I having nearly a whole day, I have undertaken to answer. I now almost regret writing the serious, long faced letter, I wrote yesterday; but let the past be as nothing. Go it while you're young! I write this in the congress of the U. R. room with persons all the things to distract me. I will resume you about eight different speeches this evening; and as to kissing—pretty give, & know one very pretty one, but I guess she won't let me kiss her.-

Yours forever
A Lincoln

Gossipy, light-hearted, even gay, Lincoln writes of youth and girls and kissing. The mood is definitely of mirth rather than melancholy

State House, Springfield, Illinois, where Lincoln delivered the House Divided speech and where he wrote part of his Cooper Union speech

U.S. Treasury women cutting greenbacks from sheets (*above*)

Sherman House, Chicago, where Lincoln stopped (*above right*)

Libby Prison, Richmond, Virginia, which was moved entire to Chicago to house museum exhibits (*right*)

Four actors in the Lincoln scene who, in their hour of fate, played powerful roles. Here they sign their names to camera registers of their faces

Unique proof from an unfinished engraving of young Mary Todd, probably 1840

Photograph from unretouched negative discarded by Alexander Hesler in Chicago and found in a wastebasket by his successor. Negative made probably June, 1860

Brady portrait of Lincoln at time of the Cooper Union speech, widely used during 1860 campaign

Alexander Hesler's photograph of Lincoln in Springfield, June 3, 1860, often having preference as the "handsomest" in Lincoln portraiture

From carte-de-visite-sized original photograph of Lincoln by Alexander Hesler, Springfield, June 3, 1860

Mary Todd Lincoln, widow

William Wallace Lincoln in Washington

Early photograph of William Wallace Lincoln in Springfield, Illinois

Tableware Mary Lincoln presented to Usher Linder for Mrs. Linder, including china gravy bowl, plates, pitcher, metal candlestick, knife and fork, spoon, and majolica pitcher

OFFICE OF

REED & SWINFORD,

CITY JEWELERS.

PARIS, ILLS.

State of Illinois.)
Edgar County.) ss

I, Denis F, Hanks, aged ninety-two years, make the following statement of Abraham Lincoln, and a watch owned by him and now in possession of Mrs. M. M. Barney a granddaughter of mine:

This watch was presented to me by Abraham Lincoln in 1864 at Washington city, D. C., where I had gone to intercede for some men who had been in a riot at Charleston, Ills. The watch he gave me is a silver "Waltham" case No. E272- Wm. Ellery movement - key-winder- No. 87013 Boston, Mass. The initials, (D. F. H.,) were engraved by Joseph Dikob, of Charleston, Ill., after I returned home.

I am a full cousin of Abraham Lincoln, and taught him to read and write.

(Signed) ....

Subscribed and sworn to before me this 14th day of May, 1891.

.... Clerk of County Court.

Lincoln's hunting-case watch, closed and open (*below*). Attest by Dennis F. Hanks to whom Lincoln gave the watch

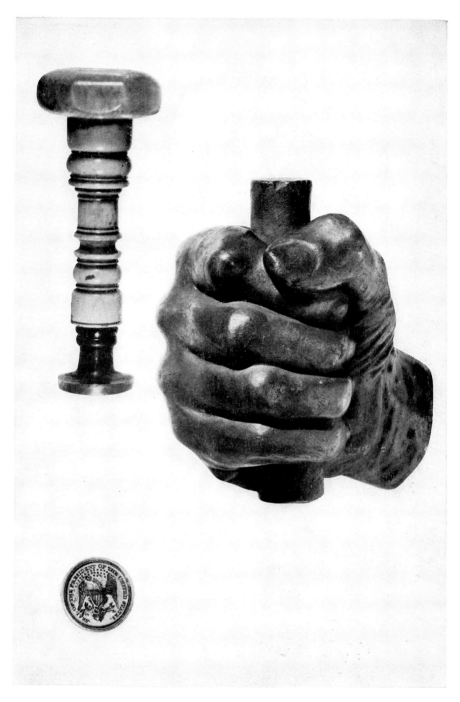

The President's seal, and the right hand of Lincoln molded from life by Leonard Wells Volk

In language dignified, chaste, and fluent came a request that Lincoln dip his quill pen and write a name:

Lowell Mass 27th Nov. 1848.

Sir.

I am engaged in collecting the autographs of American Statesmen. The high position you occupy has imparted to me a desire to possess your own. I am particularly anxious to add it to my list as you are the only Whig member from your state. If you should think proper to honor me by noticing this communication, you will confer a favor for which I shall feel grateful.

Very respectfully
Your obt. Servt.
Frank Seathe

Hon. Abraham Lincoln.

Lincoln the officeseeker of appointment to Federal office is set forth. A memorandum in Lincoln's handwriting, with his signature and that of E. D. Baker, seems to be intended to reach President Zachary Taylor, who looked with disfavor on those who were termed "ultra Whigs," in which category Lincoln and Baker put Justin Butterfield, the favored one who finally got the office. The paper reads:

He lied in his heart when he said he was not an ultra whig and he desired Gen. Taylor to be so informed. . . .

Your Obdt Serv-'ts
A. Lincoln
E. D. Baker

Out of Congress and again at home in law practice, the manipulations or "wirepulling" in which Lincoln was engaged, in the only instance in which he sought appointive Federal office, stand forth in a letter to a Hoosier politician whose influence he requested. He wrote:

Confidential

Springfield, Ills. May 25. 1849.

Hon. R. W. Thompson.

Dear Sir.

I am about to ask a favor of you—one which, I hope, will not cost you much. I understand the General Land-Office is about to be given to Illinois;

and that Mr. Ewing desires Justice Butterfield of Chicago to be the man. I will not trouble you with particulars, but will assure you, that the appointment of Mr. Butterfield will be an egregious political blunder. I believe it will gratify no single whig in the state, except it be Mr. B. himself. Now, the favor I wish of you is, that you will write Genl. Taylor at once, saying that in your opinion, either *I, or the man I recommend*, should be appointed to that office, if any one from Illinois shall be. I restrict my request to Illinois, because I think it probable that you have already recommended some one, probably from your own state; and I do not wish to interfere with that.

Yours truly

A.. Lincoln

Again actively practicing law, he wrote briefs in the lower courts and the higher, one of his most interesting being his notes for his argument in an Illinois Central case in the Supreme Court of Illinois. Besides the latter brief, and among many other legal papers written by Lincoln and part of the collection, is an award handed down by Lincoln and David Davis and John T. Stuart, serving as arbitrators, April 7, 1856. Also we meet pages whereon Lincoln wrote instructions for the judge to read to the jury. Other legal papers included go back to the first legal document drawn by Lincoln in 1833 for David Rutledge, brother of Ann. He drafted this paper long before he was licensed to practice in 1836. Also there is the instrument of April 18, 1834, served on Lincoln, which took away his surveying paraphernalia and other personal property.

Across the 1850's through the momentous year of 1858 and the nationally famous Lincoln-Douglas debates are varied papers on legal matters and law cases. In the midst of a letter in 1852 he advises a client: ". . . the signs are against us. What I mean by this is, that I have entire confidence that the law is with us on the Statute of Limitations, and yet it seems, I can not get the judge to remember that this is a question in the case at all." Farther down the letter closes, "Be patient. They have not got your land yet. Write soon."

Amid a wide variety of cases at law involving land, money, property issues, Lincoln occasionally departed into the defense of criminals and divorce contests. In one of the latter we have in the collection, as of 1856 in the Supreme Court of Illinois, in Lincoln's handwriting, "Abraham Lincoln,

Know all men by these presents that we David Rutledge. William Green Jr. and A. Lincoln are held and firmly bound unto Alexander Trent. and Martin S Trent in the penal Sum of one hundred and fifty dollars. well and truly to be paid unto them —— as witness our hands and seals, this 31st of Jany— 1833 ——

David Rutledge
William Green
A. Lincoln

First legal document drawn up by Lincoln before he was licensed to practice

being first duly sworn, states on oath that"—whereupon follow the particulars. In 1851 a decree of divorce was rendered "dissolving the bonds of matrimony" between Franklin C. Gray and Mary Anna Gray, afterward Franklin C. Gray "went through the forms and ceremonies of a legal marriage with one Matilda Caroline French, which, affiant supposes, was a valid marriage, if the decree of Divorce aforesaid, was and is valid; that still later the said Franklin C. Gray departed this life, intestate." One John Cook and Matilda C. Gray had been appointed administrators of Gray's estate in New York, and one C. J. Eaton administrator of the estate in California. There had, however, been no administration of his estate in the State of Illinois. After Gray's death "the said Matilda Caroline French or Matilda Caroline Gray . . . was delivered of a child which, in the course of nature, must have been begotten after her supposed marriage with the said Franklin C. Gray, and while they cohabited as husband and wife, and that he left no other legitimate child, so far as affiant knows, or believes; that said child is still living, a female and a minor, and that its name is 'Florence Franklin C. Gray.' " Then notice is given that "the said Mary Anna Gray wishes to prosecute a writ of error to reverse said decree of Divorce," and the parties to be defendants are named.

In a case in the Vermilion County Circuit Court, "Lincoln & Lamon for Respondent," sign the "answer of Eliza Jane Helmick to the Bill in Chancery of George Helmick." Two sentences in Lincoln's handwriting proceed, ". . . she denies that she has ever committed adultery with John Rice, or with any other person whomsoever. On the contrary thereof, she charges that said complainant, while he yet lived with her, for the purpose of contriving evidence to procure a divorce from her, at various times, and in different ways, attempted to induce different men to make attempts upon the chastity of your Respondent; and that said complainant, at one time, by threats of violence, made to her when she was alone, attempted to intimidate her to confess to her father that she had committed adultery."

The request for the payment of a fee, July 4, 1851, is here, Lincoln telling his client, that his lawsuit has been won. "As the dutch Justice said, when he married folks 'Now, vere ish my hundred tollars.' "

There are certain old poems, old stories, old books, clocks, and jack-knives, old rose and lavender keepsakes with musk and dusk in them, with a sunset smoke loitering in the faded shine of their walnut and mahogany stain and embellishment.

And we learn them by heart; we memorize their lines and outlines, and put them away in the chests and attics of our memories, keeping them as keepsakes, taking them out and handling them, reciting their feel and rhythm, scanning their lines, and then putting them back till the next time they will be wanted, for they will always be wanted again.

Abraham Lincoln had such an old keepsake, a rhymed poem with stanzas having for him the sweet pathos of a slow, quaint tune hummed by a young woman to the auburn western sky of a late winter twilight. It spun out and carried further the hymn line, "Vain man, thy fond pursuits forbear."

It came from an old country across the sea and was written like an air from an old-fashioned spinet with its rosewood touched with a yellow tarnish. It was put together like some old melodrama that measures out life so that we want to cry as we look at it.

Lincoln once wrote of it, "I would give all I am worth, and go in debt, to be able to write so fine a piece as I think that is. Neither do I know who is the author."

Lois Newhall's singing had pleased Lincoln on an evening when he was requested by the company to recite his favorite poem, "Mortality," more widely known as "O Why Should the Spirit of Mortal be Proud?"—and

Springfield, Ills. Feby. 4. 1857.

Andrew B. Chealan:

Dear Sir: I have news from Ottawa, that we win our Galatin & Saline county case. As the dutch justice said when he married folks "Now, vere ish my hundred tollars"

Yours truly

A. Lincoln

Attorney Lincoln wins the lawsuit of Andrew McCallan, and quotes for the client what the Dutch justice said when he married folks, "Now, vere ish my hundred tollars"

Above is part of a manuscript in which Lincoln wrote the twelve verses of his favorite poem, "Mortality" for Lois Newhall it was that he wrote all the twelve verses of that poem, the familiar text of the first two greeting Miss Newhall's eyes as follows:

> O why should the spirit of mortal be proud?
> Like a swift fleeting meteor—a fast flying cloud—
> A flash of the lightning—a break of the wave,
> He passeth from life to his rest in the grave.
>
> The leaves of the Oak, and Willow shall fade;
> Be scattered around, and together be laid.
> And the young and the old, and the low and the high,
> Shall moulder to dust, and together shall lie.

The verses were "adapted to music expressly composed by C. Everest" and published in 1865 in sheet-music form by Lee & Walker, Philadelphia, under the title "President Lincoln's Favorite Poem."

In the stormy career of Stephen Arnold Douglas, United States Senator from Illinois, one of his most sweeping and decisive political acts came in the launching of the Kansas-Nebraska Bill. He declared that this act would settle the slavery question for all time. The act set forth "the principle that the people of all the states & territories are to be left free to regulate their own domestic institutions in their own way, without any interference from Congress and subject only to the Constitution of the United States." We have here this statement in Douglas's handwriting. On the back of it is the notation:

> Hon. Stephen A. Douglas's original draft of the provision in his Nebraska bill that has raised the furor.
> Given to me by Senator Gwin 24ᵗʰ Mch 1854
> John S. Cunningham

When the news of the passage of the Kansas-Nebraska Bill came to Lincoln, he said that there were times he could not sleep of nights because of the terrific implications and involvements of that act of Congress.

We have here a piece of work wherein Lincoln clipped, pasted, wrote interlineations. The published text of the Lincoln-Douglas debates issued that winter was set up by the printers from a manuscript furnished by Lincoln. The labor and care of preparing this manuscript fell on Lincoln himself. From Republican newspapers favorable in viewpoint to him, Lincoln clipped the shorthand reports of his speeches. From Democratic news-

[handwritten manuscript text]

From Douglas's original draft in his own handwriting of the Kansas-Nebraska Bill which "tore the country in two," raising the issue of "Squatter Sovereignty"

papers favorable to the viewpoint of Douglas, he clipped the speeches of his opponent.

A scrapbook bound in substantial black boards, 9 inches wide by some 14 inches long, held these clippings that Lincoln pasted, on 95 pages, each numbered in Lincoln's hand. The front fly leaf and pages here and there have notes, annotations, corrections, or minor changes in Lincoln's handwriting. In scores of instances Lincoln's black lead pencil has struck out parentheses containing the words "Applause" or "Laughter" or "Cheers" and various remarks shouted from the audience.

As edited by Lincoln the reader can form no opinion as to which of the debaters got the most applause or laughter or cheers. In one deleted parenthesis came the interjection of a man in the crowd to whom Douglas had remarked that he knew this man was not going to vote for Mr. Lincoln, which the man seconded with, "I'll be d—d if I do."

Laid in this manuscript of the only book that Lincoln wrote or edited or prepared for publication may still be found the letters John Hay wrote in an effort to buy the book, which hope of Hay came to naught.

Now Lincoln's letters ran both somber and jocular. "We shall have fun again," he writes to a *Chicago Tribune* editor, along with a request for newspapers he needs for editorial work on his first book.

Second joint debate,
August 27. 1858 at Free-
port, Illinois—
Lincoln, as reported in
the Press & Tribune—
Douglas, as reported in the
Chicago Times—

A. I do not stand to-day pledged to the abolition of slavery in the District of Columbia.

Q. 5. "I desire him to answer whether he stands pledged to the prohibition of the slave trade between the different States?"

A. I do not stand pledged to the prohibition of the slave trade between the different States.

Q. 6. "I desire to know whether he stands pledged to prohibit slavery in all the Territories of the United States, North as well as South of the Missouri Compromise line."

A. I am impliedly, if not expressly, pledged to a belief in the right and duty of Congress to prohibit slavery in all the United States Territories. [Almost applause.]

Q. 7. "I desire him to answer whether he is opposed to the acquisition of any new territory unless slavery is first prohibited therein."

A. I am not generally opposed to honest acquisition of territory; and, in any given case I would or would not oppose such acquisition, accordingly as I might think such acquisition would or would not agitate the slavery question among ourselves. [Different responses.]

Now, my friends, it will be perceived upon an examination of these questions and answers, that so far I have only answered that I was not pledged to this, that or the other. The Judge has not framed his interrogatories to ask me anything more than this, and I have answered in strict accordance with the interrogatories, and have answered truly that I am not pledged at all upon any of the points to which I have answered. But I am not disposed to hang upon the exact form of his interrogatory. I am rather disposed to take up at least some of these questions, and state what I really think upon them.

As to the first one in regard to the Fugitive Slave Law, I have never hesitated to say, and I do not now hesitate to say, that I think, under the Constitution of the United States, the people of the Southern States are entitled to a Congressional Fugitive Slave Law. Having said that, I have had nothing to say in regard to the existing Fugitive Slave Law further than that I think it should have been framed so as to be free from

ence in the State of Illinois, and I believe I am saying that which, if it would be offensive to any persons and render them enemies to myself, would be offensive to persons in this audience.

I now proceed to propound to the Judge the interrogatories, so far as I have framed them. I will bring forward a new installment when I get them ready. [Laughter.] I will bring them forward now, only reaching to number four.

The first one is—

Question 1. If the people of Kansas shall, by means entirely unobjectionable in all other respects, adopt a State Constitution, and ask admission into the Union under it, before they have the requisite number of inhabitants according to the English Bill—some ninety-three thousand—will you vote to admit them? [Applause.]

Q. 2. Can the people of a United States Territory, in any lawful way, against the wish of any citizen of the United States, exclude slavery from its limits prior to the formation of a State Constitution? [Renewed applause.]

Q. 3. If the Supreme Court of the United States shall decide that States can not exclude slavery from their limits, are you in favor of acquiescing in, adopting and following such decision as a rule of political action? [Loud applause.]

Q. 4. Are you in favor of acquiring additional territory, in disregard of how such acquisition may affect the nation of the slavery question? [Cries of "good," "good."]

As introductory to these interrogatories which Judge Douglas propounded to me at Ottowa, he read a set of resolutions which he said Judge Trumbull and myself had participated in adopting, in the first Republican State Convention held at Springfield, in October, 1854. He insisted that I and Judge Trumbull, and perhaps, the entire Republican party were responsible for the doctrines contained in the set of resolutions which he read, and I understand that it was from that set of resolutions that he deduced the interrogatories which he propounded to me, using these resolutions as a sort of authority for propounding those ques-

offensive

agravate

decide

From Lincoln's one book manuscript—the debates with Douglas

Springfield, Nov, 20, 1858

Dr. C. H. Ray

My dear Sir.

I wish to preserve a Set of the late debates (if they may be called so) between Douglas and myself. To enable me to do so, please get two copies of each number of your paper containing the whole, and send them to me by Express; and I will pay you for the papers & for your trouble. I wish the two sets, in order to lay one away in the room and to put the other in a Scrap-book. Remember, if part of any debate is on *both* sides of one sheet, it will take two sets to make one scrap-book. I believe, according to a letter of yours to Hatch you are "feeling like h—ll yet." Quit that. You will soon feel better. Another "blow-up" is coming; and we shall have fun again. Douglas managed to be supported both as the best instrument to *put down* and to *uphold* the slave power; but no ingenuity can long keep the antagonism in harmony.

Yours as ever

A. Lincoln

A letter of March 4, 1859, to Mark W. Delahay of Kansas, has Lincoln's assurance that he will make an effort to get to a Republican convention in Kansas. December 7 of that same year is the date on the autograph-album leaf on which Lincoln wrote for Delahay's daughter:

Dear Mary

With pleasure I write my name in your Album— Ere long some younger man will be more happy to confer *his* name upon *you*—

Don't allow it, Mary, until fully assured that he is worthy of the happiness—Dec. 7. 1859

Your friend

A. Lincoln

At a later time when Miss Delahay asked General Ulysses S. Grant to write in her album, he thought it would be nice if he put his signature on the same page as Lincoln, and it is there, a large and smoothly flowing autograph.

Lincoln, the politician with an eye for trends and currents, yet a constructive statesman of vision, wrote to a shady Kansas politician. All of the letter, except Lincoln's signature and a few changes in text, is in the hand of Elmer Ephraim Ellsworth, Zouave officer, law student in Lincoln's office.

Dear Mary
With pleasure I write my
name in your Album — Ere long
some younger man will be more hap-
py to confer his name upon you—
Dont allow it, Mary, until fully
assured that he is worthy of the hap-
piness — Dec. 7 - 1859
Your friend
A. Lincoln

From Mary Delahay's autograph album where Lincoln and Grant signed on the same page

Springfield Ills May 14 1859

Mr. M. Delahay, Esq
My Dear Sir

I find it impossible for me to attend your Republican convention at Ossawatan on the 18th. It would have offered me much personal gratification to see your fine new country, and to meet the good people who have cast their lot there; and still more, if I could thereby contribute anything to the Republican cause. You probably will adopt resolutions in the nature of a platform; and, as I think, the only danger will be the temptation to lower the Republican Standard in order to gather recruits. In my judgement such a step would be a serious mistake—would open a gap through which more would pass *out* than pass *in*. And this would be the same, whether the letting down should be in deference to Douglasism, or to the Southern opposition element Either would surrender the o[b]ject of the Republican organization, the preventing the Spread and *Nationalization* of Slavery. This object surrendered, the organization would go to pieces I do not mean by this, that no Southern man must be placed upon our Republican National ticket for 1860. There are many men in the Slave States for any one of whom I would cheerfully vote to be either President or Vice
enable
President provided he would ~~allow~~ me to do so with *safety* to the Repub-

lican cause—without lowering the Republican Standard. This is the indispensable condition of a Union with us. It is idle to think of any other. Any other would be as fruitless to the South, as distasteful to the North, the whole ending in common defeat. Let a union be attemptede [sic] on the basis of ignoring the Slavery question, and magnifying other questions which the people just now are really caring nothing about, and it will result in gaining no single electoral vote in the *South* and losing every one in the North.

Yours very truly,
A. Lincoln

A notebook with seven pages in Lincoln's handwriting gives a list of the members of the legislature of Illinois in 1854 and 1855 with notes as to the party leanings of each man, evidently for use in his campaign for the United States Senatorship.

Out of the year 1858 and the famous Debates are two letters to Henry Asbury. In the first one, July 31, Lincoln indicates the lines he will take in the forthcoming argument. Then in less than four months the big winds die down, the fireworks end, the last handbills and procession banners have been blown from the streets to the gutters and ash heaps, the provocative discussion holding national attention becomes history. Douglas wins goal and stakes. Lincoln the loser writes to Asbury, who writes a postscript to the Lincoln letter.

Springfield, Novr. 19 1858

Henry Asbury, Esq
My dear Sir
Yours of the 13th was received some days ago. The fight must go on. The cause of civil liberty must not be surrendered at the loss of *one*, or even one *hundred* defeats. Douglas had the ingenuity to be supported in the late contest both as the best means to *break down*, and to *uphold* the Slave interest. No ingenuity can keep those antagonistic elements in harmony long. Another explosion will soon come.

Yours truly
A.. Lincoln

On the 13 I had written him a cheerful letter telling him not to give it up so the above is his glorious answer

Henry Asbury

Springfield, Nov. 19 1858

Henry Asbury, Esq
My dear Sir

Yours of the 13th was received some days ago. The fight must go on. The cause of civil liberty must not be surrendered at the end of one, or even, one hundred defeats. Douglas had the ingenuity to be supported in the late contest both as the best means to break down, and to uphold the Slave interest. No ingenuity can keep those antagonistic elements in harmony long. Another explosion will soon come.

Yours truly
A. Lincoln.

On the 13 I had written him a cheerful letter telling him not to give up &c The above is his glorious answer
Henry Asbury

Lincoln writes Asbury, who puts a memo on the letter

The boy William Wallace Lincoln, having told what he knows that is new, wastes no further words.

Springfield Apr

Dear Friend
I will write you a few lines to let you know how I am getting along. I am pretty well. The roads are drying up it is Sunday and a pleasant day I have not any more to say so I must bring my letter to an end

Wm W. Lincoln
The end

I have not any more to say so I must bring my letter to an end
Wm W Lincoln

The end

Ready to launch a boom for Lincoln for President, the Peoria, Illinois, editor, Thomas J. Pickett, bluntly suggested that all the Republican editors of Illinois should throw in with all they had on the boom—this in a letter to Lincoln asking about his giving a lecture in Rock Island. In a political hour of high tension when other candidates mentioned for the Presidency, such as William H. Seward and Salmon Portland Chase, had no hesitations about declaring themselves fit for the Presidency, Lincoln said just the opposite in his reply to Pickett. The letter:

Springfield, April 16, 1859.

T. J. Pickett, Esq
My dear Sir

Yours of the 13th is just received. My engagements are such that I can not, at any very early day, visit Rock Island, to deliver a lecture, or for any other object.

As to the other matter you kindly mention, I must, in candor, say I do not think myself fit for the Presidency. I certainly am flattered and gratified that some partial friends think of me in that connection; but I really think it best for our cause that no concerted effort, such as you suggest, should be made.

Let this be considered confidential.

Yours very truly

A.. Lincoln.

Barrett had a deep feeling about the manuscript of the autobiography that Lincoln, after his nomination for the Presidency, wrote on request of Jesse Fell of Bloomington, Illinois, and Lincoln sent to Fell with a letter. That letter had come into Barrett's hands in a purchase from the heirs of Osborn H. Oldroyd. Barrett wanted the autobiography and exchanged letters with the Fell sisters, who owned it. Their nephew, the editor of the *Bloomington Pantagraph*, came to Barrett's office one Saturday afternoon. They readily agreed on the value of the manuscript. The banks were closed. Moreover, the editor said there was another to be consulted and that he would leave the autobiography with Barrett and come back on Monday. Barrett said, "No, you bring it back on Monday," and soon after Barrett read in the paper of his sudden death. Afterwards Barrett learned that the death of the nephew had seemed almost a warning and that the Fell sisters were not going to part with the manuscript on which Lincoln had written the story of his life.

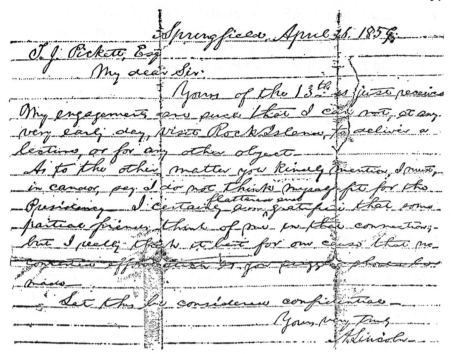

Lincoln writes short letter, every phrase significant for the hour. (*Reduced from original*)

The letter of Lincoln to Fell which Barrett later bought from the Oldroyd heirs reads:

Springfield, Dec. 20. 1859

J. W. Fell, Esq.
My dear Sir:

Herewith is a little sketch, as you requested. There is not much of it, for the reason, I suppose, that there is not much of me. If anything be made out of it, I wish it to be modest, and not to go beyond the materials. If it were thought necessary to incorporate any thing from any of my speeches, I suppose there would be no objection. Of course it must not appear to have been written by myself.

Yours very truly

A. Lincoln

M. Brayman, of Springfield, Illinois, in a letter, February 27, 1860, wrote to an old Springfield friend, W. H. Bailhache, of New York City of the day being pleasant, the sun shining, the streets improving, business getting better, and then a close-up as though the coming President-elect of the United States might be lingering in a near-by doorway. Brayman felt horsey that day. So did Lincoln. Brayman wrote of the horseplay:

I am at the Astor House. Mr. Lincoln is there, and we have spent much time together, but I am getting *crowded out*. While at Dinner to-day, he was waited upon by some admirers. He turned half round and talked "hoss" to them—introduced me as a Democrat, but one so good tempered that he and I could "eat out of the *same rack, without a pole between* us." After dinner we went to his room, then came a black republican to take him up Broadway "to show him the fine buildings," but, I guess it was to show him *to* the fine buildings. On h*is* heels came a delegation from Patterson [sic] and Orange, in New Jersey, begging him to go over and make speeches in those places. Thus you perceive, the fame of A*ncie*nt Abra*ha*m, has extended even into foreign lands. To these unsophisticated heathen he presented me, with a caution to be careful what they s*ai*d, as I was a dem*ocr*at. Then came a young man's committee of five, whereupon I bolted for the door, taking another man's coat in my haste. Calling Abraham outside long enough to assure him that he was certainly becoming *an object of* atte*nti*on, and he must have a com*mitt*ee of *recepti*on and a pri*vate Secret*ary, I made my escape into the atmosphere of Wall Street, where my politicks would be estimated according to the value of my coll*ate*rals, instead of the company I was keeping..

Mr. Lincoln speaks to-night at the Cooper Institute. For the honor of Illinois we shall all turn out [to] hear him; and I anticipate a rousing crowd. He is in fine health and spirits, and will make a telling speech—perhaps his best.

The printed report of the Lincoln-Douglas debates constituted historical material, in Lincoln's view. Whether he presented copies to similar institutions, is not known.

Hon. A Lincoln,
                                         Concord, N. H. Aug 18 1860.
Sir,
                    THE NEW-HAMPSHIRE HISTORICAL SOCIETY
Acknowledges the receipt from you of one copy of "Political Debates" as a   Donation   for the use of said Society. You will please accept

their thanks for this expression of your interest in the objects of their Institution.

> I have the honor to be
> > Your obedient servant,
> > > William F. Goodwin   LIBRARIAN

P.S. Cant you send us a "*Rail*"?

"Private & confidential" is at the top of the page of a letter Lincoln dated December 11, 1860, to Hon. William Kellogg. Closely packed, highly implicative, was this brief letter.

> ### Private & Confidential
> > Springfield, Ills. Dec. 11. 1860

Hon. William Kellogg.
My dear Sir.
Entertain no proposition for a compromise in regard to the *extension* of slavery. The instant you do, they have us under again; all our labor is lost, and sooner or later must be done over. Douglas is sure to be again trying to bring in his "Pop. Sov." Have ~~not~~ none of it, the tug has to come & better now than later.

You know I think the fugitive slave clause of the constitution ought to be enforced—to put it in the mildest form, ought not to be resisted.

> > In haste
> > > Yours as ever
> > > > A. Lincoln

Robert Todd Lincoln began to have his embarrassments over being the son of the President-elect, and was collegiate in his humor, with long excuses.

> > Phillips Exeter Academy
> > Dec 2d 1860

Dear Mother—
You see I am back at Exeter and I feel very much at home.

I am here with Dick Meconkey. We have been in a constant round of dissipation since we came. On Thursday we were at dinner at Miss Gale's. On Friday Mr Tuck gave a large party, which passed off very finely. Mr. T. thinks of going to Chicago in about three weeks and thence to St. Louis. So look out for him.

THE RAIL.

THAT OLD ABE SPLIT.

This is THE RAIL
That Old Abe split.

This is THE FENCE
That was made with
The Rail that Old Abe split.

This is THE FIELD
Enclosed by the Fence,
That was made with
The Rail that Old Abe split.

This is THE ROAD
That passed through the Field,
Enclosed by the Fence,
That was made with
The Rail that Old Abe split.

This is THE TEAM
That traveled the Road,
That passed through the Field,
Enclosed by the Fence,
That was made with
The Rail that Old Abe split.

This was THE BOY
That drove the Team,
That traveled the Road,
That passed through the Field,
Enclosed by the Fence,
That was made with
The Rail that Old Abe split.

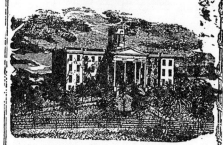

This is THE HOUSE
To be filled by the Boy,
That drove the Team,
That traveled the Road,
That passed through the Field,
Enclosed by the Fence,
That was made with
The Rail that Old Abe split.

PITTSBURGH FLAG MANUFACTORY, 45 FIFTH STREET.

Flags from 3 inches to 50 feet. ·Sandal· J. PITTOCK Agent for Co.

A Republican broadside, campaign of 1860

Tonight we are invited out to tea which will wind up our fun, as we have to commence study again tomorrow.

We have only about six weeks more before going home.

I see by the papers that you have been to Chicago.

Aint you beginning to get a little tired of this constant uproar?

I have a couple of friends from St. Louis who are going to the inauguration after vacation is over and I have invited them to stop at our house on their road. They are nice fellows and have been with me for the last year.

You will remember I wrote to Father about a fellow who is boring me considerably.

He capped the climax lately. There was a Republican levee and supper at Cambridge to which I was invited. I did not go, for I anticipated what really happened.

I was sitting in my room about 9½ ~~and~~ when two boys came up and handed me an admission ticket on the back of which this fellow had written, asking me to come over as they were calling for me. I wrote him excusing myself. He must be the biggest fool in the world not to know that I did not want to go over, when if I did, I would be expected to make a speech! Just phancy my phelinks mounted on the rostrum, holding "a vast sea of human faces" &c. I stop overwhelmed.

Yours affectionately

R. T. Lincoln

R. T. Lincoln at Phillips Exeter Academy writes to his mother

Bitter sarcasm and a toplofty manner was in a memorandum Congressman William Kellogg of Illinois left for President Lincoln in the Executive Mansion, April 3, 1861, and Lincoln's written answer had not merely patience but a truly Christian meekness:

Mr. Kellogg does me great injustice to write in this strain. He has had more favors than any other Illinois member, not excepting, I think, Judge Trumbull. Is it really in his heart to add to my perplexities now?

A. Lincoln

Patient President and greedy Congressman

A. G. Wolford, of Alton, Illinois, would have liked to tell the whole world what he wrote in a letter to his brother about the untried President. Having known "Uncle Abe" for twenty-three years, he has a positive opinion about the man. He rates him high and gives it in convincing words as of May 7, 1861, when the war was young yet:

I told Charly, in my letter to him some time ago that if Uncle Abe said the Horse was 16 feet high he would stand to it. I have known him for 23 years and he means what he says. He will do it or die you may rest assured that he will never give up untill he is left by the country to his own resources and has no aid nor backing he will take Sumpter if money and men can be found to do it or I am mistaken in the man.

Signatures to many documents, merely formal and routine, appear by scores throughout the collection, the names in other documents having an interest that for a moment stops the reader, such as the appointment of his convivial law partner in Danville, Illinois, Ward Hill Lamon, well versed in Addisonian prose and the singing of "The Blue-Tailed Fly," to be United States Marshal of the District of Columbia.

In swiftly written notes, the President would do the best he could toward getting appointments or hearings for old friends. One small sheet has the President and Mrs. Lincoln joining to say that they shall be much obliged to those who can do a favor for Mrs. Spriggs. It was at her boarding house Lincoln had lodged and eaten when a member of Congress a dozen years before and from where he had written (in a letter here preserved) to Mrs. Lincoln after she had visited him there, "All the house—or rather, all with whom you were on decided good terms—send their love to you. The others say nothing."

On the President's request to his Cabinet members to submit their opinions on whether Fort Sumter should be provisioned, the Secretary of the Navy, Gideon Welles, responded:

While it does not appear to me advisable to undertake to provision fort Sumter against the opinions of military men familiar with the circumstances, I am not prepared to say I would make no effort to reinforce the garrison and furnish it with supplies. In that event a war policy must be adopted, and we should be fully prepared for the consequences, for though it is not impossible that peace would follow the successful reinforcement of the garrison the probabilities are against it. But war once commenced, the energy

Secretary Welles writes guarded opinion for President's guidance and power of the government will be developed and the loyalty of the people displayed. I am by no means certain that, in the present condition of affairs, war with its calamities might not have a beneficent effect in uniting the people and strengthening the government.

I am not prepared to say that no effort should be made to reinforce and provision fort Sumter provided your enquiry embraced both objects. It would in all probability inaugurate a new policy with all the calamities of civil strife; but it would also develope the vigor and strength of the government, now weakened and demoralized.

Under date of September 22, 1862, the President wrote a one-sentence testimonial, with no reservations, for a young chiropodist, Isachar Zacharie, an English Jew: "Dr. Zacharie has operated on my feet with great success, and considerable addition to my comfort."

The President writes testimonial as to foot comfort

A former Governor of Kentucky and Member of Congress, Charles Slaughter Morehead, had landed, without trial, as a prisoner in Fort Warren in Boston Harbor, by order of Secretary of War Stanton. The Kentucky Legislature and Louisville Unionists had petitioned for his release on parole. After four months' confinement he was let loose. Lincoln's query read:

Might we not now let Gov. Morehead loose?

The President takes time to be homelike and chatty with a good woman living back where he came from:

Executive Mansion,
Washington, Dec. 4, 1861.

My dear Madam

I take great pleasure in acknowledging the receipt of your letter of Nov. 26; and in thanking you for the present by which it was accompanied. A pair of socks so fine, and soft, and warm, could hardly have been manufactured in any other way than the old Kentucky fashion. Your letter informs me that your maiden name was Crume, and that you were raised in Washington County, Kentucky, by which I infer that an uncle of mine by marriage was a relative of yours. Nearly, or quite sixty years ago, Ralph Crume married Mary Lincoln, a sister of my father, in Washington County, Kentucky.

Accept my thanks, and believe me

very truly

Your friend

A.. Lincoln.

Mrs. Susannah Weathers
Rossville, Clinton Co. Ind.

Here and there are pieces of writing that relate to the conduct of life. Their texts now stand on office desks and hang on schoolroom walls for what they suggest by way of instruction to the young. One instance is the letter about two young men whose mother said they "want to work." Lincoln saw it as so rare a want that he had to write about it to Major Ramsey at the Arsenal suggesting that he set them at it if possible. Possibly Lincoln at first intended to write "so rare a merit," and having written an *m*, then wrote the last three letters of the word "want" and let it go at that.

Executive Mansion
Oct. 17th, 1861

Majr. Ramsey
My dear Sir

The lady—bearer of this—says she has two sons who want to work. Set them at it, if possible. Wanting to work is so rare a want [merit?], that it should be encouraged.

Yours truly

A. Lincoln

Executive Mansion
Oct 17, 1861

Maj. Ramsay
My dear Sir

The lady — bearer of
this — says she has two sons.
who want to work. Set them
at it, if possible — Wanting
to work is so rare a merit,
that it should be encouraged

Yours, only
A. Lincoln

Lincoln's famous letter on wanting to work (*above*); his envelope address (*below*)

Maj. Ramsay
Arsenal
Washington.

One Midwest industrial concern has supplied to inquirers 20,000 facsimiles of this letter. In the many times and occasions that it has been reproduced we have here the first publication of the envelope on which Lincoln wrote the address of the recipient.

A card signed by the President requested a navy sword for Tad. In expressing his appreciation of the gift of white rabbits for his son, the father signed his full name of Abraham, possibly being absent-minded at the moment of signing.

Executive Mansion
April 2, 1862

My dear Sir

Allow me to thank you in behalf of my little son for your **present of White Rabbits.** He is very much pleased with them.

Yours truly
Abraham Lincoln

Michael Crock Esq
860 N Fourth St. Philada.

Small boy gets rabbits, father writes thanks

That form of signature "Abraham Lincoln" was as unusual on his personal correspondence as the signature of "A. Lincoln" was uncommon on an official document, as for example:

The report of the Judge Advocate General is approved & as in the state of the pleadings & in the absence of proof the court was not warranted in finding the prisoner guilty of desertion, & as he has confessed himself guilty of absence without leave only, it is ordered that the death sentence be commuted to confinement at hard labor for six months from this date.

Oct. 10. 1863.   A Lincoln

Text written by clerk, Lincoln commutes death sentence

Lincoln's anxiety for the friends of the Union in East Tennessee at times became distress. On January 6, 1862, he wrote to Brigadier General Buell his suggestion for a movement on East Tennessee.

. . . But my distress is that our friends in East Tennessee are being hanged and driven to despair, and even now I fear, are thinking of taking rebel arms for the sake of personal protection. In this we lose the most valuable stake we have in the South.

President Lincoln believed it good policy before an attempt should be made to emancipate all the slaves in the United States, that it might be worth while to see what success would attend an effort to free the chattel slaves of the District of Columbia from their shackles. On a single folio sheet he sent a message to the Senate and House recommending compensated abolishment in the District, the Federal Government to buy the slaves and manumit them. The document taking this momentous step was addressed: "Fellow Citizens of the Senate, and House of Representatives." The concluding paragraph reads:

In the matter of compensation, it is provided that claims may be presented within ninety days from the passage of the act "but not thereafter"; and there is no saving for minors, femes-covert [sic], insane, or absent persons. I presume this is an omission by mere over-sight, and I recommend that it be supplied by an amendatory or supplemental Act.

Abraham Lincoln

April 16. 1862.

GENERAL ORDERS, }   WAR DEPARTMENT,
No. 71.   ADJUTANT GENERAL'S OFFICE,
     Washington, June 21, 1862.

In every case of prisoners taken in arms against the United States, who may be tried and sentenced to death, the record of the tribunal before which the trial was had will be forwarded for the action of the President of the United States, without whose orders no such sentence, in such cases, will be executed.

BY ORDER OF THE SECRETARY OF WAR:

L. THOMAS,
Adjutant General.

OFFICIAL:

Assistant Adjutant General.

The President orders all death-sentence records forwarded to him

Back and forth, up and down, swayed the forces bringing many kinds of pressure on President Lincoln to mitigate the penalty of death imposed on one Nathaniel Gordon of Maine. This was the first and only slave-trader in the history of the United States to be tried and convicted, in accordance with the Constitution and Federal law. A ship captain, sailing from Africa and the mouth of the Congo River with some nine hundred Negroes aboard, he had been captured on the high seas. Pronouncing sentence of death, the court had declared, "Think of the cruelty and wickedness of siezing nearly a thousand fellow beings who never did you harm, and thrusting them between the deck of a small ship, beneath a burning tropical sun, to die of disease or suffocation, or be transported to distant lands, and be consigned they and their posterity, to a fate far more cruel than death. . . . As you are soon to pass into the presence of that God of the black man as well as the white man, who is no respecter of persons, do not indulge for a moment the thought that He hears with indifference the cry of the humblest of His children."

Lincoln had heard intercessors and scrutinized many respectable names on a petition for pardon. We read slowly the strange and austere language in the handwriting of the original document. The text runs as though in the background Lincoln had his contemplations: "I think I would personally prefer to let this man live in confinement and let him meditate on his deeds, yet in the name of justice and the majesty of law there ought to be one case, at least one specific instance, of a professional slave-trader, a Northern white man, given the exact penalty of death because of the incalculable number of deaths he and his kind inflicted upon black men amid the horrors of the sea-voyage from Africa to points in America." One piece of testimony indicates that Lincoln had flourished a pen over a reprieve, giving the doomed man an extra two weeks to live, saying in half a wail to a United States District Attorney, "Mr. Smith, you do not know how hard it is to have a human being die when you know that a stroke of your pen may save him." He signed the document reading:

Whereas, it appears that at a Term of the Circuit Court of the United States of America for the Southern District of New York held in the month of November A.D. 1861, Nathaniel Gordon was indicted and convicted for being engaged in the Slave Trade, and was by the said Court sentenced to death by hanging by the neck, on Friday the 7th day of February, A.D. 1862;

And whereas, a large number of respectable citizens have earnestly besought me to commute the said sentence of the said Nathaniel Gordon to a term of imprisonment for life, which application I have felt it to be my duty to refuse;

And whereas, it has seemed to me probable that the unsuccessful application made for the commutation of his sentence may have prevented the said Nathaniel Gordon from making the necessary preparation for the awful change which awaits him;

Now, therefore, be it known, that I, Abraham Lincoln, President of the United States of America, have granted and do hereby grant unto him, the said Nathaniel Gordon, a respite of the above recited sentence until Friday the twenty-first day of February, A.D. 1862, between the hours of twelve o'clock at noon and three o'clock in the afternoon of the said day, when the said sentence shall be executed.

In granting this respite it becomes my painful duty to admonish the prisoner that, relinquishing all expectation of pardon by Human Authority, he refer himself, alone to the mercy of the Common God and Father of all men.

this Fourth day of February A.D. 1862, and of the Independence of the United States the Eighty-sixth.

Abraham Lincoln

By the President:

William H. Seward
Secretary of State

Closing lines of the commutation of the death sentence

The date set for execution of sentence was the day preceding the ceremony of the inauguration of Jefferson Davis at Richmond, Virginia, as President of the Confederate States of America.

A letter of woe, distress, and reproach came to Mrs. A. Lincoln in the White House, dated "Washington, City, Feb. 21st 62," signed only "A Friend." It reads:

Washington, City, Feb. 21st 62

Silence and sadness uninterrupted reigns in and around the Executive mansion. The halls where all was merryment & gaiety but a few brief days ago, and inmates looking forward to a still brighter 22nd in commemorating a victory which had been the cause of frantick agony to mothers & wives, all changed, *now* the darkness of night holds undisputed possession, instead of the bugle and fife harbingers of glee and exultation over a down troden people, comes the muffled drum and the wail of the heart stricken mother calling after her lost one, ever and anon you hear the low voice asking where is my child! "Echo answers where." . . .

Oh! wife, mother, friend stop this sheding brother's blood— After your angel child shall have been laid in a carefully prepared grave, think of the miserable scanty covering of clay awarded to the sons of a southern mother, and when his little toys are carefully placed away in a well selected resting place, let them remain as emblems of peace, purity, and innocence, but pause and contrast them with the implements of death the sword, the bayonet, and the knife, all of which have become play-things to deal death and destruction to our southern homes. Oh! God I say again the blood that still stains the ground of our sister states still calls for vengeance.— Oh! entreat your husband to still this awful tumult and the manes of departed spirits will be appeased and mothers and orphans will rise up and call you blessed.

A Friend.

Under date of August 30, 1862, three members of President Lincoln's Cabinet signed a demand on him for "the immediate removal," the "prompt removal," of George B. McClellan "from the command of any army of the United States." They recited fearful conditions of military affairs and

Signatures of three Cabinet members to their joint demand for "immediate removal" of General McClellan placed the blame on McClellan. Three highly contrasted signatures of the Cabinet members—S. P. Chase, Secretary of the Treasury, Edwin M. Stanton, Secretary of War, Caleb B. Smith, Secretary of the Interior—are attached to this document out of plot and counterplot in the Washington labyrinths of that year.

As is well known among Lincoln students and collectors, there was a copy of the final Emancipation Proclamation of January 1, 1863, written in full in the handwriting of Lincoln and signed by Lincoln, which copy went to a Sanitary Fair in Chicago and was later burned in the Chicago fire. Another copy of the Emancipation Proclamation in the Spencerian script of a clerk, the document signed by Lincoln and attested by Seward, is in the collection.

The first and tentative Emancipation Proclamation of September 22, 1862, was followed by the second and final Emancipation Proclamation dated January 1, 1863. Emancipation, however, had been proclaimed without being enacted into law. That came January 31, 1865, in the Act passed by Congress and signed by the President, for the Constitutional Amendment abolishing slavery. The two-thirds vote of House and Senate required by the Constitution of the United States had declared a joint resolution. On heavy vellum the joint resolution was engrossed, signed by the two hundred and odd members of House and Senate who had voted for it, and with full signature of the head of the Executive Department of the Government, Abraham Lincoln.

An overly earnest student of chirography, the science which assumes to read human character by handwriting, would rise up from a scrutiny of this array of signatures and walk around in a daze. The signatures strive and clamor, they buzz and murmur.

On the death, in combat, of a great Confederate commander, the editor of the *Washington Daily Chronicle*, Colonel John W. Forney, published an editorial of respect and tribute, saying in part: "While we are only too glad to be rid, in any way, of so terrible a foe, our sense of relief is not unmingled with emotions of sorrow and sympathy at the death of so brave a man. Every man who possesses the least particle of magnanimity must admire the qualities for which Stonewall Jackson was celebrated—his heroism, his bravery, his sublime devotion, his purity of character. . . . He had one great and overmastering trait of character—a fanatical enthusiasm which overleaped all obstacles and sharpened prematurely the other qualities of his mind. He was a genuine fanatic. But for all that, we do not less admire the great and wonderful powers he possessed."

This military and naval authority thereof, will recognize and maintain the freedom of said persons.

And I hereby enjoin upon the people so declared to be free to abstain from all violence, unless in necessary self-defence; and I recommend to them that, in all cases when allowed, they labor faithfully for reasonable wages.

And I further declare and make known, that such persons of suitable condition, will be received into the armed service of the United States, to garrison forts, positions, stations, and other places, and to man vessels of all sorts in said service.

And upon this act, sincerely believed to be an act of justice, warranted by the Constitution, upon military necessity, I invoke the considerate judgment of mankind, and the gracious favor of Almighty God.

In witness whereof, I have hereunto set my name, and caused the seal of the United States to be affixed.

Done at the City of Washington, this first day of January, in the year of our Lord one thousand eight hundred and sixty-three, and of the Independence of the United States the eighty-seventh.

Abraham Lincoln.

[L.S.]

By the President:
William H. Seward
Secretary of State:

Emancipation Proclamation in Spencerian script of clerk, signature by Lincoln, attest by Seward

Executive Mansion.
Washington, May 13, 1863.

Col. Forney
My dear Sir
I wish to lose no time in thanking you for the excellent and manly article in the Chronicle on "Stonewall Jackson"

Yours truly

A. Lincoln

Executive Mansion,

Washington, May 13, 1863.

Col. Forney,
My dear Sir
I wish to lose no time in thanking you for the excellency [excellent] and manly article on the Chronicle on "Stonewall Jackson"

Yours [truly]

A Lincoln

Thanks for a nice editorial

A dozen cards have brief suggestions, often written with delicacy, occasionally sharp and peremptory, one dated October 3, 1863, reading:

Sec. of Interior, please see, hear, & oblige if you can my friend T. J. Carter.

A. Lincoln.

A request, brief and pleasant

On October 16, 1863, Lincoln addressed a letter to Major General Halleck in which after reviewing the condition of Lee's army and the prospect of an attack by Meade, the President made an extraordinary proposal for Halleck to transmit to Meade.

EXECUTIVE MANSION,
Washington, Oct. 16. 1863.

Major General Halleck

I do not believe Lee can have over sixty thousand effective men. Longstreet's corps would not be sent away, to bring an equal force back upon the same road; and there is no other ~~way~~ direction for them to have come from. Doubtless, in making the present movement Lee gathered in all available scraps, and added them to Hills & Ewell's corps; but that is all. And he made the movement in the belief that *four* corps had left Gen. Meade; and Gen. Meade's apparently avoiding a collision with him has confirmed him in that belief. If Gen. Meade can now attack him on a field no worse than equal for us, and will do so with all the skill and courage, which he, his officers and men possess, the honor will be his if he succeeds, and the blame may be mine if he fails.

Yours truly,

A.. Lincoln.

It seems that this was not the first occasion on which Lincoln had made such a suggestion to a General in the field. In a letter of Madeleine McDowell Greene, granddaughter of the General, which accompanied a letter in Lincoln's handwriting to her mother, she wrote to Mr. Barrett:

I suppose you may know our favorite Lincoln story. This is as it has been handed down to me:

When grandfather fought the battle of Bull Run he did so before the North was really ready to fight, and against his better judgment. Afterwards, when

Executive Mansion,

Washington, Oct 16. , 1863.

Major General Halleck

I do not believe Lee can have over sixty thousand effective men. Longstreet's corps would not be sent away, to bring an equal force back upon the same road; and there is no other direction for them to have come from. Doubtless, in making the present movement Lee gathered in all available scraps, and added them to Hills & Ewells corps; but that is all. And he made the movement in the belief that four corps had left Gen. Meade; and Gen. Meade's apparently avoiding a collision with him has confirmed him in that belief. If Gen. Meade can now attack him on a field no worse than equal for us, and will do so with all the skill and courage, which he, his officers and men possess, the honor will be his if he succeeds, and the blame may be mine if he fails.

Yours truly, A. Lincoln

"If Gen. Meade can now attack . . . the honor will be his if he succeeds, and the blame may be mine if he fails." (*Reduced from original*)

he was suffering considerable disgrace for the defeat President Lincoln sent for him and said that he wanted public announcement to be made, explaining how he had ordered McDowell to fight when the latter did not approve. To which my grandfather replied, "The King can do no wrong" and refused to have any such statement made. I was always proud that my grandfather had the good breeding to believe as he did and I always loved Lincoln for being so quick to take the blame and so eager to shield some one less popular from unpopularity.

ORDER OF PROCESSION

FOR THE

INAUGURATION

OF THE

National Cemetery at Gettysburg, Pa.

ON THE 19TH NOVEMBER, 1863.

Military, under command of Major-General COUCH.
Major-General MEADE and Staff, and the officers and soldiers of the Army of
the Potomac.
Officers of the Navy and Marine Corps of the United States.
Aids.   CHIEF MARSHAL.   Aids.
PRESIDENT OF THE UNITED STATES.
Members of the Cabinet.
Assistant Secretaries of the Several Executive Departments.
General-in-Chief of the Army, and Staff.
Lieutenant-General SCOTT and Rear-Admiral STEWART.
Judges of the U. S. Supreme Court.
Hon. EDWARD EVERETT, Orator of the day, and the Chaplain.
Governors of the States, and their Staffs.
Commissioners of the States on the Inauguration of the Cemetery.
Bearers with the Flags of the States.
VICE-PRESIDENT OF THE UNITED STATES and Speaker of the House of Represen-
tatives.
Members of the two Houses of Congress.
Officers of the two Houses of Congress.
Mayors of Cities.
Gettysburg Committee of Arrangements.
Officers and members of the United States Sanitary Commission.
Committees of Different Religious Bodies.
U. S. Military Telegraphic Corps.
Officers and Representatives of Adams Express Company.
Officers of different Telegraph Companies.
Hospital Corps of the Army.
Soldiers' Relief Associations.
Knights Templar.
Masonic Fraternity.
Independent Order of Odd-Fellows.
Other Benevolent Associations.
Literary, Scientific, and Industrial Associations.
The Press.
Officers and members of Loyal Leagues.
Fire Companies.
Citizens of the State of Pennsylvania.
Citizens of other States.
Citizens of the District of Columbia.
Citizens of the several Territories.

Order of procession at Gettysburg

Programme of Arrangements and Order of Exercises

FOR THE INAUGURATION

OF THE

NATIONAL CEMETERY AT GETTYSBURG,

ON THE 19TH OF NOVEMBER, 1863.

The military will form in Gettysburg at 9 o'clock a. m., on Carlisle street, north of the square, its right resting on the square, opposite McClellan's Hotel, under the direction of Major General Couch.

The State Marshals and Chief Marshal's aids will assemble in the public square at the same hour.

All civic bodies except the citizens of States will assemble, according to the foregoing printed programme, on York street at the same hour.

The delegation of Pennsylvania citizens will form on Chambersburg street, its right resting on the square, and the other citizen delegations, in their order, will form on the same street in rear of the Pennsylvania delegation.

The Marshals of the States are charged with the duty of forming their several delegations so that they will assume their appropriate positions when the main procession moves.

The head of the column will move at precisely 10 o'clock a. m.

The route will be up Baltimore street to the Emmittsburg road; thence to the junction of the Taneytown road; thence, by the latter road, to the Cemetery, where the military will form in line, as the General in command may order, for the purpose of saluting the President of the United States.

The military will then close up, and occupy the space on the left of the stand.

The civic procession will advance and occupy the area in front of the stand, the military leaving sufficient space between them and the line of graves for the civic procession to pass.

The ladies will occupy the right of the stand, and it is desirable that they be upon the ground as early as ten o'clock a. m.

The exercises will take place as soon as the military and civic bodies are in position, as follows :

Music.
Prayer.
Music.
ORATION.
Music.
DEDICATORY REMARKS BY THE PRESIDENT OF THE UNITED STATES.
Dirge.
Benediction.

After the benediction the procession will be dismissed, and the State Marshals and special aids to the Chief Marshal will form on Baltimore street, and return to the Court-house in Gettysburg, where a meeting of the marshals will be held.

An appropriate salute will be fired in Gettysburg on the day of the celebration, under the direction of Maj. Gen. Couch.

WARD H. LAMON,
Marshal-in-Chief.

Gideon & Pearson, Printers, 511 Ninth st., Washington.

Programme at Gettysburg

Federal Union was one thing, matrimonial unity another, and between the two, in this case, the President made himself clear.

Executive Mansion,
Washington, April 11, 1864.

Whom it may concern

I know nothing on the subject of the attached letter, except as therein stated. Neither do I personally know Mrs. Hunt. She has, however, from the beginning of the war, been constantly represented to me as an open, and somewhat influential friend of the Union. It has been said to me, (I know not whether truly) that her husband is in the rebel army, that she avows her purpose to not live with him again, and that she has refused to see him when she had an opportunity during one of John Morgan's raids into Kentucky. I would not offer her, or any wife, a temptation to a permanent separation from her husband; but if she shall avow that her mind is already, independently and fully made up to such separation, I shall be glad for the property sought by her letter, to be delivered to her, upon her taking the oath of December 8, 1863

A.. Lincoln

The President umpires between man and wife

One might roughly summarize a scrupulous and courteous statement of two pages that Lincoln dated August 31, 1864. Lincoln gave his belief, with particulars, to the effect that this party Louis A. Welton looked to him on the evidence, guilty of trading with the enemy and lying about it. On his own judgment the President wouldn't pardon Welton. If Thurlow Weed and H. J. Raymond, who had their own reasons for wanting Welton pardoned, would put their request in writing, and not argue with him, he would grant it. They signed, and the President pardoned.

Executive Mansion,

Washington, August 31, 1864

Mr. Louis A. Welton came from the rebel lines into ours with a written contract to furnish large supplies to the rebels, was arrested with the contract in his possession, and has been sentenced to imprisonment for it. He, and his friends complain of this, on no substantial evidence whatever, but simply because his word, only given after his arrest, that he only took the contract as a means of escaping from the rebel lines, was not accepted as a full defense. He perceives that if this had been true he would have destroyed the contract so soon as it had served his purpose in getting him across the lines; but not having done this and being caught with the paper on him, he tells this other absurd story that he kept the paper in the belief that our government would join him in taking the profit of fulfiling [sic] the contract.

This is my understanding of the case; and I can not conceive of a case of a man found in possession of a contract to furnish rebel supplies, who can not escape, if this be held a sufficient ground of escape. It is simply for the accused to escape by telling a very absurd and improbable story. Now, if Senator Morgan, and Mr. Weed, and Mr. Raymond, will not argue with me that I *ought* to discharge this man, but will, in writing on this sheet, simply request me to do it, I will do it solely in deference to their wishes.

A. Lincoln

We respectfully request the President to pardon the within named Louis A Welton, now at Fort Delaware.

Thurlow Weed.

I have read Mr. Welton's statement and if it is true, (and I know no reason for distrusting it,) his pardon would be an act of *justice*. I concur in Mr. Weed's request.

H. J. Raymond.

Gently the President adjusted a matter with the press. New York newspapers were getting news handed out by the War Department which same the newspapers at Washington were not getting, and "without harm or inconvenience to any" the President wanted it fixed.

that he kept the paper in the belief that our government would join him in to keep the profit of fulfilling the contract.

This is my understanding of the case; and I can not conceive of a case of a man found in possession of a contract to furnish relief supplies, who can not escape, if this be held a sufficient ground of escape — It is simply for the accused to escape, by telling a very absurd and improbable story.

Now, if Senator Morgan, and Mr. Weed, and Mr. Raymond, will not agree with me that I ought to discharge this man, but will, in writing on this sheet, simply request me to do it, I will do it solely in deference to their wishes.

A. Lincoln

We respectfully request the President to pardon the within named Louis A Welton, now at Fort Delaware.

Thurlow Weed.

I have read Mr. Welton's statement and if it is true, (and I know no reason for distrusting it,) his pardon would be an act of justice. I concur in Mr. Weed's request.

H. J. Raymond.

Lincoln writes record of his pardoning a criminal on request of powerful, respectable intercessors, whose statements follow letter on opposite page

Executive Mansion.
Washington, Sep. 9. 1864.

Hon. Secretary of War.
My dear Sir,
I am appealed to by the proprietors of papers here because they have to get telegraphed back to them from New York, matter which goes from the War Department. Might not this be avoided without harm or inconvenience to any?

Yours truly

A. Lincoln

General William S. Rosecrans had ordered the execution at St. Louis of a Confederate Major Enoch O. Wolf, in retaliation for the killing of a

Executive Mansion,

Washington, Sep. 9. 1862

Hon. Secretary of War.
   My dear Sir.

         I am appealed to
by the proprietors of papers here
because they have to get telegraphed back to them from New
York, matter which goes from
the War Department. Might
not this be avoided without
harm or inconvenience to any?

                    Yours truly
                    A. Lincoln

The President adjusts a matter of news handouts

Union Army Major James Wilson under extraordinary circumstances. A Baptist minister come to give consolation to Major Wolf found that the condemned man was a Mason. At once he convened the local Masonic lodge, which telegraphed President Lincoln asking mercy for Major Wolf. The President ordered Rosecrans to stay execution of sentence and to send him the record of the case. Rosecrans forwarded the record along with an elaborate argument and even demands that he be permitted to protect his men by measures of retaliation.

Rosecrans urged his points. A notorious guerrilla Colonel Tim Reeves who joined up with General Sterling Price's Confederate Army, had picked from 400 paroled Union soldiers six enlisted men from the Third Missouri Militia (cavalry), had seen to it that a firing squad shot them down to be later found with their bodies bullet-ridden and partly eaten by roving hogs. The body of a seventh man, Major James Wilson, lay with his mute comrades. The evidence was conclusive that Colonel Tim Reeves had personal motives of hate and malice toward Wilson and his State Militia cavalry, and the killings were wanton murder done on October 3, 1864. It was October 29, 1864, that six Confederate prisoners were marched out over a Missouri country road in an autumn landscape and one by one as their names were called they stepped forth and took the bullets of a Union Army firing squad—under General Rosecrans's orders. Then on November 7, 1864 when two Confederate Army majors arrived at McDowell Prison in St. Louis they met a grim welcome. Prison guards drew straws to decide which of the two majors to kill. Chance and fate picked a man and the sentence was read to him and he heard it: "In retaliation for the murder of Major Wilson, Major Enoch O. Wolf shall be shot to death with musketry on Friday next (November 11th) between the hours of 9 and 11 o'clock."

Wolf wrote to Rosecrans asking one favor, this: "If this inhuman and unsoldier like deed was committed will you please ask General Price to deliver the perpetrator of this crime, and if he turned Major Wilson over to this notorious bushwhacking Tim Reeves to be executed, he certainly will make satisfaction by delivering up to the authorities the men who committed this inhuman crime, and if he refuses to carry on an honorable warfare, I think all those officers in prison will refuse to take up arms if ever discharged." To his wife Wolf wrote it had befallen him "to be executed for the wrongs of other men."

November 10 came and a telegram to Rosecrans from Lincoln asking him to suspend the execution until further orders and meanwhile to report to the President. Nine days passed. Then came a letter to Rosecrans:

Executive Mansion,
Nov. 19th, 1864

Major-General Rosecrans.

A Major Wolf, as it seems was under sentence in your Department, to be executed in retaliation for the murder of a Major Wilson; and I, without any particular knowledge of the facts, was induced, by appeals for mercy, to order the suspension of his execution till further order. Understanding that you so desire, this letter places the case again within your control, with the remark only that I wish you to do nothing merely for revenge, but that what you may do, shall be solely done with reference to the security of the future.

Yours truly,

A. Lincoln

Closing lines of Lincoln's letter to Rosecrans. "I wish you to do nothing merely for revenge." Letter in clerk's handwriting, signature by Lincoln

Definitely now Rosecrans could do what he might decide. He could have Major Wolf, as the sentence read, "shot to death with musketry." The President had placed "the case again within your control," remarking only "do nothing merely for revenge."

Three months go by—and Major Wolf is let loose under parole while a Union Army major in a Southern prison is let loose on parole—an exchange.

And the facts as to the letter of Lincoln seem to be that he dictated it to a War Department clerk, one of the few letters he signed though another hand than his penned the letter. Also it seems definite that the letter which a clerk wrote and A. Lincoln signed is the one that went to Rosecrans, this in the Barrett Collection. Yet there exists in the Robert T. Lincoln Collection in the Library of Congress a copy of the letter in Lincoln's own hand. Why did A. Lincoln take time and bother to make a copy of this letter? Possibly for the record, though the War Department was taking rather reliable care of such documents. It could be that A. Lincoln said to himself it's a good and nice letter any way you look at it and when you truly read it, it does something to you.

Executive Mansion,

Washington, Oct 6th 1864.

Dear Gumpert

I send Thomas Cross to see you about the Carriage Bill. It was sent to me and I ant got any money to pay the man with.

And Oblidge

Thomas Lincoln

Your Friend

Tad

Young Tad Lincoln's hand is clear in its writing, and his mind is clear that he "ant got any money to pay"

Of President Lincoln's Annual Message to Congress in December of 1864, several manuscript sheets were given to various persons by the Superintendent of Public Printing, J. D. DeFrees. Three of these sheets are in the collection. One has a passage dealing with the "attempted march of three hundred miles, directly through the insurgent region," as Lincoln characterized Sherman's disappearance with his army in the state of Georgia. How little anyone knew, for sure, in the North, in that hour, about where Sherman was and what his army was doing, is suggested in Lincoln's sentence written here, "The result not yet being known, conjecture in regard to it is not here indulged."

In a message to Congress, Lincoln draws a line through one sentence

Preceding this short sentence was a long one and Lincoln drew his pen through the whole of it, struck it out, better not say it. The sentence read, "We must conclude that he feels our cause could, if must be, survive the loss of the whole detached force; while, by the risk, he takes a chance for the great advantages which would follow success."

Another of these sheets which came from DeFrees gives us in the handwriting of Lincoln his declaration to Congress, the nation, and the world that the Emancipation Proclamation would stand as first issued and with no changes. It reads:

In presenting the abandonment of armed resistance to the national authority on the part of the insurgents as the only indispensable condition to ending the war on the part of the government, I retract nothing heretofore said as to slavery. I repeat the declaration made a year ago, that "while I remain in my present position, I shall not attempt to retract or modify the Emancipation Proclamation, nor shall I return to slavery any person who is free by the terms of that proclamation, or by any of the acts of Congress."

The largest and most important single classification in the collection consists of upward of two hundred pieces of paper, all having the handwriting of Abraham Lincoln, and twelve early-period documents signed by forebears or kinfolk. In another group are some thirty letters written by Mary Todd Lincoln, this including three letters before her marriage to Lincoln, which seem to be the only ones surviving out of that period. These hold many girlish passages having bloom, charm, melancholy. She wrote the three letters from which excerpts follow to Mercy Levering:

July 23rd, 1840.

. . . Your *risibles* would have undergone a *considerable state* of *excitement*, were you to have seen the "poetry of motion" exercised in the dance. Had our grandfathers been present in the festive halls of mirth, they would undoubtedly have recognised the familiar airs of their youthful days, all the old Virginia reels that have been handed down to us by *tradition*, were played. Your cousin Sep methinks would have enjoyed the danse, no insinuations meant, save his extreme fondness for this fascinating amusement, and the rapid manner they hurried through the figures. At the end of each cotillion, I felt exhausted after such *desperate exertions* to keep pace with the music . . . I would such were not my nature, for mine I fancy is to be a quiet lot, and happy indeed will I be, if it is, only cast near those, I *so dearly love*. My feelings & hopes are all so sanguine that in this dull world of reality tis best to dispell our delusive day dreams as soon as possible. Would it were in my power to follow your kind advice, my ever dear Merce and turn my thoughts from earthly vanities, to one higher than us all. Every day proves the fallacy of our enjoyments, & that we are living for pleasures that do not recompense us for the pursuit. . . .

December 13—20—1840

. . . The icy hand of winter has set its seal upon the waters, the winds of Heaven visit the spot but roughly, the same stars shine down, yet not with the same liquid, mellow light as in the olden time. . . . We have a pleasant jaunt in contemplation, to Jacksonville, next week there to spend

I believe I need
no escort, and un-
less the Sec. of War
directs, none need
attend me.
                A. Lincoln
July 4. 1864

I would be glad, if
convenient, for Isaac
G. Wilson of Ill. to see
an Engineer at West
Point.
April 12. 1865.   A. Lincoln

Allow this young lady, Miss
Annie P. Shephard to pass
with Paymaster Carpen-
ter to Point Lookout &
see there, Charles Skink-
er, Thomas Golay, and
Frank. Shephard, pris-
oners at that place.
                A. Lincoln
June 30. 1864

Allow Edward C. Car-
rington, District Attorney
of this District, to bring
his Mother with him
from Harper's Ferry to
his own home in Washington
June 30. 1864 A. Lincoln

Will Gen. Wallace please
allow these two ladies
to visit their brother,
Walter Lenox in Pris-
on at Fort. McHenry?
Sep. 1. 1864   A. Lincoln

Will the Sec. of
State please call and
once?
                A. Lincoln
Dec. 14. 1864

Passes, requests, inquiries, on small cards Lincoln wrote a wide variety of messages.
Texts at bottom of opposite page

a day or two, Mr. Hardin & Browning are our leaders the van brought up by Miss E. my humble self, Webb, Lincoln & two or three others whom you know not. We are watching the clouds most anxiously trusting it may snow, so we may have a sleigh ride.—Will it not be pleasant?

Then the engagement with Lincoln was broken and he suffered from a severe cold. She wrote again after the breaking of the wedding arrangements to Mercy Levering. This letter of Mary Lincoln to Mercy Levering in June 1841 indicates that Mary is no disconsolate woman at all but possessed of a curious serenity:

The last two or three months have been of interminable length. After my gay companions of last winter departed, I was left much to the solitude of my own thoughts and some *lingering regrets* over the past, which time can alone overshadow with its healing balm. Thus has my *springtime* been passed. . . .

. . . Mr. Speed, our former most constant guest has been in Kentucky for some weeks past, will be here next month, on a visit *perhaps*, as he has some idea of deserting Illinois. His mother is anxious he should superintend her affairs. He takes a friend's privilege, of occasionally favouring me with a letter, in his last he spoke of his great desire of once more inhabiting this region & of his possibility of soon returning. . . .

His worthy friend [Lincoln] deems me unworthy of notice, as I have not met *him* in the gay world for months. With the usual comfort of misery,

---

I believe I need no escort, and unless the Sec. of War directs, none need attend me.

I would be glad, if convenient for Isaac G. Wilson of Ill. to be an Examiner at West-Point.

Allow this young lady, Miss Annie P. Shepherd to pass with Paymaster Carpenter to Point Lookout & see there, Charles Skinker, Thomas Gold, and Frank Shepherd, prisoners at that place.

Allow Edward C. Carrington, District Attorney of the District, to bring his mother with him from Harper's Ferry to his own house in Washington.

Will Gen. Wallace please allow these two ladies to visit their brother, Walter Lenon in Prison at Fort. McHenry?

Will the Sec. of State please call at once?

imagine that others were as seldom gladdened by his presence as my humble self, yet I would that the case were different, that he would once more resume his station in Society, that "Richard should be himself again." Much happiness would it afford me.

A short note of a far later date, November 24, 1864, portrays a politically active woman, not merely interested but excited over the games of office and patronage. The note is addressed to "Mr. Halstead," presumably the Cincinnati journalist Murat Halstead, reading: "I write you in great haste, to say, that after all the excitement, Gen. Banks, is to be returned to his command, at New Orleans, and the *Great Nation*, will be comforted with the idea, that he is not to be in the Cabinet." Also among her political letters is one in which she went out of her way to use her influence in behalf of Kentucky horses being taken for cavalry use:

. . . Being a native of Kentucky, it would be a great pride to me, to know that this selection had been made. I ask this as an especial favor. Lieut Watts, is going to Baltimore this evening, and it would give me great pleasure, if he could hand the order to Major Belger. In the battle for the Union, it would gratify me, to see the horses used, from my native state. Hoping I will receive a favorable answer, I remain.

Yours very sincerely
Mary Lincoln.

Closing lines of a Mary Lincoln letter

There appear, after the assassination of her husband, letters of grief, indications of an overstrained mind. "My heart is indeed broken, and without my beloved husband, I do not wish to live." There are letters as to her personal needs, financial embarrassments—and one peremptorily brief note to "Mrs. Sally Lincoln," widow of Thomas Lincoln, the beloved stepmother of Abraham Lincoln.

An authority on Hebraic lore reads the upper inscription of a signet ring seal of Mrs. Lincoln as spelling *Yerushalaim.* Of symbols in the center, the two six-pointed stars would appear to be the conventional symbols of Judaism, the center crosses Maltese. The building at the right can be taken for the Mosque of Omar and at the left the Holy Sepulchre. In overall intent the design seems to affirm Jerusalem as the seat of all religion, but supremely of Christianity, the Cross dominant and the name of the Virgin as the foundation stone. The spelling "Mary" would indicate British or American workmanship. If Mary Lincoln ever sealed the name of Mary on a letter page, it is not known that such a page exists. She gave the seal to Mrs. Myra Bradwell of Chicago, a friend helpful to Mrs. Lincoln in her illness after her husband's death. To Mrs. Bradwell, Mrs. Lincoln also gave the manuscript of Lincoln's definition of Democracy and other valued possessions now owned by Margreta Pritchard, from whom Mr. Barrett bought Mrs. Lincoln's bloodstone seal.

Seal in Hebraic characters from signet ring of Mary Lincoln, "Mary" spelled backward

Yale University had, on a wall more or less hallowed, for many years, a telegram Lincoln sent to Grant in an hour when there was hell to pay. And here was Barrett offering them rare letters written by sons of Old Eli, besides other items—so they gave him the Lincoln telegram and more in exchange.

U. S. MILITARY TELEGRAPH

——————————————1865

By Telegraph from   City Point,   March 29,   1865

To————————————————————————

Gen. Grant.

Your three despatches received. From what direction did the enemy come that attacked Griffin? How do things look now?

A Lincoln

U. S. MILITARY TELEGRAPH.

1865

By Telegraph from City Point, Monday, 1865

To

Gen. Grant.
Your three despatch, received — From what direction did the enemy come that attacked Griffin? How do things look there?

A. Lincoln

The Commander-in-Chief queries his general

Possibly the light of a new smile came over the haggard face of President Lincoln as he wrote a telegram at Head Quarters Armies of the United States, dated City-Point, April 2, 8:45 P.M. 1865, addressed to Lieutenant General Grant:

Head Quarters Armies of the United States,
City-Point, April 2, 8.45 P.m. '65.

Lieut. General Grant.

Allow me to tender to you, and all with you, the nations grateful thanks for this additional, and magnificent success — At your kind suggestion, I think I will visit you to-morrow.

A. Lincoln

Message written by Lincoln twelve days before his death

Head Quarters Armies of the United States,
City-Point, April. 2. 8/15 P.M. 1865.

Lieut. General Grant.

Allow me to tender to you, and all with you, the nations grateful thanks for this additional, and magnificent success. At your kind suggestion, I think I will visit you to-morrow.

A. Lincoln

When the boy Tad wanted something very special his father often wrote a card addressed to whosoever it was that might have what Tad was wanting. On April 10, 1865, such a card requested the Secretary of War to let Tad have some flags. On the back of the card three different officials took pen in hand and flung their personal hieroglyphics on the card indicating that they favored what Tad wanted.

In the year 1896 a letter came to Charles F. Gunther, the Chicago candy man, on a letterhead of the Russian Nurseries, Baraboo, Wisconsin, dated May 27, and reading:

I have in my possession, a passport written in Abraham Lincoln's own handwriting, also a long cipher message, written on the last day of Lincoln's life, and I think the last message he ever wrote. If there is any value in them, I would like to sell them, I have become blind and paralyzed & need funds. The way I came to be in possession of these relics—was through my uncle, Albert B. Chandler, now President of the Postal Telegraph Co., N. Y. City and who was at the time of Lincoln's death, an employe in his office, serving in the capacity of Telegraph Operator. If you wish to have me send them to you for examination, I will be pleased to do so, but wish them promptly returned, if you do not accept them

Please make me an offer

Respectfully

Don Carlos Chandler.
Baraboo
Wis

Care of H. H. Howlett.

In this same year of 1896 Gunther purchased from the above-mentioned Don Carlos Chandler a manuscript of the dispatch, the "cipher message," described in Chandler's letter. The dispatch is dated April 12, 1865. The text of it is that of the last letter known to have been written by Lincoln before his death two days later.

Hon. Sec. of War.

Tad wants some flags — can he be accommodated.

April 10. 1865. *A Lincoln*

Let It have the bearer have four flags for the Priest's House 4 mes.

Mr. Brearley, chief clerk. Please comply with President's request D. C. Thomas M. S. K. N. Y. Sq.

This request of the President was sent to the Secy. of War on the 10th of April 1865. on the receipt of the news of the capt. of Lee and his army. T.E.

Let Master Tad have a Navy sword.

A Lincoln

When the boy Tad wanted flags or a Navy sword, the Government saw that he got them

Eleven years after Gunther's purchase of the dispatch came publication of the book *Lincoln in the Telegraph Office* by David Homer Bates, a cipher-operator in the War Department Telegraph Office. The book has been generally accepted as exceptionally well written, strict in its fidelity to Lincoln and its reports of his visits to the telegraph office. On pages 362-63 of the book is published the complete text of the dispatch written by Lincoln on April 12, 1865, to Major General Godfrey Weitzel at Richmond. Preceding the text of the dispatch we read:

Lincoln then wrote his last telegraph despatch, using for the purpose a Gillott's small barrel pen—No. 404—borrowed from Albert Chandler.

Following the text of the dispatch, we read:

When this despatch was passed over to us, we quickly transcribed its contents in the cipher-book, line after line and column after column, little thinking that it was the last message we should ever receive from his hands. Soon it was in form for transmission to the cipher-operator at Richmond, and then the end of our association with the great President had come.

Thus it happened that a letter, in part purporting to be written in behalf of a man blind, paralyzed, and needing funds, set forth also that the owner of the despatch was a nephew of Albert B. Chandler, who had handled cipher telegrams for Lincoln and had in 1896 become president of the Postal Telegraph Company. Perhaps, too, notice should be taken that David Homer Bates wrote as though he, Bates, was a participant of the scene in the telegraph office when Lincoln wrote the dispatch on April 12, 1865—"this dispatch was passed over to us, we quickly transcribed its contents in the cipher-book," wrote Bates. The pronouns "us" and "we" make clear the impression in Bates's mind that, to his best recollection some forty years after, he was in the room either during or immediately after Lincoln wrote the dispatch.

Some twenty years after Gunther's purchase of the dispatch from the reportedly blind and paralyzed Don Carlos Chandler, the document passed into the Barrett Collection. More than thirty years went by, and then in June of 1949 came a revelation. It happened that Roy P. Basler, executive secretary of the Abraham Lincoln Association at Springfield, Illinois, and chief editor of a projected definitive edition of the Lincoln letters, speeches, and papers, had gone to Cape Girardeau to attend the funeral of his father, who met death buried in the rubble of a tornado that swept that Missouri

Time

Office U. S. Military Telegraph,
WAR DEPARTMENT,

"Cypher"

Washington, D. C. *April 12.* 1865

Major General Weitzel
            Richmond, Va

                    I have just seen your Judge Camp-
bell's letter to you of the 7th. He assumes, as appears to me, that
I have called the insurgent Legislature of Virgin-
ia, together as the rightful Legislature of the State, to settle
its all differences with the United States. I have

applicable, let my letter to you, and the
paper to Judge Campbell both be withdrawn 'or countermanded,
and he notified of it. Do not now allow
them to assemble; but if any have come,
allow them peaceable return to their homes.

                                A. Lincoln

Last letter written by Lincoln (*middle portion omitted*)—original in National Archives, Washington, D. C.

Copy of last letter written by Lincoln—unknown copyist included all errors and corrections in Lincoln original (*middle portion omitted*) area. Answering a letter from Barrett to Basler, at this time, his secretary wrote that Basler was away at his father's funeral.[1] Only incidentally did she give Barrett the information that Basler in his recent researches had found in the National Archives in Washington a copy in Lincoln's hand of Lincoln's letter to Weitzel of April 12, 1865.

Barrett wrote at once for a photostatic copy and on receiving it immediately notified Basler not to credit the Barrett Collection with the Lincoln letter to Weitzel. As Barrett's eye ran over the familiar flowing quill-written handwriting of Lincoln, he realized that a document that he had long cherished as an original was only a copy, the copy executed by some other hand than that of Lincoln, and as Barrett had occasion to write, "It is now interesting only as a curiosity that could arouse but never answer the queries as to whether the sale of the copy as an original came about through a mistake or a series of mistakes or was brought about by design. The printed heading of the telegraph blank was of a form used by the Government and carefully guarded in wartime. The copier, although he used the government telegraph form, copied mistakes and corrections just as Lincoln had written them except in a few instances where he misread them. Because of lapse of time and other factors, it is probably impossible ever to determine whether the sale of the letter as an original was by mistake, with malice aforethought, or hope of gain."

Death struck, a fame arose. A tradition, running in labyrinths, grew in fact and fable. Here in a single division of manuscripts are appraisal, commentary, reminiscence, and tribute from upward of one hundred persons of the Lincoln generation, many having had personal acquaintance with Lincoln. They range from the scrupulous account of the Hampton Roads "Peace Conference" by John A. Campbell to short luminous impressions of the poets Walt Whitman and Algernon Swinburne. They range from a masterly campaign address of Carl Schurz in 1864, expository of Lincoln and his policies, to two pages of vehement Copperhead doctrine by Clement L. Vallandigham. Edwin M. Stanton, David Davis, John Dix, Isaac N. Arnold, are here, Edward Bates, Frank P. Blair, Jr., the poet Bryant, the

---

[1] Basler later wrote to Barrett: "Mother was also buried under the rubble where she had fled to the basement, but miraculously escaped, physically, with scarcely a bruise. Dad stayed on the porch watching the storm approach, a fraction of a minute too late—with characteristic curiosity."

painter Carpenter, the Cabinet member Chase, many more whom Paul M. Angle designates as "Others in the Cast."

When Osborn H. Oldroyd solicited comment on Lincoln from public men for publication in the book *Immortelles* in 1882 the manuscripts of opinion and testimony ran upward of two hundred, of which all but two or three are here in the Barrett Collection. Former President Rutherford B. Hayes wrote his observation: "Now, all men begin to see that the plain people who at last came to love him, and to lean upon his wisdom and firmness with absolute trust, were altogether right." Charles Francis Adams, Minister to Great Britain under appointment by Lincoln, wrote with interesting candor: "Personally I never saw President Lincoln more than twice in my life, and then for a very few minutes. He then frankly told me that my mission to Great Britain had not been altogether his selection, but I believe he became well satisfied afterwards. So on the other hand I became from a very lukewarm admirer of his, one of the most appreciative of his high qualities, and mourned his great loss. I shall never forget the moment when in London the tidings of this loss were brought to me. It seemed as if we were all afloat in the midst of a boundless ocean."

Senator Benjamin Harrison of Indiana, later President of the United States, gave Oldroyd a fine sweet blunt answer. "One should be very careful of his words when he attempts to say anything worthy of the illustrious Lincoln. I am sure if I were to attempt to write I should fall below the great theme." General William Tecumseh Sherman was brief with a touch of the peremptory: "I will state that it would take more than this scrap of paper for me to word my sentiments of the life & services of Abraham Lincoln." At Menlo Park, New Jersey, Thomas A. Edison paused amid his electrical toils and conjurations to say that he could only write what others had written better and then gave out on June 17, 1880, with a one-sentence paragraph:

Menlo Park N.J.
June 17—1880

The writer can only reiterate what has been much better said by others, that the life and character of Abraham Lincoln and his great services to this Country during the war of the rebellion will stand as a monument long after the granite monuments erected to his memory have crumbled in the dust.

Thomas A Edison

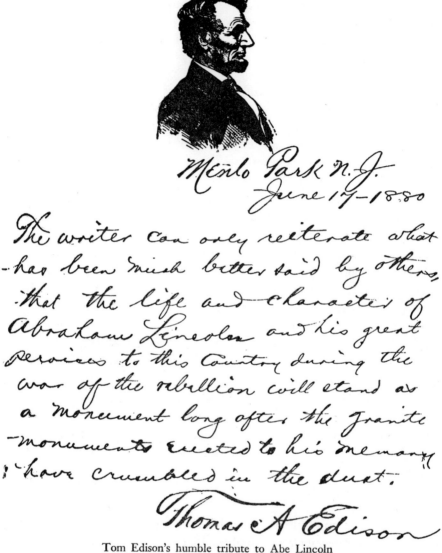

Menlo Park N.J.
June 17 – 1880

The writer can only reiterate what
has been much better said by others,
that the life and character of
Abraham Lincoln and his great
services to this country during the
war of the rebellion will stand as
a monument long after the granite
monuments erected to his memory
have crumbled in the dust.

Thomas A Edison

Tom Edison's humble tribute to Abe Lincoln

One of Barrett's few modest ventures in verse-writing compresses his feeling about Lincoln in a four-line meditation:

Slow, oft with faltering step that seemed to stray,
A homely man, but plain in truth and right, pursued his troubled way.
Unsought, unknown, the fame that waited close beyond those years of woe
    and blood,
He only knew, he wished and sought, mankind and country's good.

7. Photographs and Relics

LINCOLN was the first President of the United States to be elaborately and distinctively photographed. Across the 1850's and through to April 9, 1865, the camera record is extraordinary. The best photographs of that time are as good as the best photographs of the present day, competent living photographers have testified. The leading photographers of the Lincoln era, Mathew Brady, Alexander Gardner, and others, have respect and salutations from the modern generation for their camera work. The photographer Hesler has a friendly name for what he did with Lincoln's face and figure. Naturally, too, the Lincoln face and figure enter as a factor. Either the smooth-faced Lincoln or the bearded one, the length of limb, the easy hang of arm or curve of shoulder—these were a challenge to all the good photographers.

Here are many of the master photographs of Lincoln in prints from original negatives. The Brady photograph at the time of the Cooper Union speech is here, clear and undimmed. The two rather incomparable camera registers of Lincoln at Antietam, one with McClellan in a tent, the other with McClellan and staff, are here as likenesses to be cherished by all Lincoln students. Here are ambrotypes, photographs cabinet size and card size, tintypes, stereographs, rather sweetly and appropriately companioning the many letters and documents personally signatured.

Here, too, as the camera caught them are the street and block in Springfield where Lincoln's office was located, the Capitol building, a funeral crowd at the Lincoln home in mourning, Lincoln's horse in front of his old home, the funeral car, a small photograph of remarkable clarity and definition of line taken of a fringe of crowd at the second inauguration of Lincoln. The Lincoln sons are here, the cousin Dennis Hanks in a silk hat, and a series of Mary Todd Lincoln, the wife and the widow. Ford's Theatre,

Mr. John T. Ford himself, the conspirators who were later executed, seven different poses of John Wilkes Booth, these have their place.

And in the realm of documentation rather than the sphere of art, definitely, are the bronze life mask of Lincoln from an early cast made by the sculptor Leonard W. Volk, and bronze casts of the right hand and the left hand of Lincoln.

Then in the realm of the ingenious, often flamboyant and risen out of bathos, are cards with angels, wreaths, immortelles, the naked slave in sculpture kneeling in gratitude before the sculptured Emancipator, George Washington and Abraham Lincoln shoulder to shoulder with a Stars and Stripes background. One spurious photograph—or montage, if you choose—gives us Lincoln side by side with his wife, though it is known they never faced the camera together.

On the north wall of Oliver Barrett's law office hangs a massive gilt-framed painting in oil, a portrait of Lincoln, three-quarter length seated, 44 by 54 inches in size. It was painted from life by James R. Reid Lambdin in Washington, in March of 1863. Lambdin was a director of the Pennsylvania Academy of Fine Arts in Philadelphia and Professor of Fine Arts at the University of Pennsylvania, bearing the distinction of having painted portraits of every President of the United States from John Quincy Adams to James A. Garfield, usually painting his subject in the Executive Mansion as he did with Lincoln.

On the south wall of the Barrett office is a Lincoln portrait in oils, 24 by 28 inches in size, painted from life by W. T. Matthews, late in 1864.

Published color reproductions of the Lambdin portrait have brought in the Barrett mail an extraordinary series of comments in appreciation of its quality. Besides the Lambdin and Matthews paintings there are three others of earlier periods, two of them portraits of the beardless Lincoln.

Thirty-nine relics meet the eye. What is the "association value" of a pair of beaded moccasins with the initials "A. L." inwrought, wherein the feet of Lincoln trod about the White House on his various errands? From what basis of values would an appraisal begin as to the price figure to be set on a silver watch carried by Lincoln, a gold watch chain, a silver watch chain, a pearl-handled pocket knife with "A. Lincoln" silver-inlaid in the pearl? The watch is a Waltham Case No. E 279, a William Ellery movement No. C 7613, Boston. An affidavit of Dennis Hanks attests that the watch was given him by Lincoln when he visited the President in the White House in 1864. The well-known gold watch chain, as heretofore noted, was presented to Lincoln by a delegation from California in 1863. The silver watch chain, bought by one A. Boyd from Dennis Hanks in 1869, was worn by Lincoln in his early years. Various bidders might go either high or low for the bloodstained fan carried by Mrs. Lincoln on the night of April 14, 1865, and a certificate of authentication by Elizabeth Keckley, Negro seamstress and friend of Mrs. Lincoln. A small box with three locks of hair indicates "No. 1. Willie Lincoln's hair"; "No. 2. Abraham Lincoln's hair taken from his head after death"; "No. 3. Abraham Lincoln's hair clipped from his head at the tomb."

Two items once exhibited in the Libby Prison Museum, Chicago, are pieces of the pillow on which Lincoln died, the bloodstains visible. From the box at Ford's Theatre where Lincoln sat the night death struck are a key, a piece of wallpaper, and one of the curtains of the box. One description cards reads: "Bloodstained shawl on a piece of the silk dress worn by the leading lady, Miss Laura Keene, on the night of April 14, 1865." One may view also part of a bloodstained towel that lay under the head of the dying President. Accompanied by their various authentications are such further tokens as a small piece of an undershirt sleeve, a piece of the flag that covered the remains, a bloodstained piece of paper from the Peterson house where death occurred, a piece of the American flag that draped Lincoln's box, a pass to Ford's Theatre, Lincoln box tickets saying "RESERVED," one having bloodstains.

RESERVED

Among other mortuary tokens are a piece of coffin lining and a glove worn by a pallbearer at Lincoln's funeral. A spoon with arms and eagle on the handle, two blue pitchers with Lincoln's portrait on them, a China plate with Lincoln's portrait, a White House table plate, a set of jet mourning jewelry worn by Mrs. Lincoln at the time of the death of her son Willie, Lincoln's spectacles, a quill pen used by Lincoln, a piece of the tablecloth from the home of Illinois' Governor Edwards on which Lincoln's wedding breakfast was served, a set of jewelry having gold set with diamonds and the engraved inscription "Presented to Mrs. Lincoln from her friend William Mortimer, September 12, 1863"—these have their betokenings.

Accompanying the Lincoln watch we have the naïve declaration of Dennis F. Hanks, which he had often made orally and in writing: "I am a full cousin of Abraham Lincoln, and taught him to read and write."

From original photograph by Brady, February 9, 1864. He wears a watch chain of fine-spun, woven strands of gold presented by California delegation, now in Barrett Collection

Photograph of 44 by 54 inch portrait of Lincoln painted from life by James Reid Lambdin in March of 1863

A Lincoln portrait in oils, 24 by 28 inches, painted from life by W. T. Matthews late in 1864

Marcy   *McClellan*   *Lincoln*   *Meade*   *Fitz-John Porter*

Most notable and informing photograph of the standing Lincoln, Army of the Potomac Headquarters, October, 1862—from Alexander Gardner Album No. 1

President Lincoln Showing Sojourner Truth the Bible Presented Him
by the Colored People of Baltimore.

Executive Mansion, Washington, D. C., Oct. 29, 1864.

Photo montage and retouching to achieve photographer's conception of a
famous White House scene

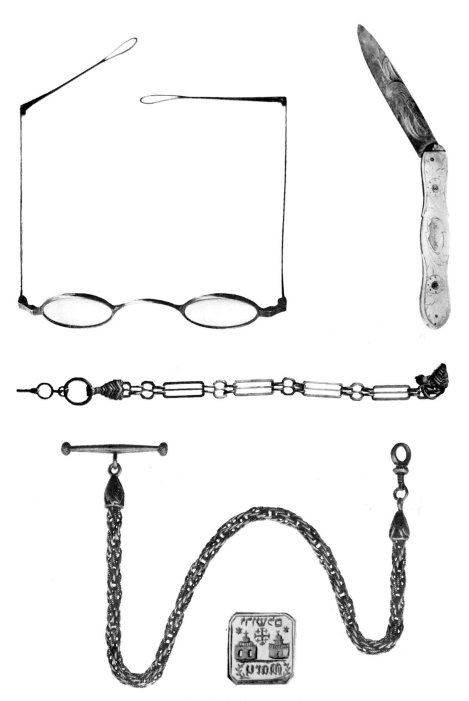

Lincoln's spectacles (*top left*); Lincoln's knife (*top right*); watch chain presented by Lincoln to Dennis F. Hanks (*center*); spun-gold watch chain presented to Lincoln by California delegation; bloodstone seal from signet ring of Mrs. Lincoln

From original photograph by Alexander Gardner, November 15, 1863, four days before speech at Gettysburg

Seated, humble, aware, Lincoln confers with McClellan, commanding the Army of the Potomac after Antietam, October of 1862—photograph by Brady

Lincoln medals minted when he was President or immediately after death

A quality of the festive is there in a group of tableware presented by Mrs. Lincoln to Usher F. Linder for Mrs. Linder when the Lincolns were making ready to move to Washington. Here is a china pitcher with a moss-rose pattern on it, a majolica pitcher, a large serving dish, a gravy boat, four small plates, knife and fork, a spoon, a candlestick, the ensemble being, as was noted, rather festive. Here also are two canes of Lincoln's and a mahogany chair used in the Executive Mansion, which came to Barrett from the daughter of Lincoln's personal guard William H. Crook.

More than two hundred broadsides, cartoons, lithographs, give moments of political tumult, of emotional high pressure, of a variety of actions and follies.

"By the way this puts me in mind of a little Story in Esop's Fables"

There once was a Copperhead vile,   who attempted to damage a file,
So he tried it in truth,   but soon broke every tooth
On that rusty and crusty Old File.

Campaign broadside

An advertisement for a runaway slave touches deep misery, as also does a "Democratic Cataclysm of Negro Equality."

John Leverett of Boston sells to Job Lane of Waldon "a negro boy called mercury," price 35 pounds, June 12, 1667—one of the earliest of New England documents of slave buying and selling.

Know al men by these presents that I Job Lane of Walden in the County of Midl sex in New Engld Carpenter acknowleg my self to be indebted unto John Leverett of Boston in the County of Suffolke, in the Massachusetts

Philadelphia Post Office, June 16th, 1863.

I have just received the following dispatch from the Governor of this State, with a request that it be conspicuously posted in the City.

C. A. WALBORN, P. M.

Harrisburg, June 16th, 1863.

THE ENEMY

is

APPROACHING!

I MUST RELY UPON THE PEOPLE FOR THE

DEFENCE OF THE STATE!

AND HAVE

CALLED THE MILITIA

FOR THAT PURPOSE.

The term of service will only be while the danger to the State is imminent.

Send forward Compancis

AS SOON AS POSSIBLE.

Signed,

ANDREW G. CURTIN.

Pennsylvania's Governor prepares for Gettysburg

Glory to God in the Highest: Peace on Earth, Good will amongst men.

EXTRA DISPATCH.

LEE'S SURRENDER¡

FULL PARTICULARS.

Correspondence between Gens. Grant & Lee.

The Army of Northern Virginia Surrendered ! !

The *Evening Dispatch* of St. Louis, Missouri, headlines end of the war

$200
REWARD

Ranaway from the subscriber, on Sunday night, the 16th of December, negro boy Gusty, who calls himself GustavusSi mms,he is about twenty years of age, five feet six inches high, dark ginger-bread color, large flat nose, which he almost hides with upper lip when he laughs. He carried away with him one black and one grey coat and a brown over-coat and a pair of drab fulled cloth pants and blue comfort, he also had an oil-cloth clothes bag.

I will pay $50 for his apprehension in the state of Maryland or in the District of Columbia, and $200 if taken in a free State.

ANN P. EVERSFIELD.

Bladensburg Po., Prince George's Co., Md.

H. Polkinhorn's Steam Job Printing Office, D street. bet. 6th & 7th sts., Washington, D C.

Handbill advertising reward for fugitive slave

Know all men by these presents that I Job Lane in the County of middlesex in New Engld Carpenter acknowledge my selfe to be indebted unto John Osburett of Boston in the County of Suffolke in the massachusetts Colony in New Engld Esqe for a negro boy called mercury the sume of thirty pounds of currant money of new Engld the which I the shop fell bond to pay ... unto the ... at his new dwelling house in Boston, or in either pay ... his ... ... as for money or to his heyres ... for the true performance of the same to pay my heyres executors ... in ... ... of fifty pounds of like currant money in witnes whereof ... I haue hereunto set my hand & seale this 12 the day of June 1667.

witnes:
William Browne
Isaac ...

Job Lane

Job Lane of Waldon, Massachusets, buys a Negro boy called Mercury and promises to pay "thirty pounds of corrant money of New Engld" for the aforesaid Negro boy—above handwriting was in style in 1667

Collony in aforesayd New Engld for a negro boy called mercury the sum of thirty pounds of Corrant monney of New Engld the which sum I the sayd Jobe Lane promise to pay unto the sayde Leverett at his Now dwelling house in boston, or in other pay to his Content as for monnoy or to his heyres execcutors or assignes for the true performance of the same I doe here by fyrmely bynd my selfe my heyres successors & assignes in the penalty of Sixty pounds of like currant monnoy in witness whereof I have hereunto sot my hand & seal this 12th day of june 1667

Job Lane

(Seal)

Witnes:
William Sedgwicke
X Isaac   ?

PUBLIC SALE!!

AS TRUSTEE FOR JAMES VANMETER, I WILL SELL ALL OF THE property of James Vanmeter at his residence, known as the Wright place, on the Hornback Mill Road, on Friday the 11th day of September 1863.

CONSISTING OF

THREE SLAVES

Charles, Mary and her child, the man is about 24 years old, a good farm hand, the woman is an excellent cook and washer.

HORSES, MULES, CATTLE, SHEEP, HOGS

AND CROP. CORN IN THE FIELDS,

OATS, WHEAT, TOBACCO

Kitchen Furniture, &c., Farm Implements of every kind. Terms of Sale, a credit of 4 months will be given on all sums of $10, and over carrying interest from day of sale. The purchaser to execute Notes with good security.

Winchester August 24th 1863.   **JAS. H. C. BUSH,** Trustee.

Handbill (*reduced size*) of sale of livestock and other property

A bill for services rendered in dealing with slaves reads:

August 2, 1759 To summonsing two Magistrates one not at home
and four free holders one evidence at 7/6 pr—   2- 5- 0
To taking two Negroes & summonsing one Do as Evidence_____1- 2- 6
To whipping & Branding one Negroo at 20 pr   2- 0- 0
To milige for same thirty six miles 15 pr   1-17-16

The above account is approved on by John Pamor   J P

Impressive is the broadside of John, Bishop of Buffalo, on the draft and race riots of 1863, to be "read in every church on the Sunday after its reception." Festive, gay, and gustatory, nothing less, is the array of victuals, dishes plain and fancy, swank and bon-ton dining-table embellishments, set forth in the printed menu of the Tremont House in Chicago, May 2, 1865—and we hope each and all brought good appetites.

In New Orleans, Louisiana, a large assembly of Negroes celebrated the anniversary of the Emancipation Proclamation and sent a committee to Washington to present Lincoln with an elaborately wrought book inscribed to "A. Lincoln, President of the United States, By the Colored People of New Orleans." The volume is bound in red morocco, has silver bosses gold-pegged, and on a heavy block of gold is the inscription to the President.

This book in the Barrett Collection goes with a group of books having some direct personal association to Lincoln, several having Lincoln's signature, one being pencil-marked by him at passages he rated noteworthy. One conspicuous volume in this group is a printed copy of the Constitution of the United States, bound in black cloth, the front cover having the name Abraham Lincoln lettered in gold. This came to Lincoln when he was a Member of Congress, each member then receiving a copy similar except for the name on the front cover. The earliest item of these personal association books goes away back to *The Kentucky Preceptor*. In this corner also is a copy of the printed text of the complete Lincoln-Douglas debates, Lincoln inscribing in ink this copy to a Springfield, Illinois, physician, W. J. Fox.

A surprising number of Lincoln medals were struck while he was alive, sixty-four specimens of these and twenty-five in commemoration after death, as we may handle them here. One is an Indian Peace Medal from the United States Mint as ordered by Congress for distribution to the chiefs of Indian tribes. On one side is a draped bust of Lincoln, on the other a land-

A NATION IN TEARS.

TREMONT.

ONE O'CLOCK ORDINARY

Tuesday May 2, 1865.

Soup.

Vegetable Soup,   Vermccilli Soup.

Fish.

Boiled Trout Lobster Sauce.

Boiled Dishes.   Roast Dishes.

Boiled Dishes	Roast Dishes
Beef Tongue,	Duffield's Ham, Champagne Sauce,
Jole and Spinach,	Beef,
Corned Beef and Cabbage	Loin of Veal,
Duffield's Sugar Cured Ham, Cold,	Stuffed Chickens,

Cold Dishes.

Cold Roast Beef   Corned Beef and Cabbage,   Cold Roast Ham.

Potted Beef with Onions,   Spare Ribs, with Chopped Lettuce,

Lamb Steaks Jelly Sauce.

Side Dishes.

Mutton Chops, with Spinach,
Chickens, Fricaseed, Gardner Sauce,
Shoulder of Mutton, a la Borgouise,
Macaroni, Spanish Style,
Ribs of Beef, Brazie with Carrots,
Sliced Lamb, Sautee with Fine Herbs,
Beef Kidneys, Broiled Steward's Sauce,
Ham Fritters Egg Sauce,
Fricandeau of Veal, Tomato Sauce,
Roulade of Lamb, Parsley Sauce.

Relishes.

Worcestershire Sauce.   Olives.   Apple Jelly,
French Mustard,   Horseradish,   Lettuce.

Vegetables.

	Mashed Potatoes,		Mashed Turnips.
Boiled Potatoes.	Boiled Hominy	Spinach,	Boiled Onions
Beets,	Green Corn,		Fried Parsnips
Boiled Rice.			

Pastry.

Apple Pies,   Sago Pies,   Tapioca Pudding,
Spanish Meringues,   Lady Fingers,   Rum Cakes.

Dessert.

Almonds,   Apples,   Raisins,
Hickory Nuts,   Prunes,   Filberts.

Coffee.

Tremont Hotel, Chicago, menu card, May 2, 1865

scape with an Indian plowing a cornfield, four children playing near a schoolhouse, ships at a wharf, a steamship, church, and mountain in the background, all in a circular disk. Obverse are two Indian warriors, one with a scalping knife over a dead nude enemy, and below a squaw's head, and between, a quiverful of arrows, a bow, and a calumet. These were a "peace offering" from the "Great White Father" at Washington. Among some Indians they were highly prized and worn on a chain around the neck. Being of silver, they were not lacking in tangible value.

On another medal a profile bust of Lincoln facing left has the inscription "The President of the U.S. 1861." The other side shows the young Lincoln in the backwoods splitting a log, inscribed "The rail splitter of 1830." A large proportion of these medals portray the young rail-splitter. Also the larger part of the medals set forth Lincoln as a candidate in the year 1860 and again in 1864. One favorite slogan on the medals: "Abraham Lincoln * _ * free land, free speech & free men.," the obverse side with a spread eagle holding an olive branch and three arrows in his talons, the slogan: "Union of the States." The militant youth organization of the Republican Party had their name large on one medal, "Wide Awakes."

From the Philadelphia Mint came a medal with two draped flags on each side of a broken column having a shield and tablet inscribed "A. L.," and the inscription, "He is in glory and the nation in tears." Below the base were three lines reading: "Born Feb. 12, 1809 Assassinated Apr. 14, 1865." Another pictured a coffin inscribed "Medal Struck From a Portion of the Lead Which Lined the Coffin of Prest Abrm Lincoln, Assassinated Apl 15 1865." Other medals had sentiments reading "Martyr to liberty," "The great statesman and beloved president," "His memory is enshrined in every loyal heart," "With malice toward none, with charity for all, with firmness in the right as God gives us to see the right."

Among accounts by persons present in Ford's Theatre on the night of the assassination is one by Jenny Gourlay Struthers, who was playing Mary Meredith in *Our American Cousin*. Perhaps the most vivid narrative from persons in the audience is that of Julia Adelaide Shepard, in a letter written to her father and saying on the next day, "Sleeping or waking that terrible scene is before me." There is the letter of Anson G. Henry, of Springfield, Illinois, writing to his wife a nine-page letter on the day of the funeral, April 19, 1865. As a family friend and at one time physician to Lincoln, Dr. Henry had stayed over to do his best to console Mrs. Lincoln. He writes of her explanation of how they came to go to Ford's Theatre that night, the President saying, "if he stayed at home he would have no rest, for

[Handwritten letter in cursive script]

Part of letter of Dr. A. G. Henry reporting last words of Lincoln as given by Mrs. Lincoln

he would be obliged to see company all the evening as usual." She sat close to him, leaning, and recalled asking him, "What will Miss Harris [a companion in the box] think of my hanging onto you so?" Then with a kindly smile to her came his last words, "She won't think any thing about it." Thus Dr. Henry related hearing it from Mrs. Lincoln.

[Handwritten signature: J. M. Booth & Lady — Boston   3]

The handwriting of J. Wilkes Booth and his signature are here in rhymes and doggerel, his script on the register of Aquidneck House, April 5, 1865; "J. W. Booth & Lady, Boston, Apt. 3. Time B." The range of plays and roles in which Booth starred is indicated in twelve playbills of 1863-64 naming various theaters and cities, with J. Wilkes Booth as:

Shylock in *The Merchant of Venice*   Phidias in *The Marble Heart*
Pescara in *The Apostate*   Claude Melnotte in *Lady of Lyons*

Duke of Gloucester in *Richard III*   Romeo in *Romeo and Juliet*
Alfred Evelyn in *Money*   Raphael, *The Sculptor*, etc. etc.
Charles De Moor in *Robbers*

One playbill of October 20, 1863, announcing Wilkes Booth as Richard
the Third has altered and italicized lines of Shakespeare drama intimating

THIS (Tuesday) EVENING, Oct. 20,
Will be acted Shakspeare's Great Historical Tragedy, in 5 acts, entitled

RICHARD III

OR, THE BATTLE OF BOSWORTH FIELD!

" *Let's muster men : my counsil is my shield ;*
We must be brief when traitors brave the field ! "

RICHARD, { Duke of Gloster, afterwards }   MR. J. W. BOOTH
          { King Richard III., }
Henry, Earl of Richmond..Mr Sutton
King Henry VI..Mr S. James
Prince of Wales..Miss Marie Boniface
Duke of York...Miss Laura Le Brun
Duke of Buckingham...Mr W. W. Pratt
Lord Stanley...Mr Page
Tressel..Mr Page
Duke of Norfolk...Mr S. Parker
Sir William Catesby..Mr Wilson
Lord Mayor of London..Mr Herndon
Sir Richard Radcliff..Mr H. Russell
Sir Walter Blunt..Mr Sandford
Earl of Oxford...Mr Barron
Lieutenant of the Tower..Mr Clifton
QUEEN ELIZABETH....................Mrs. BARROW
Lady Anne..Miss Fanny Brown
Duchess of York...Mrs E. Le Brun

Act 1—Death of King Henry VI.
Act 2—Gloster's Wooing.
Act 3—Reception of the Princes.
Act 4—Coronation of Richard III.
Act 5—BATTLE OF BOSWORTH FIELD!
" *Let them not live to taste this land's increase*
That would with treason wound this fair land's peace!"
TERRIBLE BROAD-SWORD COMBAT between RICHARD & RICHMOND
Triumph of Richmond, and Death of King Richard III.

Admission, ...50 Cents

Playbill with "Mr. J. W. Booth" as star. (*Reduced size*)

violence against "traitors," and the vague threat: "Let them not live to
taste this land's increase That would with treason wound this fair land's
peace." Also in this grouping of material is perhaps the fullest series of photographs of John Wilkes Booth being shown in a variety of roles and costumes
as an actor and in poses and apparel he wore offstage. Handbills and posters
offering rewards for the capture of "the murderer," broadsides and newspapers giving the contemporary accounts of the crime, the escape of the
assassin and the hunt for him, the lingering hours in which the victim never
returned to conscious life. Of newspapers there are 62 issues from cities
North and South in the days immediately following the assassination, portraying shock and grief as it struck great masses of people in a way not
having parallel with anything else in American history. The elaborate text
of one poster reads (the line of three photographs across the top being
omitted):

War Department, Washington, April 20, 1865.

☞ $100,000 REWARD!

THE MURDERER

Of our late beloved President, Abraham Lincoln,

IS STILL AT LARGE.

$50,000 REWARD

Will be paid by this Department for his apprehension, in addition to any reward offered by Municipal Authorities or State Executives.

$25,000 REWARD

Will be paid for the apprehension of JOHN H. SURRATT, one of Booth's Accomplices.

$25,000 REWARD

Will be paid for the apprehension of David C. Harold, another of Booth's accomplices.

LIBERAL REWARDS will be paid for any information that shall conduce to the arrest of either of the above-named criminals, or their accomplices.

All persons harboring or secreting the said persons, or either of them, or aiding or assisting their concealment or escape, will be treated as accomplices in the murder of the President and the attempted assassination of the Secretary of State, and shall be subject to trial before a Military Commission and the punishment of DEATH.

Let the stain of innocent blood be removed from the land by the arrest and punishment of the murderers.

All good citizens are exhorted to aid public justice on this occasion. Every man should consider his own conscience charged with this solemn duty, and rest neither night nor day until it be accomplished.

EDWIN M. STANTON, Secretary of War.

DESCRIPTIONS.—BOOTH is Five Feet 7 or 8 inches high, slender build, high forehead, black hair, black eyes, and wears a heavy black moustache.

JOHN H. SURRAT is about 5 feet. 9 inches. Hair rather thin and dark; eyes rather light; no beard. Would weigh 145 or 150 pounds. Complexion rather pale and clear, with color in his cheeks. Wore light clothes of fine quality. Shoulders square; cheek bones rather prominent; chin narrow; ears projecting at the top; forehead rather low and square, but broad. Parts his hair on the right side; neck rather long. His lips are firmly set. A slim man.

DAVID C. HAROLD is five feet six inches high, hair dark, eyes dark, eyebrows rather heavy, full face, nose short, hand short and fleshy, feet small, instep high, round bodied, naturally quick and active, slightly closes his eyes when looking at a person.

NOTICE.—In addition to the above, State and other authorities have offered rewards amounting to almost one hundred thousand dollars, making an aggregate of about TWO HUNDRED THOUSAND DOLLARS.

Handbill (*reduced size*) offering reward

Among materials related to the assassination are nineteen letters by Louis J. Weichmann, some handwritten and some typewritten, all from Anderson, Indiana, to Osborn H. Oldroyd. Weichmann was a clerk in the office of the Commissary General of prisoners—a wavering, suspicious, and careful young man who had been associated with members of the group of conspirators who sought to take the lives of government heads. The hardened young soldier of giant physical frame, Louis Payne, who in his attempts to stab Secretary Seward in the jugular vein was foiled by the surgical steel apparatus with which surgery encased Seward's head after runaway horses had thrown the Cabinet member from his carriage—Payne, the conspirator and desperado, is represented here by a Latin textbook once owned by his associate in crime, David Herold. Also Payne is seen here in a portrait sketched and signed by General Lew Wallace, author of *Ben Hur*, and a member of the military commission which tried the conspirators.

As the four years of Civil War progressed, those using the United States mails had a choice of many envelopes, mostly in color, the designs patriotic. In the collection are 650 different specimens, all unused, many of them mounted in old albums. On one sheet are nine rare Lincoln postage stamps.

The death of Lincoln, and the events of the aftermath of that death, shape into a story that can be told as high and sacred tragedy or as lurid incredible melodrama or a brief pitiful folk tale known to mankind from generation to generation around the earth. In the Barrett Collection we meet accounts, vestiges, documents, relics, that render the atmosphere of the fatal night and the days that followed. The strange clockticks from hour to hour of Lincoln's last night on earth are traced by an army surgeon who was in the theater at the time of the shot and in the house across the street when death came and in the performance of an autopsy. Charles Sabin Taft was the surgeon, and he titled his manuscript, *The Notebook of an Army Surgeon Present at the Assassination, Death and Autopsy*. He wrote his notes the day after the death "and immediately after the official examination of the body," this "by direction of Secretary Stanton for the purpose of preserving an official account of the circumstances attending the assassination in connection with the medical aspects of the case."

8. Newspapers

ATYPEWRITTEN list of newspapers in the Barrett Collection, naming and dating the journals, would require some five letter-sized sheets. They would span Lincoln's political career from an issue of the *Alton* (Illinois) *Spectator* of December 13, 1838, giving a full account of the House of Representatives of the Illinois Legislature electing a Speaker—Lincoln 38 votes, Ewing 43 votes—continuing through the April 25, 1865, issue of the *Salt Lake* (Utah) *Daily Telegraph* and its obituary biographical sketch of Lincoln. The list would include many journals defunct, gone to limbo—the *People's Advocate* of Carrollton, Illinois, 1843; the *Daily Cavalier* of Chicago, 1846; the *Chicago American* of 1839; the *Chicago Republican* of 1843; the *Miners Journal* of Galena, Illinois, 1829; the *Illinois Statesman* of Jacksonville, 1843; the *Monmouth Atlas* of 1847; the *Rushville Phoenix* of 1838; the *Battle Axe* of Winchester, Illinois, 1842; the weekly *St. Louis Intelligencer* of 1856; the *Indiana Statesman* of 1851; the *Log Cabin* of Albany, New York, 1840; the *Egyptian Spy* of Tamaroa, Indiana, 1860; the *Richmond Enquirer* of Richmond, Virginia, 1862—all of them, to use a phrase not uncommon in recent years, gone with the wind.

Death has not been unkindly to these newspapers out of the rag-paper era preceding modern mass-production pulp and newsprint. Many of these well-preserved journals touch the Lincoln career, the *Chicago American* in 1839 in its reference to "A. Lincoln [this perhaps the first time Lincoln was mentioned in a Chicago newspaper] and Cyrus Walker, Esqs., Whig candidates for State Electors"; the good old *Sangamo Journal* at Springfield, November 11, with a news item of Lincoln's wedding, the same journal on February 14, 1842, announcing a celebration by the Washington Society, whose members believed in the example of George Washington with reference to the use of alcoholic liquors: he drank but he knew when to quit:

he was a temperance man. In the announced address of "A. Lincoln, Esq." he made himself clear on the liquor question of that hour.

The same issue of the *Sangamo Journal* reported the death by apoplexy of an old friend and valued counselor of Lincoln, Bowling Green, the *Journal* saying: "This intelligence will excite an emotion of sorrow throughout all Southern and Middle Illinois. In every neighborhood of these regions, a witness will be found to testify to his universal goodness of heart, and to his dauntless bravery, in that period of our history, when the blows of the ruthless savage were to be warded off of the heads of helpless families. From his old companions, in arms and early hardships and privations, we claim the generous tear of sympathy." Also in this issue were reported two decisions as to rights of Negroes by Judge Treat in Circuit Court. A Negro named Daniel had been jailed, lacking "an authenticated certificate of freedom." In a habeas-corpus action the court declared a legislative act of 1829 requiring such a certificate of freedom to be unconstitutional, and Daniel was granted his freedom. In another case, Judge Treat heard a citizen from Arkansas who brought witnesses to prove that he was the owner of one James Poster, who had lived in Springfield two or three years. The court ordered the slave to be given over to its lawful owner.

In the June 7, 1839, issue of the *Sangamo Journal*, with its usual legend under its front-page name, "Published Every Friday::::Office North East Corner of the Public Square," in a column of business and professional cards, down below the dry-goods dealers, grocers, hat-makers, saddle and harness makers, druggists and doctors, including an "Indian and German Root Doctor," arriving amid the lawyers we find the modest card:

STUART & LINCOLN
Attorneys & Counsellors at Law
Springfield, Ill.
Office No. 4 Hoffman's Row, up stairs.

Amid the cards of other lawyers, and alongside hotel advertisements, in the *Illinois Daily Journal* of December 29, 1848, was the card of Lincoln & Herndon, "Attornies," and so spelled.

In this same month is belittlement of one Robert Owen, Jr., who later became a Congressman to exchange letters and actively co-operate with President Lincoln. The paragraph headed "Infidelity in England," reads:

A Bath (English) paper says that Mr. Robert Owen, the founder of the Society System, met with a signal defeat last week, at Reading. Mr. Owen had challenged the clergy of that town to a public discussion of the relative merits of Socialism and Christianity. The Rev. Mr. Legg took up the glove, and before an assembly of upwards of 800 breathless, quiet auditors, he nobly vindicated the divinity of our faith, and rendered the wretched infidel who was opposed to him literally speechless. Mr. Robert Owen is the father of the well known, or much known Robert Dale Owen, who formerly edited an infidel paper in New York. He is now in Indiana, the owner of a large property, purchased by his father, and given to his sons.—Robert Jr. is also a member of the Legislature of Indiana.

Plain as a pikestaff was it that the *Illinois State Register* didn't like Mr. Lincoln, either his political or his oratorical style. In its issue of November 23, 1839, it put new loaded questions to Mr. Lincoln and asked why he had not answered its previous old ones. Also Mr. Lincoln publicly acts like a clown, doing it for effect, the *Register* telling its readers:

Mr. Lincoln, another Federal candidate for Elector, followed in the evening. His argument was truly ingenious. He has however, a sort of *assumed clownishness* in his manner which does not become him, and which does not truly belong to him. It is *assumed*—assumed for effect. Mr. L. will sometimes make his language correspond with this *clownish* manner, and he can thus frequently raise a loud laugh among his Whig hearers; but this entire game of buffoonery convinces the *mind* of no man, and is utterly lost on the majority of his audience.

We seriously advise Mr. Lincoln to correct this *clownish* fault, before it grows upon him.

But we have digressed. The main object of calling in Mr. Lincoln, was to raise up Mr. Walker, who had been actually demolished by Mr. Douglass [sic] in the afternoon. Lincoln made out to get Walker rather unsteadily on his legs again, and between the two Whig speakers, our Democratic "little giant," as Walker called him, had a rough time of it. Lincoln misrepresented Douglass, as was apparent to every man present. This brought a *warm* rejoinder from Mr. Douglass. Mr. Walker then rose, complained of Mr. D. for his *warmth*, and went on for an hour starting new points. Thus a concerted plot of *"two pluck one,"* began to show itself. But under all these disadvantages, Mr. Douglass literally swamped his adversaries.—His arguments were *not answered;* while his opponents were driven from every ground which they assumed.

On Wednesday evening, Mr. Douglass took the floor, before a large audience, and delivered one of the most powerful arguments against an United States Bank that we ever listened to. It sunk deep into the hearts of his hearers. There was a profound silence upon his conclusion, and a settled gloom covered the countenances of the Whigs.—They saw how utterly hopeless must the attempt to answer him. Mr. Lincoln was, however, again put forward; but he commenced with embarrassment and continued without making the slightest impression. The Mr. Lincoln of Wednesday night, was not the Mr. Lincoln of

Tuesday. He could only meet the arguments of Mr. Douglass, by relating stale anecdotes and old stories, and left the stump literally whipped off of it, even in the estimation of his own friends.

In this issue of the *Register* of November 23, 1839, we find one A. R. Skidmore announcing he "will pay for hogs weighing from 175 to 200 lbs. $2.50, nett; from 200 to 300, $3." George Gregory, near the Land Office, will shoe your oxen. Thirty-three horses in and about Springfield have strayed from their owners, and all of them have been "taken up" by citizens who describe the horse for the owner to come and get him, this certifying that the one who has "taken up" aforesaid animal is a good neighbor rather than a horse thief. A sorrel stud, a roan mare colt, an iron-grey stud colt, a black mare, a grey roan, a dark iron-grey mare, a sorrel filly, a black gelding colt, a dark brown mare, right hind foot white, a small star on forehead, a small snip on the right side of her nose, a natural trotter— you'll know your horse if you lost him.

Then amid the printed word of "three work steers strayed away" and "Durham cattle for sale" is an advertisement headed "$50 Reward," reading:

Ranaway from the subscriber, living in Lewis county, Mo. 4 miles from Tully, a slave named Charles, about 20 years of age, five feet six or seven inches high, well made, free spoken among whites, and pleasant in conversation, had a white speck in the ball of the eye, which may be perceived upon close inspection, a scar at the extremity of the left eye-brow, also, a scar on the right wrist, and one between the neck and collar-bone; had also, scars on his back. He took away a blue cloth, long napped hunting coat, trimmed with black braid; also a pair of cowhide boots,—had cassinett pantaloons. The above reward will be paid for said boy if caught out of the State, and if taken up in Missouri, a suitable reward, and all reasonable charges will be paid. Any person securing said slave in jail, or having information, will forward it to Andrew N. Sutherland, Wingville P.O., Grant co. Wisconsin Territory, or to John Sutherland, Tully, Mo.   Andrew N. Sutherland.

In this same period the *Vandalia Free Press and Illinois Whig* issue for July 17, 1840, prints the Illinois ticket of Electors for Harrison for President, naming, as spelled, "Abram Lincoln, of Sangamon." There is light on how the color line was drawn by members of Lincoln's party in the editor of this Whig paper, William Hodge, making an issue of it in two columns on the front page. The headline runs, "A Most Extraordinary Act of Mr. Van Buren," and the subhead in italics, "Negro Servants allowed by him to testify in Court against White Men." A lieutenant of the United

States Navy, G. M. Hooe, of the West India Squadron, after a trial and a reprimand in General Orders by the Secretary of the Navy, entered the complaint:

There is one other point in the proceedings of the Court (touching their legality) to which I invite the particular attention of your excellency.—It respects a matter to which all southern men are deeply sensitive, and if not overruled by your Excellency, will assuredly drive many valuable men from the Navy. In the progress of the proceedings of this Court, two negroes, one the cook, and the other the private steward of Commander Levy, were introduced as witnesses against me. I protested against their legal competency to be witnesses in the territory of Florida, on the ground that they were negroes. The Court disregarded my exception, and as the record shows, they were allowed to be examined, and to testify on my trial. This I charge as a proceeding illegal and erroneous on the part of the Court, and, if so, according to established law and precedent must vitiate and set aside their whole proceedings.

This was signed by George Mann Hooe. It was returned to the Navy Department after examination and the written endorsement:

THE PRESIDENT FINDS NOTHING IN THE PROCEEDINGS IN THE CASE OF LIEUT. HOOE, WHICH REQUIRES HIS INTERFERENCE.

M. Van Buren.

Lincoln's generation was near that of the American Revolution. They could touch hands with living men who had fought through that Revolution. We get a glimpse of it in a six-line item in this 1840 issue of this Vandalia newspaper, the item headed, "*Room for the grey hair'd veterans*":

At a late Harrison meeting in Madison County, Ohio, Geo. Hempleman, aged 108, presided. One of the vice presidents was 99 years of age, another 81, and a third 79.—They were all soldiers of the revolution.

After considerable partisan temper and much of strut and swashbuckling on national issues we find the Vandalia editor in the bottom right-hand corner of the front page enjoying with his readers this item:

An eastern lady of fashion stepped into a shop not long since and asked the keeper if he had any "matrimonial baskets," she being too polite to say *cradles*.

Ten years earlier we have an issue of the *Kaskaskia* (Illinois) *Democrat* throwing light on times and customs meeting the eye of the twenty-one-year-old Abraham Lincoln. Two columns are given to a discussion as to who are Sabbath-breakers and whether the Sabbath can be broken. Stage-coaches could be run on the Sabbath and good Christians could ride in them

on the Sabbath, also good Christians could on the Sabbath plant the land
of the good earth made by the Lord, according to an argument by a Massachusetts clergyman, John Leland. He approved a report favoring complete individual liberty on the Sabbath: "It breathes the language of John
Milton, Roger Williams, William Penn, Thomas Jefferson, &c. and I think
it is in perfect accordance with the letter and spirit of the New Testament."

A two-column discussion follows on reductions of the price of public
lands. Then the editor briefly informs his readers that a bill has passed the
state senate cutting the price of public lands "to the general purchaser, *to
One Dollar An Acre, and to the actual settler, to Seventy-five Cents Per
Acre.*" Then comes denunciation of the political opposition. They are "hired
assassins of character who conduct the 'Illinois Intelligencer'" resorting to
"base and scandalous means" portraying our candidate as "the legitimate
father of knaves, counterfeiters & horse thieves." But "their daggers are of
lath." The public will be convinced that the opposition newspaper "is the
most abusive, scandalous, and *filthy* public journal in the western country . . . a stain on our State—an unseemly *wart*, that should be taken out by
the roots." As this was a not uncommon editorial performance, we may be
sure that the growing young Lincoln was not unfamiliar with the violent
art of invective.

Swinging to the *Chicago Republican*, January 11, 1843, we find amid
much uneven miscellany, a quirk of humor almost startling, headed "The
Western Girls," reading:

Mr. Marshall, in a recent speech in Kentucky, after alluding to causes that induced him to challenge Col. Webb, adds: "If, under all these circumstances of
wanton aggression on the part of Col. Webb, I had not called him out, there
is not a Presbyterian lady in my district, who would not have whipped me with
her *garters*, in scorn and contempt, from her presence."

At Kingston, New York, the *Ulster Rail Splitter*, calling itself "A Lincoln
Campaign Paper," in an issue of August 9, 1860, prosperous and bulging with
advertising, gives a three-column speech of Congressman John Sherman,
saying in part:

Why, then, my fellow-citizens, can't we all join together and elect Abe
Lincoln? . . . He is a man of tried ability and of conservative ideas; a man who
can give a reason for his opinions, and if you don't think so read that famous
speech he made in the Cooper Institute in New York; a man moderate and
conservative, but determined. When Old Abe (he is not so very old and I like
to call him so) puts his foot on a rail it has to be split [Voice—"Hurrah for
Old Abe!" and cheers.]

On page 3 of the same journal we meet quotations from a stump speech of Horace Greeley, who had not favored the nomination of Lincoln for President and who was later to bitterly oppose Lincoln policies and methods and the nomination of Lincoln to a second term. In this 1860 campaign, however, Greeley is quoted as favoring

the election of that honest man and pure patriot, Abraham Lincoln . . . that good man will be in a position to reform abuses and restore the Government to its ancient purity . . .

Some twelve years since I was sent to Congress by accident. I there met Mr. Lincoln and have enjoyed his acquaintance since that time. He is a practical, well informed man, who has grown up under the discipline of adversity, and I do not believe a better man than he could have been selected at Chicago. Even Douglas—for I will give him what credit I can—said he was a foeman worthy of his steel; and when informed of the nomination made at Chicago, he exclaimed, "Well, they have settled one question; the next President must come from Illinois!"

The same journal prints a "straw" poll taken among "the unfortunate inmates of the Auburn (New York) Prison," which resulted:

Abraham Lincoln,	0
Stephen A. Douglas	682
John C. Breckinridge,	200

A remarkable campaign paper, in news, entertainment, political enthusiasm, is the *Rail Splitter* published at Chicago, copies very scarce, Barrett's copy, dated October 6, 1860, being No. 16 of Vol. I.

In a four-column account of a Republican Party rally in Chicago and speeches by William H. Seward and Owen Lovejoy, we get a vivid impression of the activity and the extent of membership of the Wide Awakes in the Middle West. They were a militant organization, many of them drilled in military formations, instructed in weapons, and not entirely vaguely representing the idea that if certain undefined events came to pass they, the Northern youth, would fight. An evening procession had five thousand marchers carrying lighted torches. Leading were three units of Mounted Rangers from Chicago, Aurora, and Du Page County. Then came Wide Awake companies, all with flags, some with brass bands, lanterns shining with the motto "Freedom is our Watchword," and "We will not rest till the victory is won." An indefinable prophecy, a forecast vague yet terrible to some who witnessed it, was in the marching companies of Wide Awakes from Chicago, Springfield, Batavia, Michigan City, Sandwich,

South Chicago, Mendota, Urbana, Decatur, Chicago Central, Sycamore, Ottawa, Lisbon, La Salle, Mt. Palatine, Morrison, McHenry County, West Side of Chicago, Woodstock, Rockford, Downer's Grove Plow Boys in red shirts and white pants, Waukegan, Libertyville, North Side of Chicago, Elgin, St. Charles, Geneva, Belvidere, Blackberry of Kane County, Fremont of Lake County, Byron, Lyons, Jacksonville, and from outside of Illinois, Wide Awakes from Lyons, Iowa, from Kenosha and Milwaukee, Wisconsin, from Michigan City and St. Joseph, Michigan.

In this copy of the *Rail Splitter* is set forth the claim that in Maryland a grandson of Charles Carroll of Carrollton, signer of the Declaration of Independence and great friend of religious freedom, is for the Lincoln ticket. A half-column article shadow-boxes, perhaps rather unfairly, around the question whether Stephen A. Douglas is a Roman Catholic. The campaign rhymers were in their element, this being one specimen, from the *Bath* (Maine) *Sentinel*, which the *Rail Splitter* of October 6, 1860, gave its readers:

THE PRESIDENTIAL CHAIR.

"A Douglas Song."

To gain the Presidential chair
 I've toiled for many a day;
I've tried to get New England men
 To help me on my way;
But—judging from appearances—
 The people everywhere
Are bound to give Old Abraham
 The Presidential chair.

———

At every station, on each road
 Where I could hearers find,
I told them Squatter Sovereignty
 Meant—"Your own business mind."
I stuffed them well with anecdotes,
 And stories rich and rare,
But still they said Old Abe should fill
 The Presidential chair.

———

I thought the good old Pine Tree State
 Would hug me to her heart,
And take my Squatter Sovereignty
 As pledged by Mr. SMART!

But now I find I've been deceived,
　For all the people there
Say honest Abraham must fill
　The Presidential chair.

———

These "*Rowdies*" and these "*Vagabonds*"
　I now can plainly see,
Have played the joke on Mr. Smart
　That he has played on me.
They must have heard of me before,
　Or else they would not swear
That none but honest Abe should fill
　The Presidential chair.

———

I'll leave those bleak New England hills
　And travel in the South;
And if I'm not successful there,
　For ever shut my mouth.
I'll settle down in Illinois,
　And never more will dare
To hope that I was born to fill
　The Presidential chair.

———

And when I'm laid beneath the sod
　My epitaph shall be:
"Here lies the man who lived and died
　On Squatter Sovereignty,"
And my good democratic friends,
　A monument will rear
To him whose heart was broken on
　The Presidential chair.

In the same issue, more felicitous, carrying what is termed a love interest, and moving toward a surprise ending, is "The Maiden's Soliloquy" by one unidentified Jessie:

THE MAIDEN'S SOLILOQUY.

By Jessie.

A maiden sat in her cozy room,
　The blinds all carefully closed;
"I wonder who loves me best!" she sighed,
　"Of gentlemen who've proposed.

There's MONEY with John, and HEART with George,
    While Charlie is full of FUN,
Ah! if I could tell who loved me best,
    He'd be the favorite one. . . .

But I wish to weigh the matter well,
    Ere choosing a man for life;
Ah! who is the man that loves me best?
    And when shall he call me 'WIFE?'

My Mother often prayed a man
    With honor within his breast,
Should prove the one to offer his hand,
    And love her daughter the best.

For this is the man for a girl to choose,
    A husband to be respected,
But I guess on the whole I'll remain as I am
    TILL ABRAHAM IS ELECTED."

As of this date of October 6, 1860, the *Rail Splitter* refers to "the Texas Scare" and subheads: "No Wells Poisoned—No Strychnine in Possession of Negroes—a Panic without a Cause." Then come paragraphs ascribed to the *New Orleans Picayune*, saying "not half of what has been confessed seems to be borne out by later facts," though "it reveals enough to warn and instruct the entire South." That Texas should have such a scare, that a leading New Orleans newspaper should give it such close attention and a Lincoln campaign paper in Chicago reprint from the New Orleans paper, this while militant Wide Awakes marched before immense crowds in Chicago—it all signified a growing national tension.

A well-preserved eight-page copy of the *New York Herald*, December 17, 1860, has in its news and editorial columns the quivers of an excitement that all who share it are aware is to go higher, that not far ahead may come a leap into chaos beyond prediction. Two news letters from Springfield, Illinois, headed, "Important From Springfield," try to indicate by rumor and guesswork what may be the course of Lincoln's policy when some eleven weeks later he is inaugurated President of the United States. More than three columns on the editorial page are aimed chiefly at Lincoln, one editorial of a column and a half, headed, "The Duty of the President Elect at This Crisis Considered." The mood and spirit of the editorial is indicated in two sentences:

Democracy was rent asunder and prostrated before and during the contest at the election. The crisis created by the black republicans has called up a spectre of such frightful mien that they have fled in all directions, and have no rallying point; and Mr. Lincoln stands to-day as the President of the whole republic, with all ties to "party" severed, and free to act as his exalted position and responsibility demand he should act, viz: to create from the ruins of two obsolete and adverse parties one—a Union party—strong, nay, overwhelming in its power; for its source will be the affection and loyalty of citizens, breathing a prayer for the perpetuity of the Union at large, and whose ambition is to create a new era of fraternal peace and universal prosperity.

The opposition Mr. Lincoln may expect if he tries to use "coercion" will be overwhelming, the *New York Herald* predicts. The implication is direct that if Lincoln on taking office tries to use force, in other words to fight for the Union, he will be beaten at the start. The exact language of the *Herald* editorial reads:

But when it is taken into account that in the Presidential election on the 6th of November the popular vote stood 2,821,874 against the republican programme, with only 1,858,200 in its favor, it may be fairly asked, from what source does Mr. Lincoln expect to derive the means of coercion, or what two-thirds of the people will be doing while he, with the aid of one-third, is inaugurating a bloody civil war, which, if it ever should be commenced, must signally fail in its object.

What Lincoln had to deal with here was the most daring, the most enterprising, the most widely circulated daily newspaper in America, and one not lacking foreign influence. Owned and edited by James Gordon Bennett, it was beyond doubt Bennett's personal opinion, arrived at deliberately, that stood forth from the closing sentence of an editorial urging various moderates to measures of reconciliation between the South and the North. This one sentence, however, read: "It may be too late to save the Union from dismemberment, but it is not too late to save us from the horrors of civil war." Perhaps Mr. Bennett could not possibly have more directly implied that he would rather see the Union wrecked than to try any measures of force toward saving it. In these many columns of reasoning and counsel, we get a view of the heavy and fierce pressures brought on President-elect Lincoln to speak out, many weeks before he would be President, what he would then do.

That life went by then somewhat as it does now, that violence and hate had their daily toll, that the recitals of human distress day by day ran much in the past era as in the present—this is registered in *Herald* items of a worker at the Metropolitan Gas Works falling to dislocate hip and knee joints, ending in death at Bellevue Hospital—of a fifteen-year-old boy jumping for his father's cart, missing his hold, falling under the wheels to his death—of a drunken man losing balance and falling downstairs to his death—of a saloonkeeper caught endeavoring to eject a couple of drunken customers from his premises, receiving stab wounds in the abdomen—of two Negroes fighting, and one with a knife slashing the face and head of the other—of two tenement-house women, one German and the other Irish, in a quarrel over the payment of three dollars, and on the German woman getting a black eye, her husband sending a bullet spinning into the Irish woman's husband's leg, police arriving to arrest the German.

On his journey to Washington for inauguration Lincoln was as nearly completely noncommittal on what he would say or do as he had been for many months. The *Salem* (Illinois) *Advocate*, continuously bitter against Lincoln, editorialized:

The illustrious Honest Old Abe has continued during the last week to make a fool of himself and to mortify and shame the intelligent people of this great nation. His speeches have demonstrated the fact that although originally a Herculean rail spliter and more lately a whimsical story teller and side splitter, he is no more capable of becoming a statesman, nay, even a moderate one, than the braying ass can become a noble lion. People now marvel how it came to pass that Mr. Lincoln should have been selected as the representative man of any party. His weak, wishy-washy, namby-pamby efforts, imbecile in matter, disgusting in manner, have made us the laughing stock of the whole world. The European powers will despise us because we have no better material out of which to make a President. The truth is, Lincoln is only a moderate lawyer and in the larger cities of the Union could pass for no more than a facetious pettifogger. Take him from his vocation and he loses even these small characteristics and indulges in simple twaddle which would disgrace a well bred school boy.

Similar utterance, reeking with rancor, continued throughout the years of the war. For the three years 1861-63 the three bound volumes in the Barrett Collection are lacking only five issues of the *Salem Advocate*. Two of these volumes were bound for John A. Merritt, editor of the paper.

Across the years of the war some thirty-five newspapers are represented with one copy, ten of them by more than one, or several, copies. More often than not these newspapers touch on some action or phase of Lincoln. The numerous copies of leading newspapers of the country, on the days immediately following the death of Lincoln, are of more than ordinary interest as portraits and studies of Lincoln's personality.

The excitement and the ever changing expectations from hour to hour till midnight and past on April 14 and 15, these are chronicled almost as on a thermometer in the series of dispatches from Washington published in the newspapers of April 15. The *New York Daily Tribune* of that date printed:

> Washington, Friday,
> April 15 [1865]
> The President was shot in a theatre to-night, and is perhaps mortally wounded.

After which came more in sequence to the eleventh dispatch which had a commentary, ending:

> *Later.*—The accounts are confused and contradictory. One dispatch announces that the President died at 12½ p.m. Another, an hour later, states that he is still living, but dying slowly. We go to press without knowing the exact truth, but presume there is not the slightest ground for hope.

There was groping for accurate and detailed information, tension resulting from the definite report that the President had been assassinated, but not yet any news forthcoming on the questions: "Who killed Lincoln? What kind of man could have done this deed?" In its issue on the morning of April 15 the enterprising *New York Herald* closed an editorial: "The assassin had not been arrested up to the hour of our latest dispatches. Who he is is not positively known, though suspicion points strongly to a certain individual."

Later came a flood of detailed fact and surmise. Horses took on personality and importance. An excitement of horses, saddles, stables, and riders ran from the pencils of *Herald* reporters:

> The horse supposed to have been ridden by the man who made the assault on the Sewards was a roan, well known in the city, of peculiar pacing gait, and very fast. He belongs to Thompson Naylor, livery stable keeper, on E Street. This horse had been let on Friday, to be returned at eight o'clock in the evening. Not coming at the time stated the hostler was on the lookout for him near Willard's. He knew the horse by the peculiar sound of his hoofs upon the pavement. As a horseman came down the avenue the boy stated to a friend, "There's the pony, now!" Observing that he did not turn down Fourteenth Street to the stable, he ran towards him to question him. At that moment the horseman turned, and from some cause or other—perhaps the commotion on the streets—and, riding back to the corner, passed rapidly up Fourteenth Street and down F Street. The boy, now fearing that the man intended to steal the horse, ran to the stable, and, mounting another fleet horse, started in pursuit. Know-

ing that the man had given his residence as Port Tobacco, Md., he went toward the Navy Yard bridge, across the eastern branch. Near the Capitol he met an old man who informed him that a man on a roan horse had just passed up the hill. He then pushed on to the Navy Yard bridge, where he inquired of the guard if a man on a roan had just crossed over, and was answered in the affirmative, and the man gave his name to the guard as Smith. The boy then explained to the guard his fears that the horse was stolen, and asked if he could pass over. The guard said he could, but could not return that night. Not caring to be out over night, and knowing nothing of the tragic scenes which had just been enacted in the city, he returned to the stable.

This person who hired the roan horse had been keeping one or two horses at Naylor's stables during the last two weeks. One of them, a stallion, had been sold. The other, a brown one-eyed pacer, whose gait and speed were quite similar to those of the roan, he had taken away, and reported that he had sold him. It now appears that this horse was the one taken on the street on Friday night by the police, after having fallen with his rider, who escaped. Naylor's foreman identifies the saddle which was on the horse as the same which had formerly belonged to the one-eyed brown horse. He also identified his photograph, now in the hands of the authorities. When he kept his horses at Naylor's he gave his name as Atzerard, and his residence as Port Tobacco. When he hired the roan horse on Friday he left Pumphery's brown mare at the stable, with directions that she should be fed, groomed and saddled by ten o'clock precisely.

This was the mare which, on the same day, had been hired of Pumphery by Booth. At ten in the evening a man, who gave his name as Earle, called for the mare. The stable boy asked him what had become of the man with the roan? "Oh," said he, "he will be back directly," and when mounting to ride away he remarked, "You will hear of great news before morning." The boy thought nothing of that, as we had been hearing of great news every day for some time, but, feeling uneasy about the roan, he watched to see which way the rider of the mare went and saw him turn up Tenth Street, toward Ford's theatre.

Neither Pumphery's mare nor the roan have yet been returned.

In two columns of printer's type, so fine it is wearing on the eyes to read it, the *Illinois State Journal* of May 5, 1865, gives the Springfield address of Bishop Matthew Simpson of the Methodist Episcopal Church on the day they buried Lincoln in his home town. Touching on Lincoln's religious faith, the Bishop gave an anecdote having the mixture of humor and wisdom familiar to many of the Springfield folk. Said the Bishop:

As a ruler, I doubt if any President has ever showed such trust in God, or in public documents so frequently referred to Divine aid. Often did he remark to friends and delegations that his hope for our success rested in his conviction that God would bless our efforts, because we were trying to do right. To the address of a large religious body, he replied, "Thanks be unto God, who in our National trials, giveth us the Churches." To a Minister who said "he hoped the Lord was on our side," he replied, "that it gave him no concern whether the Lord was on our side or not," for he added, "I know the Lord is always on the side of right," and with deep feeling added, "But God is my witness that it is my constant anxiety and prayer that both myself and this nation should be on the Lord's side."

In this same burial sermon, in one passage of high and solemn meditation on the role of the American Republic among nations of the earth, Bishop Simpson spoke, in measurable degree, as an interpreter and a foreteller:

There are moments which involve in themselves eternities. There are instants which seem to contain germs which shall develope and bloom forever. Such a moment came in the tide of time to our land when a question must be settled, affecting all the powers of the earth. The contest was for human freedom. Not for this republic merely. Not for the Union simply, but to decide whether the people, as a people, in their entire majesty, were destined to be the Governments or whether they were to be subject to tyrants or aristocrats, or to class-rule of any kind.

This is the great question for which we have been fighting, and its decision is at hand, and the result of this contest will affect the ages to come. If successful republics will spread in spite of monarchs all over this earth. [Exclamations of Amen, thank God.]

Here a variety of newspapers report in column after column the units forming the procession in each of the series of cities where the Lincoln funeral car stopped. To name the organizations, delegations, guards of honor, troop bodies from Army and Navy and State Militia, representatives from Federal, state, county, and municipal governments, churches of every faith and denomination, besides many fraternal societies represented—this required more than four columns in the *New York Herald*. Spread over scores of newspaper pages were the orations of dignitaries, prelates, speakers of the day. The funeral oration of the Reverend Dr. Phineas D. Gurley, Pastor of the Presbyterian Church where the Lincoln family had a pew, as delivered in the White House April 19, 1865, required two and one-quarter columns of fine type in the newspapers. Protestant, Catholic, and Jewish churches were represented in sermons spread over entire pages in the metropolitan daily journals. The *New York Herald* of April 24, 1865, gave more than a column to the lavish dithyrambic utterance of Henry Ward Beecher:

Rear to his name monuments, found charitable institutions and write his name above them, but no monument will ever equal the universal, spontaneous and sublime sorrow that in a moment swept down lines and parties, covered up animosities, and in one hour brought a people into unity of grief and fellowship of anguish. . . . He fell by the bullet like the soldier in battle, and yet there was not a drummer boy or private for whom the great heart of Lincoln would not have bled. . . . And now the martyr is moving in triumphal march, mightier than when alive. The nation rises up at every stage of his coming. Cities and States are his pallbearers, and the cannon speaks the hours with solemn progression. Dead, dead, dead, he yet speaketh. Is Washington dead? Is Hampden dead? Is David dead? Is any man that was ever fit to live dead? Disenthralled of flesh, risen to the unobstructed sphere where passion never comes, he begins his illimitable work. His life is now grafted upon the infinite, and will be fruitful, as no earthly life can be. Pass on, thou that hast overcome! Your sorrows, Oh people, are his paeans; your bells and bands and muffled drums sound triumph in his ears. Wail and weep here; God makes it echo joy and triumph there. Pass on! Four years ago, Oh Illinois, we took from thy midst an untried man, and from among the people; we return him to you a mighty conqueror. Not thine any more, but the nation's; not ours, but the world's. Give him place, Oh ye prairies. In the midst of this great continent his dust shall rest, a sacred treasure to myriads who shall pilgrim to that shrine to kindle anew their zeal and patriotism. Ye winds that move over the mighty places of the West, chant his requiem! Ye people, behold the martyr whose blood, as so many articulate words, pleads for fidelity, for law, for liberty!

The *World*, a New York daily newspaper, on April 19, 1865, had an editorial page of remarkable miscellany for the day they were taking the coffin of Lincoln out of the White House. This was the newspaper that in May of 1864 had been suppressed, not allowed to print or sell, by the order of President Lincoln, at the instigation of Secretaries Seward and Stanton. As a leading Copperhead journal it had satirized and belittled the President. Now it gave to its readers the farewell speech of Lincoln on leaving Springfield, Illinois, in February of 1861, with its sentiment now recalled: "I know not how soon I shall see you again. A duty devolves upon me which is, perhaps, greater than that which has devolved upon any other man since the days of Washington." Reprinted, too, was a fragment from the flag-raising ceremony at Independence Hall, Philadelphia, four years before, wherein the President-elect referred to the hope and promise of the Declaration of Independence, "that in due time the weights would be lifted from the shoulders of all men, and that *all* should have an equal chance," and with this the curiously prophetic sentence, "But if this country cannot be saved without giving up that principle, *I was about to say, I would rather be assassinated upon the spot than surrender it.*" Here, too, was a reminiscence of the painter F. B. Carpenter, resident in the White House while doing his large painting of Lincoln reading the Emancipation Proclamation to his Cabinet. The President at a table had pushed aside his pen and papers, and talked to Carpenter about Shakespeare, then reading aloud favorite passages from Shakespeare, and Carpenter's recollection ran:

Then half closing his eyes he repeated to me the lines which I enclose to you ["Oh! why should the spirit of mortal be proud?"]. Greatly pleased and interested, I told him that I would like, if ever an opportunity occurred, to write them down from his lips. A day or two afterward he asked me to accompany him to the temporary studio of Mr. Swayne, the sculptor, who was making a bust of him at the Treasury Department. While he was sitting for the bust I was suddenly reminded of the poem, and said to him that then would be a good time to dictate it to me. He complied, and sitting upon some books at his feet, as nearly as I can remember, I wrote the lines down, one by one, from his lips.

This was signed by Carpenter, "With great regard, very truly yours," after which he gave the twelve stanzas of "Oh! Why Should the Spirit of Mortal Be Proud?"

In an adjoining column of the *World* was a long letter from Judge J. W. Edmonds to the brother of Lincoln's assassin, Edwin Booth, who had voted for Lincoln and was in complete political disagreement with his crack-brained brother. The letter to Edwin Booth ended:

So far as your inner anguish is concerned, I can but commend you to that God whose overruling Providence you so fully realize, and so far as the world around you can affect you, I bid you be of good cheer, for all will be well, and you may be assured of the earnest sympathy of the good and true everywhere.

To this Edwin Booth responded:

My Dear Judge: Your kind letter of this morning overwhelms me. It so fully expresses the inmost sentiments of my heart that I can only say God bless you. Come and see me.

Most notable of all, however, on this April 19 editorial page of the *World* was its announcement that on this day of "The Funeral of President Lincoln" the office of the *World* would be closed from 10 A.M. to 6 P.M. and no evening edition issued, this followed by an editorial titled "The Obsequies of President Lincoln," which read in full:

But once before in our history has such a genuine and universal sorrow marshaled the funeral obsequies of an eminent American as will lend to the mournful pageant of to-day its most imposing feature.

In our own times we have seen the feverish heart of Paris stand still to honor the dead NAPOLEON, borne back in a solemn triumph from the tomb of his exile; and London silence for a day its multitudinous clamors before the open grave of England's greatest soldier. The funeral of the first Emperor was the formal restoration to France of all that she had lost of national pride and national self-respect in the great catastrophe of 1815. The burial of WELLINGTON rounded and consummated for England the most splendid epoch in her annals. For us no similarly symbolic and impressive scene has been possible since the first President of the Republic, the founder of our independence, the soldier-statesman upon whose virtues the fabric of our liberties had been stayed throughout the dark and dangerous beginnings of the nation, was borne amid the tears of a whole people to his rest.

Forgetting in the long years of our national prosperity and progress the trials and perils of our fathers, we had come at last to esteem the great commonwealth which they established as quite beyond the reach of ruin from human passions and human folly. The terrible event which this day mourns, and the lessons of which the mourning of this day, if it be worthy, noble, and sincere, must write as with the finger of Heaven upon all our hearts, chastens our vainglorious and reckless age with a new and vivid sense of the wisdom of our ancestors. Once more we stand with them in the presence of the perils of anarchy, and may this day comprehend, if four years of civil war have failed to make us do so, the force and fullness of the gratitude and the reverence with which they honored in George Washington those simple and sublime civic virtues of justice, temperance, moderation, and loyalty to duty, which alone made the foundation of the Republic possible, and by which alone its stately fabric can be restored and perpetuated.

All that the pomp and circumstance of a nation's sorrow can do to testify to a nation's horror of the atrocious crime which has snatched the sixteenth President of the Union from the midst of his labors, and the harvest of our hopes will this day be done. The tolling of bells, the doleful boom of artillery, the trappings of woe investing all homes, "sonorous metal blowing martial sounds," nothing will be wanting; and all will but feebly utter the deep universal sense that, while in the loss of our President we have suffered a grievous political calamity, in the manner of that loss every principle of our national system, every tradition of our honorable past, every hope of future peace and glory for us as a nation, has been most wickedly and most wantonly outraged.

In that deep universal sense of the grander impersonal aspects of this day's solemnities, their highest and most vital significance must be found. Grief, above all the grief of a nation, should be, like a nation's joy,

"Majestic, equable, sedate,
Confirming, cleaning, raising, making free."

Wise men were troubled most when WASHINGTON died, the orb of his life sinking calmly and gently through its golden west, to reflect how greatly the nation had owed to him alone, to the personal qualities and virtues of his single nature, its safety and its peace.

Standing, as we do to-day, about the tomb of his successor, upon whom, after he had scorned delights and lived laborious days in the service of the state he was called to rule and guide, came

"The blind Fury with the abhorrèd shears,"

and split his thin-spun life in the very hour of the approaching fruition of his efforts and his devotion; the temper and the measure of our mourning must determine whether we sorrow as men without hope, or wisely and to some ripe end.

In the grave of our murdered President, just men of all parties and shades of opinion this day bury, so far as he is concerned, the bitternesses and extravagances born of political conflict about his measures and his policy.

They remember only that he loved his country; that he earnestly, humbly, and bravely labored for its salvation, according to the light which Heaven gave him, and that the assassin's blow which struck him down struck us all in whatever is most dear to us as citizens and as men. With such memories, and with the fame which springs from them, green and undying, the name of ABRAHAM LINCOLN passes to-day into American history.

That history remains with us. To love our country as well as he; to labor as earnestly, as humbly, as bravely, for its salvation, each of us according to his light; to maintain all that is dear to us as citizens and as men, is the lesson which this day reads to us, that so, out of this cloud of sorrow, the nation may pass on and up again into a new and nobler peace, prosperity, and glory.

So sinks the day-star in the ocean-bed:
And yet, anon. repairs his drooping head.
And tricks his beams, and with new spangled ore
Flames in the forehead of the morning sky.

In its issue of April 26, 1865, the *New York Herald* gave its readers a report of twenty columns, possibly a book of 30,000 words, on the arrival in New York the day before of the mute body of Abraham Lincoln and the ceremonials and demonstrations attendant thereon. In the dead march paying tribute to a vanished leader were "nearly 100,000 people in line," witnessed by another "three-quarters of a million of silent spectators," the procession holding "all nationalities, all religions, all trades, all classes, all politics, all

Four books above, each with signatures or inscriptions of Lincoln family members. The large volume, *City and Suburban Architecture* by Samuel Sloan; three volumes at right, *Among the Hills* by J. G. Whittier, *Pioneer Boy* by William Thayer, *Elements of Character* by Mary C. Chandler. *Below,* copy "The Constitution," presented each member of Congress, Lincoln's name in gilt on the front cover. Bloodstained fan carried by Mrs. Lincoln on the night of the assassination

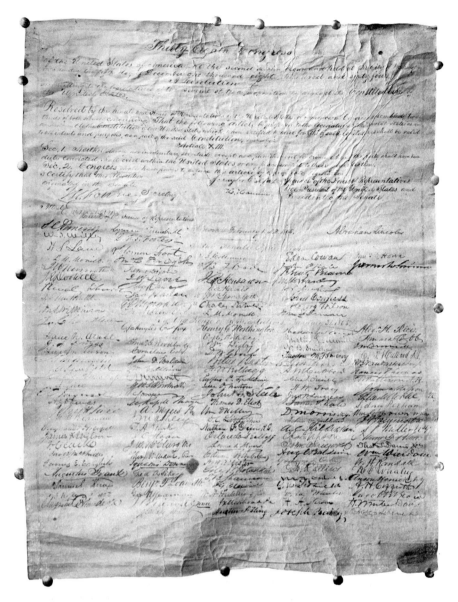

Engrossed parchment of the act of constitutional amendment for abolishment of slavery, passed January 31, 1865, massing in five long columns these signatures of President Abraham Lincoln, Vice-President Hamlin, and Senate and House members voting for the measure

Lincoln home in Springfield, Illinois, in mourning garb, May, 1865

Funeral car which carried Lincoln's body from Washington, D.C., to Springfield, Illinois, witnessed day and night by millions of people

Original photograph of crowd gathered at Lincoln's tomb

colors," and when the funeral car passed "the multitude uncovered," said the *Herald*. Free swing and unlimited play of mind and feeling were allowed a rare reporter, transcriber, interpreter. His moving fingers shoved a lead pencil over copy paper for the opening paragraphs of the most spectacular day the American metropolis had ever witnessed:

New York never before saw such a day as it witnessed yesterday. Rome in the palmiest days of its power never witnessed such a triumphal march as New York yesterday formed and looked upon. When four years ago Abraham Lincoln passed through the city to be armed with authority as the nation's leader, Broadway sufficed to contain the crowd which, with varied sentiments, cheered, and scoffed, and scowled him a doubtful welcome. When yesterday the same people, inspired with a common, universal sorrow, sadly followed his body, crowned with more glorious honors as the nation's savior, the same wide street held hardly a fraction of them. Then he was going to be crowned chief magistrate of a divided people and disrupted nation on the eve of a great, bloody and uncertain war. Yesterday he was the great martyr of a nation united under his guidance and that of God, by the successful close of that gloomy war. Then he passed through almost unknown, and the crowd that followed his coach with cheers were actuated by curiosity as much as admiration. Yesterday it was different; yesterday witnessed the real triumphal march of Abraham Lincoln; for he had conquered the prejudices of all hordes and classes, and the hearts of the people who honored him beat with love and veneration of the man. Better for his fame that it should come thus late than too soon. This test of his success and his greatness can never be doubted or disputed.

It was not the occasion that drew the people to the streets yesterday. The city had witnessed nobler occasions than this, exciting grander passions and sublimer thoughts, but none more hallowed. Four years and a fortnight ago its people rallied spontaneously to avenge the insult thoughtlessly given at Sumter, but fearfully avenged on a hundred fields; but then the people gathered in excited groups to listen to excited words and give their approving voice to high resolves, and their hands to noble deeds. They have risen to the cry of "invasion" to repel the advancing hordes that desolated a sister State, but it was amid the wild excitement generated by the grand passion of revenge for burned cities and slaughtered friends. A little month ago they left labor and commerce and speculation to rejoice at the cry of "Victory," and its echo "Peace!" But amid that glad rejoicing there were mixed some feelings unworthy of the people of a great metropolis. Yesterday they met in sorrow to pay the last honors to their noble dead, and the great multitude that, with uncovered heads, saw Abraham Lincoln's funeral car pass by were actuated and moved by a single sentiment of profound sorrow and veneration, and a high resolve and calm determination that he who had perished should not die in vain. The gloom of their sorrow shrouded the city. The calm determination lay underneath the surface. It broke from no lips, and was expressed in but few mottoes. It slept, indeed, unsuspected in the depths of many a heart, but none the less for the want of expression in words did the countenances of the people declare that determination to be that "though the President dies the nation shall live." On all former occasions the city has risen in its might to the signaling of the flag of Stars and Stripes, but yesterday in the national metropolis was unfolded a flag of black, upon which that resolution was emblazoned in letters of unfading white. The spirit of the good man whom they honored will rest the better to know that no feeling of hate or vengeance marred his people's high resolve, but that they had taken his last advice to heart, and bent only upon justice and right, had determined to pursue their purpose and his own "with malice towards none, with charity for all."

That which follows from the pens of our reporters tells in detail how a hundred thousand freemen followed their martyr's body, watched by more than half a million hearts. Many of our readers will make a summary of the details we give in their own minds, and deduce some interesting facts therefrom. Those who have not the moments nor the disposition to do so will be surprised at the calculations, which are easily deducible from the well established premises which are stated.

In the twenty-four hours of daylight and darkness during which the body lay in state, not one moment elapsed that did not present a visitor to see the face of the dead. At midnight the line of those plodding their way slowly to the City Hall was as long as when it first started. Women and children rose at midnight from their beds to take their place in the line, and the whole city was alive to the desire to look upon their martyr's features. During the time in which the body remained in state it is calculated that not less than one hundred and fifty thousand persons looked upon the body.

The part of the procession composed exclusively of the military, which, when drawn up in line along the sidewalk to salute the hearse as it passed by, extended from the Hudson River depot to Union square, a distance of at least two miles, contained fifteen thousand men under arms, while in the entire procession, the head of which reached the depot, four miles distant from City Hall, fully two hours before the several hundred freedmen, who brought up the rear, started from the place of their rendezvous, were not less than seventy-five thousand souls. And before those men of sable hue, who bore the banner that termed Abraham Lincoln their "emancipator," had reached the depot, the cadets of the Military Academy at West Point had fired the salute and presented their arms to the passing funeral train. In the procession there was represented the people of every State in the North, of every clime, and almost every nationality on the face of the globe; and all felt that in joining in this last tribute to a man who

was "not for one
one nation b...

A c...
an...

age, but for all time," they also mourned a benefactor of not
...at of the world.

...ommentary on Lincoln the man, and an appraisal of him as statesman
...d warrior, an original personality prophetic of an incalculable new era,
this was bodied forth in the April 17, 1865, issue of the *New York Herald.*
It ran two columns in length, its style and thought extraordinary, taking
Lincoln as a type of world hero of irreckonable import not only to his own
country but to the world outside of America. Carrying the title "The Great
Crime—Abraham Lincoln's Place in History," the editorial in full read:

Abraham Lincoln, in the full fruition of his glorious work, has been struck
from the roll of living men by the pistol shot of an assassin. That is the un-
welcome news which has, for the last two days, filled every loyal heart with
sadness, horror and a burning thirst for retribution. That is the news which
has swept away from the public mind every sentiment of leniency or conciliation
towards the conquered brigands of the South, and in whose lurid light, as by the
phosphorescent flames recently enkindled in the crowded hotels of this city
by men with rebel commissions in their pockets, we are again terribly reminded
of the absolute barbarity and utter devilishness of the foemen we have now
tightly clutched in our victorious grasp. The kindliest and purest nature, the
bravest and most honest will, the temper of highest geniality, and the spirit of
largest practical beneficence in our public life, has fallen a victim to the insane
ferocity of a bad and mad vagabond, who had been educated up to this height of
crime by the teachings of our "copperhead" oracles, and by the ambition of
fulfilling those instructions which he received "from Richmond." Of him, however, and the bitter fruits to the South and to all Southern sympathizers which
must follow his act as inevitably as the thunder storm follows the lightning flash,
we do not care in this moment of benumbing regret and overwhelming excitement to allow ourselves to speak. The deliberations of justice must be held in
some calmer hour; while, for the present, we can but throw out some few hurried reflections on the character of the giant who has been lost to our Israel, and
the glorious place in history his name is destined to occupy.

Whatever judgment may have been formed by those who were opposed to
him as to the calibre of our deceased Chief Magistrate, or the place he is
destined to occupy in history, all men of undisturbed observation must have
recognized in Mr. Lincoln a quaintness, originality, courage, honesty, magnanimity and popular force of character such as have never heretofore, in the annals
of the human family, had the advantage of so eminent a stage for their display.
He was essentially a mixed product of the agricultural, forensic and frontier life
of this continent—as indigenous to our soil as the cranberry crop, and as
American in his fibre as the granite foundations of the Ap[p]alachian range. He

may not have been, and perhaps was not, our most perfect pr[...]duct in any one branch of mental or moral education; but, taking him for all in [...] all, the very noblest impulses, peculiarities and aspirations of our whole people—what [...] may be called our continental idiosyncrasies—were more collectively and vividly re[...]ro-duced in his genial and yet unswerving nature than in that of any other public man of whom our chronicles bear record.

If the influence of the triumph of popular institutions in our recent struggle prove so great over the future destiny of all European nations as we expect it must, Mr. Lincoln will stand in the world's history, and receive its judgment, as the type of man of a new dynasty of nation-rulers—not for this country alone, but for the whole civilized portion of the human family. He will take his place in a sphere far higher than that accorded to any mere conqueror; and, indeed, without speaking profanely, we may well say that, since the foundation of the Christian era, no more remarkable or pregnant passages of the world's history have been unfolded than those of which Mr. Lincoln on this continent has been the central figure and controlling influence. It is by this measurement he will be judged, and by this standard will his place be assigned to him. Under his rule our self-governing experiment has become, within the past four years, a demonstration of universal significance that the best and strongest rule for every intelligent people is a government to be created by the popular will, and choosing for itself the representative instrument who is to carry out its purposes. Four years ago it appeared an even chance whether Europe, for the next century at least, should gravitate towards democracy or Caesarism. Louis Napoleon was weak enough to hope for the latter, and has destroyed himself by the folly of giving his hope expression. The triumph of the democratic principle over the aristocratic in our recent contest is an assurance that time has revolved this old earth on which we live into a new and perhaps happier—perhaps sadder—era; and Jefferson Davis, with his subordinate conspirators, flying from their capital before the armed hosts of the nation which had elected and re-elected Abraham Lincoln, may be regarded as a transfiguration of imperialism, with its satellite aristocracies, throwing down the fragments of a broken sceptre at the feet of our American—the democratic—principle of self-rule.

The patriarchal system of government was, we may presume, as simple as the lives of those over whom it was exercised, and has left but very imperfect traces of its existence. Of the theocratic or priestly form of government, we have had types in the characters of Moses and Mohammed—both powerful and original men, and true representatives of the ambitions, needs and poetically superstitious temperaments of the nations they respectively ruled. With Rome came the full development of the imperial system, based on military subjugation and absorption; the system which Louis Napoleon believes is about being revived—wholly oblivious, apparently, that his volume of moody and fantastic dreams is printed on a steam press, and not copied painfully from waxen tablets, as were the memoirs of Julius Caesar, by the stylus of a single copyist. With the spread of Catholicity came the feudal system, of which Charlemagne was but an accident and by no means the creator—that system having been a necessity for the perpetuation of Church property and the protection of the non-belligerent religious Orders. With the discovery of printing, immediately followed by Luther's insurrectionary upheaval in the religious world, commenced the mental and moral preparation of mankind for the acceptance of popular institutions and the right of self-government—in a word, for the democratic principle of which Cromwell was the first forcible expression, and Napoleon Bonaparte, in his earlier triumphs over kings and empires, the armed and irresistible assertion. False to the ideas which caused his elevation, this Napoleon was hurled from the throne he sought to build on the ruins and with the materials of prostrate popular liberty; and it was thus reserved by an All-wise Providence for this latest found of the continents of our earth, to give the first successful example of that truly popular system of government—soon to be in control of all nationalities—which had the moral sublimity and practical virtues of George Washington to guide it through its experimental stage; and the perhaps externally grotesque, but morally magnificent, figure of Abraham Lincoln to be both its representative and martyr in the present supreme moment of its permanent crowning.

This estimate of the place inevitably to be occupied in the world's history by the great National Chief whose loss we mourn may not prove either a familiar or pleasant idea for the mere partisans of the present day to contemplate; but it will be found none the less a true and philosophical estimate. In the retrospective glance of history the "accidents," as they are called, of his elevation will all have faded out of sight; and the pen of the historian will only chronicle some such record as the following:—From the very humblest position in a family subsisting by agricultural labor, and himself toiling for daily bread in his early youth, this extraordinary man, by the gifts of self-education, absolute honesty of purpose, perfect sympathy with the popular heart and great natural endowments, first rose to eminence as a lawyer; then graduated in Congress; was next heard of as the powerful but unsuccessful rival for national Senatorial honors of the democratic candidate for the Presidency, over whom he subsequently triumphed in 1860; and four years later we find him, in the midst of overwhelming financial embarrassments, and during the uncertain progress of the bloodiest and most desolating civil war ever waged, so completely retaining the confidence of the American people as to be triumphantly re-elected to the first office in their gift. They will claim for him all the moral influences, which—acting through material forces and agencies—have led to the abolition of slavery, and the permanent enthroning of popular institutions on this continent; and, in their general summing up of this now unappreciated age in which we have our feverish being, and in their pictures of those events wherein the clamorous partisans of the past week were prone to urge that Mr. Lincoln had been but a passive instrument, his name and figure will be brought forward in glowing colors on their canvass [sic], as the chief impelling power and central organizer of the vast results which cannot fail to follow our vindication of the popular form of government.

And surely some hundred years hence, when the staid and scholarly disciples of the historic Muse bring their grave eyes to scan and their brief tapelines to measure the altitude and attitude, properties and proportions of our deceased Chief Magistrate, their surprise—taking them to be historians of the present type—will be intense beyond expression. It has been for centuries the tradition of their tribe to model every character after the style of the heroic antique. Their nation-founders, warriors and lawmakers have been invariably clad in flowing togas, crowned with laurel or oak wreaths, and carrying papyrus rolls or the batons of empire in their outstretched hands. How can men so educated—these poor, dwarfed ransackers of the past, who have always regarded greatness in this illusory aspect—ever be brought to comprehend the genius of a character so externally uncouth, so pathetically simple, so unfathomably penetrating, so irresolute and yet so irresistible, so *bizarre*, grotesque, droll, wise and perfectly beneficent in all its developments as was that of the great original thinker and statesman for whose death the whole land, even in the midst of victories unparalleled, is to-day draped in mourning? It will require an altogether new breed and school of historians to begin doing justice to this type-man of the world's last political evangel. No ponderously eloquent George Bancroft can properly rehearse those inimitable stories by which, in the light form of allegory, our martyred President has so frequently and so wisely decided the knottiest controversies of his Cabinet; nor can even the genius of a Washington Irving or Edward Everett in some future age elocutionize into the formal dignity of a Greek statue the kindly but powerful face of Mr. Lincoln, seamed in circles by humorous thoughts and furrowed crosswise by mighty anxieties. It will take a new school of historians to do justice to this eccentric addition to the world's gallery of heroes; for while other men as interesting and original may have held equal power previously in other countries, it is only in the present age of steam, telegraphs and prying newspaper reporters that a subject so eminent, both by genius and position, could have been placed under the eternal microscope of critical examination.

As to the immediate effect of Mr. Lincoln's death, our institutions are fortunately of a character not depending on the life of any individual for their maintenance or progress. We shall miss his wise guidance and the radiations of that splendid wit which has illumined so many of our darkest hours during the past four years of struggle. We shall forever execrate "the deep damnation of his taking off," and may doubtless—for we are but human—more rigorously press upon the vanquished in this contest who have been prompters of the bloody deed the full penalties of their heinous crimes. Nevertheless the progress of the American government is upward and onward casting flowers as it passes upon

the grave of each new martyr, but never halting in the march of its divine
and irresistible mission. In Vice President Andrew Johnson—henceforward President of the United States—we have a man of similar origin with Mr. Lincoln;
equally a child of the people, equally in sympathy with their instincts, and perhaps better informed as to the true condition and governmental necessities of
the Southern States. Self-educated, and raised by personal worth through years
of laborious industry and sacrifice, no accident of a moment can be accepted
by the judgment of our people as reversing Mr. Johnson's claims to the confidence and respect of the country. In Secretary Stanton and General Grant he
has two potent and reliable advisers, who will give the first steps of his administration such wise support and guidance as they may need; and while we all
must mourn with sad and sickened hearts the success of the great crime which
has removed our beloved and trusted President from the final scenes of the
contest he had thus far conducted to a triumphant issue, let us not forget that
by the circumstance of death the seal of immortality has been stamped upon his
fame; nor is it any longer in the power of changing fortune to take away from
him, as might have happened had he lived, one of the most solid, brilliant and
stainless reputations of which in the world's annals any record can be found—its
only peer existing in the memory of George Washington.

Thus spoke the *New York Herald*, a newspaper surpassing all others in
the country in circulation, enterprise, and profits. A few weeks before Lincoln was inaugurated it called on him to resign and let a more competent
and experienced man be chosen in his place. Over and again it bore down
on the President with sarcasm, satire, ridicule, personal belittlement. Early
in 1864 the *Herald* did its utmost, went the limit in news reports and edi-
torials, to name another candidate and stop Lincoln from re-election and a
second term. Later its policy shifted to one of neutrality. Then on the death
of Lincoln it gave him keen appraisal, lavish tribute, a timeless place in history, in a surpassing portrait-study.

9. The Cold War of 1860-61—
the Later War—Aftermath

ALONE stood South Carolina. Alone she led off. Alone she was to tell the world she was a sovereign State, completely and independently sovereign, never having yielded any smallest slice of her sovereignty to the Government of the United States.

On December 20, 1860, in secret session, the unanimous vote of 169 delegates forming a State Convention, "dissolved" the bonds holding South Carolina a part of the United States. The delegates one by one signed the Ordinance of Secession. Governor F. W. Pickens of South Carolina on December 22 wrote to the president of the Convention:

I have rec^d from the Convention as yet no official notification of the purpose of the ordinance. I would most respectfully suggest that such notice be given in order that I may issue a proclamation announcing the fact to the World, that we are a free & independent Republic & as such authorized to negotiate treaties & do all other acts that appertain to a free & independent Republic.

A free and independent republic, a sovereign nation that has surrendered none of its sovereignty to any power outside itself, can appoint Ministers, Ministers Plenipotentiary, envoys or special envoys. Governor Pickens named a "Special Envoy," I. W. Hayne, to go to the capital of "a foreign power," Washington, D.C., there to call on the Chief Magistrate, there "to make a demand." Hayne carried a letter of instructions, an important document.

President Buchanan refused an interview to "Special Envoy" Hayne and sent word that any communication must be in writing, under the old theory that "a written paper is the best witness." After days of waiting and of

Lower half of letter of Governor Pickens to president of South Carolina Convention, December 22, 1860. (*Reduced from original*)

conference with Southern colleagues, Hayne delivered his important document of January 12, 1861, into the hands of President Buchanan. What the President read, if it had to be put in short and simple words, carried the notice: "We don't want war but you can be sure we are ready to make war if we don't hear the right answers." He read:

STATE OF SOUTH CAROLINA,
EXECUTIVE OFFICE, STATE DEPARTMENT,
CHARLESTON, JANUARY 12, 1861.

Sir.

The Governor has considered it proper, in view of the grave questions which now affect the State of South Carolina and the United States, to make a demand upon the President of the United States, for the delivery to the State of South Carolina of Fort Sumter, now within the territorial limits of the State, and occupied by troops of the United States.

The Convention of the people of South Carolina authorized and empowered its Commissioners to enter into negotiations with the Government of the United States, for the delivery of forts, Magazines, light houses and other real Estate within the limits of South Carolina.

The circumstances which caused the interruption of that negotiation are known to you, with the formal notification of its cessation, was the urgent expression of the necessity for the withdrawal of the troops of the United States from the harbor of Charleston.

The interruption of these negotiations left all matters connected with Fort Sumter and troops of the United States within the limits of this State; affected by the fact that the continued possession of the Fort was not consistent with the dignity or safety of the State, and that an attempt to reinforce the troops at that fort, would not be allowed. This therefore became a state of hostility in consequence of which the State of South Carolina was placed in a condition of defence. During the preparation for this purpose, an attempt was made to reinforce Fort Sumter and repelled.

You are now instructed to proceed to Washington, and there in the name of the Government of the State of South Carolina, enquire of the President of the United States whether it was by his order that troops of the United States were sent into the harbor of Charleston to reinforce Fort Sumter; if he avows that order, you will then enquire, whether he asserts a right to introduce troops of the United States within the limits of this State to occupy Fort Sumter: and you will, in case of his avowal, inform him that neither will be permitted, and either will be regarded as his declaration of War against the State of South Carolina.

The Governor to save life, and determined to omit no course of proceeding usual among ~~Sena~~ civilized Nations, previous to that condition of general hostilities, which belongs to War; and not knowing under what order, or by what authority Fort Sumter is now held; demanded from Major Robert Anderson, now in command of that Fort, its delivery to the State. That officer, in his reply, has referred the Governor~~ment~~ to the Government of the United States at Washington. You will therefore demand from the President of the United States, the withdrawal of the troops of the United States from that fort, and its delivery to the State of South Carolina.

You are instructed not to allow any question of property claimed by the United States, to embarrass the assertion of the political right of the State of South Carolina, to the possession of Fort Sumter. The possession of that Fort by the State is alone consistent with the dignity & safety of the State of South Carolina: but such possession is not inconsistent with a right to compensation in money in another Government, if it has against the State of South Carolina any just claim connected with that Fort. But the possession of the Fort cannot in regard to the State of South Carolina be compensated by any consideration of any kind from the Government of the United States, when the possession of it by the Government is invasive of the dignity and affects the safety of the State; that possession cannot become now a matter of discussion or negotiation. You will therefore require from the President of the United States a positive and distinct answer to your demand for the delivery of the Fort. And you are further authorized to give the pledge of the State to adjust all matters which may be, and are in their nature, susceptible of valuation in money, in the manner most usual, and upon the principles of Equity and Justice, always recognised by Independent Nations, for the ascertainment of their relative rights and obligations in such matters.

You are further instructed to say to the President of the United States that the Governor regards the attempt of the President of the United States, if avowed, to continue the possession of Fort Sumter; as inevitably leading to a bloody issue; a question which in the judgement of the Governor h can
conclusion,
have but one ~~solution,~~ reconcilable with a due regard to the State of South Carolina, the welfare of the other States which now constitute [the United States, and] that humanity which teaches all men, but particularly those, who in authority control the lives of others, to regard a resort to arms, as the last which should be considered. To shed their blood in defence of their rights is a duty, which the Citizens of the State of South Carolina fully recognize. And in such a cause the Governor while deploring the stern necessity which may compel him to call for the sacrifice, will feel that his obligation to preserve inviolate the sacred rights of the State of South Carolina will justify the sacrifice necessary to secure that end. The Governor does not desire to remind the President of the responsibilities which are upon him.

Respectfully
Your obt. Servt.
A. G. Magrath

To Hon. I. W. Hayne.
Special Envoy from the State of South Carolina to the President of the United States.

Lone-handed, a little sovereign state by herself, South Carolina was playing her role as a nation. Was she too sure of herself? Could it be that 'most any day she would train her cannon on Fort Sumter, pull down the United States flag and run up her own, and bring on a war? There were Senators from Southern states not sure what the defiant and belligerent men at Charleston might do. Ten of these Senators signed a letter to Hayne, asking delay. "Until you have received and communicated his [Governor Pickens's] response to the President, of course your State will not attack Fort Sumpter [sic], and the President will not offer to reinforce it."

Signatures of ten Senators from southern states, not yet seceded, in letter to South Carolina's Envoy Hayne proposing delay of attack on Fort Sumter

A second letter was signed by the same Senators, except three "now on their way back to their respective States." The new Confederate States of America was on the way to being born in a few days. The Senators' message to Governor Pickens could be briefed: "Don't start shooting now—if you'll wait we'll be shooting with you." Their cool and measured way of saying this read:

We take this occasion to renew the expression of an earnest hope that South Carolina will not deem it incompatible with her safety, dignity, or honor to refrain from initiating any hostilities against any power whatever, or from taking any steps tending to produce collision until our States which are to share her fortunes shall have an opportunity of joining their Counsels with hers.

Not for long was South Carolina to stand alone. Her awareness of the preparations of other states to join her is phrased in Hayne's response to the Senators.

Washington Jan 1861.

Gentlemen;

I have just rec^d your communication, dated the 15th inst. You represent, you say, States, which have already seceded from the United States, or, will have done so, before the 1st of Feb^r. next, and which will meet South Carolina in Convention, on, or, before the 15th of that month: that your People feel they have a common destiny with *our* People, & expect to form with them in that Convention a new Confederacy, and provisional Government: that you must, & *will* share our fortunes, suffering with us the evils of War, if it cannot be avoided, and enjoying with us the blessings of peace, if it *can* be preserved.

I feel, GENTLEMEN, the force of that appeal, and so far as *my* authority extends, most cheerfully comply with your request.

I am not clothed with power to make the arrangements you suggest, but provided you can get assurances, with which you are entirely satisfied, that *no* reinforcements will be sent to Fort Sumter in the interval, & that public peace shall *not* be disturbed by any act of hostility towards South Carolina—, I will refer your communication to the Authorities of S°. Carolina, & withholding their communication, with which I am at present charged, will await further instructions.

MAJOR ANDERSON & his Command, let me assure you, *do* now obtain all necessary supplies, of food, (including fresh meat, & vegetables), and I believe, fuel & water—, & *do* now enjoy free communication by Post, & special messengers, with the President, & will continue to do so, certainly, until the door of negotiation shall be closed.

If your proposition is acceded to, you may assure the President that no attack will be made on Fort Sumter, until a response from the Governor of South Carolina has been received by me, and communicated to him.

> With great consideration, and profound
> Esteem,
> Your *Obedient Servant*,
> (Signed) *Isaac W. Hayne*
> Envoy from the Governor, &
> Council of South Carolina

Foreign powers were to be told that their consuls or other representatives whom they sent to South Carolina would not be recognized if they came under the approval of the United States Government. The Court of Spain had withdrawn its consul at Charleston, and the State Department of South Carolina served notice, in an eight-page letter to the departing consul, that his successor, or any like servants of foreign powers, could act as officials only by recognition of the Governor of South Carolina. In foreign affairs as in domestic matters no sovereignty was to be yielded. In the new political set-up South Carolina held "the power to establish political or commercial relations between this State & any other Power or Nation. The representative therefore of any Foreign Power or Nation exercises its functions within the limits of this State, by the permission & authority of the Government of the State . . . he [the Governor of South Carolina] will with pleasure afford your Successor, upon the presentation of his papers, the recognition which will admit him to the discharge of his Consular duties within this State."

Under the date of February 6, 1861, Joseph Holt, Secretary of War for the United States Government, offered a reply of nine pages to the January letter Hayne delivered to President Buchanan. A postscript added on a tenth page omitted the title of "Special Envoy" and designated the Hon. I. W. Hayne by his other and equally correct title of "Attorney General of the State of South Carolina." Secretary Holt dismissed the proposal of the January letter as "simply an offer on the part of South Carolina to buy Fort Sumter and contents as property of the United States." In an elaborate legal argument Holt contended Fort Sumter was not in ordinary "public domain"; the "incontestable" authority of the United States over the fort came from "the peaceful cession of South Carolina herself, acting through her Legislature, under a provision of the Constitution of the United States." The basic idea of Fort Sumter in the first place, Holt urged, was that the United States Government should use it for the defense of Charleston and its people. For the Federal Government to hand it back now to South Carolina would be the same as the State of Maryland putting in a claim for the District of Columbia and getting back what she once ceded to the Federal Government.

War Department,
February 6th. 1861

Sir,

The President of the United States has received your letter of the 31st. Ult°. and has charged me with the duty of replying thereto.

In the communication addressed to the President by Governor Pickens, under date of the 12th of January, and which accompanies yours now before me, his Excellency says "I have determined to send to you the Hon. I. W. Hayne, the Attorney General of the State of South Carolina, and have instructed him to demand the surrender of Fort Sumter in the harbor of Charleston, to the constituted authorities of the State of South Carolina. The demand I have made of Major Anderson and which I now make of you, is suggested because of my earnest desire to avoid the bloodshed which a persistence in your attempt to retain the possession of that fort will cause, and which will be unavailing to secure to you that possession, but induce a calamity most deeply to be deplored." The character of the demand thus authorised to be made appears—under the influence, I presume, of the correspondence with the Senators to which you refer—to have been modified by subsequent instructions of his Excellency, dated the 26th, and received by yourself on the 30th of January, in which he says, "If it be so that Fort Sumter is held as property, then as property, the rights whatever they may be, of the United States, can be ascertained, and for the satisfaction of these rights, the pledge of the State of South Carolina, you are authorised to give." The full scope and precise purport of your instructions as thus modified you have expressed in the following words: "I do not come as a military man to demand the surrender of a fortress, but as the legal officer of the State—its Attorney General—to claim for the State, the exercise of its undoubted right of eminent domain, and to pledge the State to make good all injury to the rights of property which arise [sic] from the exercise of the claim." And lest this explicit language should not sufficiently define your position, you add, "The proposition now is that her (South Carolina's) law officer should under authority of the Governor and his Council, distinctly pledge the faith of South Carolina, to make such compensation, in regard to Fort Sumter and its appurtenances and contents, to the full extent of the money value of the property of the United States delivered over to the authorities of South Carolina by your command." You then adopt his Excellency's train of thought upon the subject, so far as to suggest that the possession of Fort Sumter by the United States "if continued long enough must lead to collision," and that "an attack upon it would scarcely improve it as property, whatever the result, and if captured, it would no longer be the subject of account."

The proposal then, now presented to the President, is simply an offer on the part of South Carolina to buy Fort Sumter and contents as property of the United States, sustained by a declaration, in effect, that if she is not permitted to make the purchase, she will seize the fort by force of arms. As the initiation of a negotiation for the transfer of property between friendly governments, this proposal impresses the President as having assumed a most unusual form. He has however investigated the claim on which it professes to be based apart from the declaration that accompanies it. And it may be here remarked that much stress has been laid upon the employment of the words "property" and "public property" by the President in his several messages. These are the most comprehensive terms which can be used in such a connection and surely when referring to a fort or any other public establishment, they embrace the entire and undivided interest of the Government therein. The title of the United States to Fort Sumter is complete and incontestable. Were its interest in this property purely proprietary, in the ordinary acceptation of the term, it might probably be subjected to the exercise of the right of eminent domain; but it has also political relations to it, of a much higher and more imposing character than those of mere proprietorship. It has absolute jurisdiction over the fort and the soil on which it stands. This jurisdiction consists in the authority to "exercise exclusive legislation" over the property referred to, and is therefore clearly incompatible with the claim of eminent domain now insisted upon by South Carolina. This authority was not derived from any questionable, revolutionary source, but from the peaceful cession of South Carolina herself, acting through her Legislature, under a provision of the Constitution of the United States. South Carolina can no more assert the right of eminent domain over Fort Sumter, than Maryland can assert it over the District of Columbia. The political and proprietary rights of the United States in either case, rest upon precisely the same ground.

The President, however, is relieved from the necessity of further pursuing this inquiry, by the fact that whatever may be the claim of South Carolina to this fort, he has no constitutional power to cede or surrender it. The property of the Untied States has been acquired by force of public law, and can only be disposed of under the same solemn sanctions. The President as the head of the Executive branch of the Government only, can no more sell and transfer Fort Sumter to South Carolina, than he can sell and convey the Capitol of the United States to Maryland or to any other State or individual seeking to possess it. His Excellency the Governor is too familiar with the Constitution of the United States, and with the limitations upon the powers of the Chief Magistrate of the government it has established, not to appreciate at once, the soundness of this legal proposition.

The question of reinforcing Fort Sumter is so fully disposed of in my letter to Senator Slidell and others, under the date of the 22d of January— a copy of which accompanies this—that its discussion will not now be renewed. I then said, "At the present moment, it is not deemed necessary to reinforce Major Anderson, because he makes no such request. Should his safety however require reinforcements, every effort will be made to supply them." I can add nothing to the explicitness of this language which still applies to the existing status. The right to send forward reinforcements, when in the judgment of the President the safety of the garrison requires them, rests on the same unquestionable foundation as the right to occupy the fortress itself.

In the letter of Senator Davis and others to yourself, under date of the 15th ultimo, they say, "We therefore think it especially due from South Carolina to our States—to say nothing of other slaveholding States—that she should, as far as she can consistently with her honor, avoid initiating hostilities between her and the United States or any other power," and you now yourself give to the President the gratifying assurance that "South Carolina has every disposition to preserve the public peace"; and since he is himself sincerely animated by the same desire, it would seem that this common and patriotic object must be of certain attainment. It is difficult, however, to reconcile with this assurance, the declaration on your part, that "it is a consideration of her (South Carolina's) own dignity as a Sovereign, and the safety of her people which prompts her to demand that this property should not longer be used as a military post by a government she no longer acknowledges," and the thought you so constantly present, that this occupation must lead to a collision of arms, and the prevalence of civil war. Fort Sumter is in itself a military post and nothing else, and it would seem that not so much the fact as the purpose of its use, should give to it a hostile or friendly character. This fortress is now held by the Government of the United States for the same objects for which it has been held from the completion of its construction. These are national and defensive, and were a public enemy now to attempt the capture of Charleston, or the destruction of the commerce of its harbor, the whole force of the batteries of this fortress would be at once exerted for their protection. How the presence of a small garrison actuated by such a spirit as this, can compromise the dignity or honor of South Carolina or become a source of irritation to her people, the President is at a loss to understand. The attitude of that garrison, as has been often declared, is neither menacing, nor defiant nor unfriendly. It is acting under orders to stand strictly on the defensive, and the Government and people of South Carolina must well know that they can never receive aught but shelter from its guns, unless in the absence of all provocation, they should assualt it and seek its destruction. The intent with which this fortress is held by the President is truthfully stated by Senator Davis and others in their letter to yourself of the 15th of January, in which they say, "It is not held with any hostile or unfriendly purpose towards your State, but merely as property of the United States which the President deems it his duty to protect and preserve."

If the announcement, so repeatedly made, of the President's pacific purposes in continuing the occupation of Fort Sumter until the question shall have been settled by competent authority, has failed to impress the government of South Carolina, the forbearing conduct of his administration for the last few months, should be received as conclusive evidence of his sincerity, And if this forbearance, in view of the circumstances which have so severely tried it, be not accepted as a satisfactory pledge of the peaceful policy of this administration towards South Carolina, then it may be safely affirmed, that neither language nor conduct can possibly furnish one. If with all the multiplied proofs, which exist, of the President's anxiety for peace and of the earnestness with which he has pursued it, the authorities of that State shall assault Fort Sumter and peril the lives of the handful of brave and loyal men shut up within its walls, and thus plunge our common country into the horrors of civil war, then upon them and those they represent, must rest the responsibility.

Very Respectfully
Your Ob^t Servant
J. Holt.
Secretary of War.

The Hon. I. W. Hayne
Attorney General
of State of South Carolina

P. S. (over)

P.S. The President has not, as you have been informed, received a copy of the letter to yourself from the Senators, communicating that of Mr. Holt of the 22d of January.

JH

Closing lines of J. Holt's argument against assault on Fort Sumter

Three days after the date of the Holt letter to Governor Pickens of South Carolina, another letter went to the Governor over the signature of Robert Toombs, United States Senator from Georgia, resigning to become Secretary of State of the Confederate States of America. "We think we have the right to insist," wrote the abrupt and forthright Toombs, "that you follow the present status at Charleston." Congress at Washington, it was believed, would adjourn "without voting men or money," which, as Toombs and mutual friends saw it, "would give us the advantage of a whole Campaign, and would be of inestimable value to us."

The question of who should fire the first gun and on what grounds and authority, problems as to delegated powers and jealousies between "sovereign States," on these the South Carolinian William Porcher Miles, a former United States Congressman, reports to Governor Pickens from the Confederate States capital at Montgomery, Alabama.

Montgomery Feb. 9th/61

Honble F. W. Pickens
Dear Sir

We have just elected M^r. Jeff. Davis President and M^r. Alex. H. Stephens Vice President of the Provisional Gov^t. It seems to me that we ought not to attack Fort Sumter without authority from the Confederate Gov^t. I cannot see that the short delay compromises the honour of the State in the least, if—when the attack is ordered—South Carolina troops *alone* engage in it. We do not ask our Confederate States *to help* us take it. But our attack necessarily plunges the new Gov^t. into a war with the U.S. and that before *they* (our Confederates) are prepared This would be the inevitable consequence for surely the U.S. Gov^t. so soon as we open our batteries upon Sumter will be bound by every consideration to send relief and assistance to Major Anderson and his handful of men who is holding his post by the express orders of his Government. *Might* not our attack be considered as "making war" which the Provisional Constitution restrains a State from doing except in case of invasion? Is Anderson's *presence with the troops which he had before the secession* of our State an act of invasion?

But now as to our pressing the subject of our situation in Charleston upon the Congress here assemblied. We cannot with due consideration for the dignity of South Carolina seem to implore our brother delegates to come to our aid in any way. They know the condition of things with us. They have many of them seen your telegraphic despatches and Hayne's. It is for them to suggest action of some sort not for us. But moreover there are great objections to our electing a General. The general opinion is that the President as Commander in Chief should nominate his own General. It is feared that a General of our appointment might not be acceptable to the President elect and thus jealousy and distraction and inefficiency would result. M^r. Memminger and all of our delegation (except Messr^s. Rhett & Barnwell) concur in these views. Toombs and many others of the truest, *perpetual* separation men and all of the *pluckiest* school to boot *warmly* concur in them. Toombs deems it of so much consequence that he will write you this evening on the subject.

The *Courage* of South Carolina has been too amply and too habitually proved to require us now to do *anything merely* to demonstrate it further.

Her wisdom and good sense have been oftener called in question let us now show that she possesses both.

Very faithfully yours
Wm Porcher Miles

The furtive conduct so often required in either a revolution or a cold war stands out in the letter of Jefferson Davis, the first President of the newly organized Confederate States of America. Not yet had there been time for printing official stationery, so the letter began with the handwritten words at the top of the first page:

Executive office
Confederate States

Montgomery Feb. 22. 1861.

Davis in his letter notifies Governor Pickens of South Carolina that the Congress of the Confederate States of America by resolutions passed on February 15 and February 22 requested Davis to let the Governors of South Carolina and Florida know that the Congress favored "immediate steps" to take over Fort Sumter at Charleston and Fort Pickens at Pensacola, Florida, "either by negotiation or force, as early as practicable." It was no pleasant holiday affair and Davis wrote, "The injunction of secrecy, you will perceive has been removed only so far as to authorise me to communicate in the manner deemed expedient; and I must therefore ask that you consider it as confidentially done."

Indications are definite that the writing of this letter was neither by Davis himself nor by a clerk or underling. The handwriting unmistakably is that of the moderate and unwarlike Secretary of the Treasury of the Confederate States, a Charleston lawyer and politician, Christopher Gustavus Memminger. The text reads:

His Excellency
F. W. Pickens.
Dear Sir

After writing to you today the subjoined Resolution was received. The injunction of secrecy, you will perceive has been removed only so far as to authorise me to communicate in the manner deemed expedient; and I must therefore ask that you consider it as confidentially done.

The Resolution suggests two methods by which possession of the Forts may be had. It was not intended however that the progress of the one should retard or affect the preparations for the other. While therefore steps are being taken for negotiation, earnest efforts have been made to procure men of military science and experience, and to seek for munitions and machinery suitable to remedy the supposed or known deficiencies in the existing supplies.

Congress probably did not design to interfere with the progress of constructions which had been commenced by state authority, the instruction of troops or other preparations which will be useful in future operations; and

Closing lines of February 22, 1861, letter signed by Jefferson Davis, all else in the letter in handwriting of Christopher G. Memminger

I hope you will continue thus to prepare for whatever exigency may arise. As soon as a skilful Engineer is available, he will be sent to make examination of the Fort within your State and to aid in the works needful to the execution of the Resolution of Congress, should force be the means to which we must resort.

Very Respectfully
& Truly Yours
Jefferson Davis

Copy
Resolutions.

Feb. 22, 1861. Congress. "Resolved that the President of the Confederate States be requested to communicate in such manner as he may deem expedient to the Governors of South Carolina and Florida the resolution of Congress concerning Forts Sumter and Pickens.["]

The resolution above referred to is as follows:

Resolved by the Confederate States of America in Congress assembled, that it is the sense of this Congress, that immediate steps should be taken to obtain possession of Forts Sumter & Pickens by the authority of this Government either by negotiation or force, as early as practicable, and that the President is hereby authorised to make all necessary military preparations for carrying this Resolution into effect.

Passed February 15. 1861.

Events had been moving fast. The Confederacy got organized. In quite a different tone, in almost vocal quavers, Anderson wrote to a friend in the North.

Fort Sumter S. C.
March 4. 1861

P. D. Mickler Jr.
Syracuse
N. Y.
Dear Sir:

I thank you for your favor of the 27th Feby.

Every thing moves on, in this region, in the beaten track—both sides making every preparation for a conflict, which I pray God will avert, and

Thanking you for
your kind wishes, and wishing
you prosperity, I am

Very Respy
Robert Anderson
Col.

Closing lines of a letter of Major Robert Anderson in his handwriting (*above*); part of an Anderson letter with text probably in another's writing (*below*)

I have the honor to

Acknowledge the receipt of your communication
of to day, and to say that, under the cir =
cumstances, I have deemed it proper to refer
the entire matter to my Government

which, I trust, there is now good grounds for a hope, will not take place. My command, thank God, continues well, and is in fine heart. The New Commander of this portion of the Southern Army—a graduate of the Mily. Academy—a gentleman and a fine soldier, Genl. P. G. T. Beauregard, is, to day, making an inspection of the Forts of this harbour (omitting Ft Sumter).

Thanking you for your kind wishes, and invoking your prayers for us

I am,

Yours Respy

Robert Anderson

USA

Meantime Major Robert Anderson, in command of Fort Sumter, had played a waiting game. On January 9, 1861, he wrote a letter to Governor Pickens replying to a demand of the Governor that he and his United States troops move out of the fort.

Head Quarters Fort Sumter S.C.

January 9th 1861

To his Excellency

F. W. Pickens

Governor of the State of South Carolina

Sir

I have the honor to acknowledge the receipt of your communication of to day, and to say that, under the circumstances, I have deemed it proper to refer the whole matter to my Government, and that I intend deferring the course indicated in my note of this morning, until the arrival from Washington of the instructions I may receive. I have the honor also to express a hope that no obstructions will be placed in the way of, and that you will do me the favor of giving every facility to, the departure and return of the bearer Lieut T. Talbot U.S. Army who has been directed to make the journey.

I have the honor to be

Very respectfully

(Signed) Robert Anderson

Major U.S.A.

Comd

Comparison of the handwriting of the two letters suggests that the January one was written by a member of Major Anderson's staff. Perhaps this is not the original, but a copy.

The punctuation of the period marking the end of the cold war may be seen, in part, distinctly in two telegrams in the Barrett Collection. On April 12, 1861, the Confederate Secretary of War, L. P. Walker, put on the wires the message, "Our batteries opened upon Sumter at four thirty this morning." And the next day, April 13, the message, entire, "Sumter is ours."

THE PENSACOLA TELEGRAPH COMPANY,

CONNECTING WITH EVERY LINE IN NORTH AMERICA.

Dated _Montgomery, Apr. 13, 1861._

Rec'd, Pensacola, _Apr. 14, 1861. _____o'clock, _____min. M._

To _Genl. Bragg_

Sumter is ours.

L. P. Walker

Having telegraphed General Bragg, April 12, 1861, "Our batteries opened upon Fort Sumter at four thirty this morning," the Confederate Secretary of War the next day telegraphed Bragg, "Sumter is ours," the incident marking the end of the cold war between North and South

The negotiations and manipulations of the cold war ended this April of '61. Life in the army was reported in letters to home folks.

Samuel Garland, Jr., was thirty-one years of age when he wrote this, with the rank of Colonel. Later, as Brigadier General, he led the van of Lee's army in the Maryland campaign, and was killed in action in the Battle of South Mountain.

Camp of The Eleventh V^a

My dear Mother,

Dec. 11th 1861.

Writing sometimes to you & sometimes to Nannie, I lose the count & cant tell when I am in arrears. No matter. I must ask you all to do—as I do—& that is write as often as you have opportunity, and at least often enough to prevent uneasiness. We are sometimes so short of candles as to be compelled to spend our evenings chatting around my stove—which renders my tent so comfortable, that it is the loafing place of my friends, when I am not occupied. Our situation here is very annoying, from the fact, that the expected advance of the enemy has kept us from perfecting any plans for the winter!—and the middle of December finds us shivering in our tents, at the bleakest place in Eastern V^a, while the Yankees are taking it after their own fashion, & building nice quarters about Washington & Alexandria. I cannot speak with any certainty of getting home even in January, for the rule of the Generals is still unrelaxed and my vigorous health gives no prospect of a sick leave. The life here is now growing monotonous—relieved only by an occasional review, and a military execution. This last I could not make up my mind to attend, nor would the painful details be interesting. The condemned were two of Wheat's Tigers, who assailed with weapons the officers & Guard of the 7th L^a. & rescued some prisoners condemned by Court-Martial to the ball & chain. You will be glad to know that the Episcopal Church here, which had been defaced by the Vandals & then occupied as an Hospital by our Army, has been restored to sacred uses, the marks of occupation & desecration removed as far as possible. For several Sundays now, I have listened to the Rev^d. Col Pendleton, with his full Regimentals only partially concealed by an overcoat. The attendance is good & the service read with 'onction,' Rev^d. Mr. Powell assisting.

General Lee's daughter (Mary Lee) who was a great belle in the old Army has been here. At the request of my present Brigadier (Ewell) I spent an evening with her at his H^d.Q^{rs}. & another at Meacham's—finding her quite an elegant & interesting woman. Not long since, Mrs Campbell Brown & daughter of Nashville (the mother of the General's Aid) paid him a visit both very nice people & I passed an evening with them. I also see a good deal of Kirby Smith & in fact all the Generals. They treat me very cordially & converse freely. I am really more intimate with Ewell, than I was with Longstreet:—The old fellow is infatuated about Miss Lee & talks to me about the affair.

Don't let your quiet be disturbed about my poor Uncle's matters. My

Private

Hd. Qrs Richmond Va
May 29th 1862

His Excellency F. W. Pickens
Gov. of South Carolina
Gov:

Your letter of May 23d has been received. I thank you most cordially for the freedom with which you have made your suggestions about the state of affairs at Charleston and will assure you that they are duly considered. I am sure that we both estimate alike the importance of defending the city

last

of Charleston to the ~~utmost~~ extremity. To loose [sic] this City now would as you remarked Close our only Channel of cummunication [sic] with the foreign world. Through which we have and still hope to receive many valuable cargoes of munitions of war.

The dissentions [sic] which have arisen among the officers who have been called to the defence of Charleston are truly to be regreted [sic]. Steps have been taken as far as practicable at present, to remedy to some extent this evil. Genl. Ripley has been relieved from duty in Charleston and ordered elsewhere and another competent officer will be sent to replace him. I will have insert[ed] for your information. A copy of my instructions to Genl. Pemberton. "General, It is desired that you give particular attention to the condition of the fortifications in Charleston harbour. Not only as regards the Armament and supplies, but also as regards the condition and feeling of the garrisons. This is particularly important as any disatisfaction might be attended by irreparable mischief. Since the example of Fort Jackson we cannot be too particular in guarding against mutiny."

"Since your forces have been to some extent reduced and may be still further diminished, it becomes necessary for you to make up in vigilance any want of Physical force you may have to contend against. The importance of defending both Charleston and Savannah to the last extremity particularly Charleston is earnestly brought to your attention. The loss of Charleston would cut us off almost entirely from communication with the rest of the world and close the only channel through which we can expect to get supplies from abroad, now almost our only dependence. You will therefore make use of every means at your command to put these cities in the most perfect State of defence. Your attention is particularly called to the river and harbour obstructions. These should be rendered as strong as it is possible to make them. Spare no labor or expense upon them. It is also of the greatest importance that the discipline of the garrisions of the different works should be brought to the highest state of perfection.

"Let it be distinctly understood by everybody, that Charleston and Savannah are to be defended to the last extremity. If the harbours are taken, the cities are to be fought street by street and house by house as long as we have a foot of ground to stand upon. The State authorities of both South Carolina and Georgia will doubtless lend us every means at their command to aid you in your operations."

I feel well assured of your hearty cooperation with confederate forces serving in your State. Harmonious action between the State and Confederate authorities is greatly to be desired and must result in promoting the general good.

There are now in position in the different works about Charleston over two hundred guns many of them of the most improved class. I feel confident that this number of guns, if properly manned and fought will render Charleston impregnable. If it however be found that other guns are needed and they can be procured they shall be sent to Charleston. There are none available at this place now.

In regard to Genl. Hayes—just at this time it is impossible to comply with your suggestions. He commands a division of Genl. Johnston's Army around this City, having commanded it many months, knowing its condition and being accustomed to the Commission he cannot be relieved without injury to the service. I esteem him very highly and he has always been regarded as an officer of great merit especially as an Artillerist. I do not know how far the cause you mention might impair his usefulness in Carolina

I am Gov:　very Resptly

Your Obt Servant

R E Lee

It was under date of April 28, 1862, that Governor John Letcher of Virginia wrote to Governor F. W. Pickens of South Carolina that the war outlook had changed and after one year of it the people were losing interest in it: ". . . when we shall wake up to a full sense of the peril which now stares us in the face, and when the people shall demand with irresistible voice to be led into the enemy's country—then, and not till then can we hope to compel them to terms of peace."

By thousands in prison camps North and South, Confederate and Union soldiers in 1864 lived near starvation, hoped for exchange, prayed for the war to end. They dug tunnels toward escape and saw men shot and hanged for being caught. The pocket diary of James Burton of Syracuse, New York, is often telegraphic in brevity. His entries could be elaborately annotated, but any reader can get the main thread of his story. Thousands of prisoners took a longer prison stretch than Comrade Burton. One day he resents his Government's not getting him exchanged. Another day, near the November election of 1864, he believes his Government is afraid of prisoners' votes if they should be exchanged. Still another time, and this near Charleston, South Carolina, he finds: "Many Union people here especially among the females, who would take pleasure in distributing eatables among us if the scamps (Rebs.) would allow." This may have been a hunger hallucination. Gaunt however are the brief entries where he tells of "many" Union soldiers taking the oath of allegiance to the Confederacy, and if he comes to it he will not consider the oath binding. Parts of his diary follow:

Entries from the Pocket Diary of James Burton,
Syracuse, New York, for the year 1864

Sunday, [April] 17.
Attack on Plymouth commenced about 4.00 A.M. Said to be a heavy force. Citizens and Darkies all called out and under arms.
[April] 18.
General attack all round. Shot & shell fly around town very lively. . . .
[April] 20.
Skirmishing all day mostly by Heavy guns, but attack renewed at ½ past nine, lively musketry firing down the river, Rebs stormed into the East End of the town and took the Redoubts and came down through the streets pell mell at about 5 o.C. A.M. and of course all citizens & troops outside of the Main Fort were forced to surrender. We were marched out the east End of the Town about two miles and remained until the Fort gave in about 10 O.C. A.M. and then we marched back to town and out the Southwest road about a mile for the night.
Thursday, [April] 21.
Morning passed off in recovering *rations*. 8 Hard Tack & a piece of *our* Pork pr. ration. Started at noon.
Friday, [April] 22.
On the march to Hamilton, and a hard march too, feet badly used up and very painfull, blistered on the bottom. Most of the Darkies captured at P. said to be shot. About 300.

[April] 25.

Arrived at Tarborough at noon hot and dusty feet sore &c. Everybody hungry and no rations.

[April] 30.

Arrived at Macon at 8 o.C. A.M. Stopd about an hour & left for Andersonville, Ga. Arrived about 3 o.C. P.M. after being counted off, were shoved into the Hog Pen with ten thousand other poor miserable dirty human beings

Sunday, [May] 1.

The enclosure called "Camp Sumpter" of about 12 Acres now contains at least 10,000 prisoners, a majority from "Belle Island" (Richmond). Some without shirts, shoes, hats or blankets, with little holes dug into the ground and covered with brush for habitations, looking more like living skeletons than human beings. The nights so cold that they are compelled to hover around a few smoking Embers to keep Life in them, and as the morning sun begins to shed its ever welcome warmth, they crawl into their holes for sleep, and new comers are even worse off, in that respect, not having any holes to crawl into.

Man shot for being over the "Dead Line."

Tuesday, [May] 3.

Last night I woke up soon after laying down (11 o'C) and could not sleep being so cold; so after lying until 3 o'C. got up and sought a little fire the same as the other Demon looking Objects.

The balance of our Plymouth friends have just arrived, making now at least 12000 uf us huddled together in this miserable Sheep pen. Our ration is pint & half of corn meal and about ¼— of poor (live) raw bacon. Just paid *a dollar* for one half of a Canteen for a frying pan. *Greenback* are worth five dollars confederate for one, in Camp, and more outside.

[May] 5.

About 40 said to have escaped last night, some through a tunnel & others scaled the Stockade. This morning (Thursday) all kept standing in the ranks at roll call, untill the *leakage* could be found.

This Camp opened the 23ᵈ of February & up to last night 940 have died. Mostly prisoners that suffered so severely at "Belle Island" (Richmond).

[May] 23.

900 New Prisoners came in today from the "Army of the Potomac" taken between F. Burgh & Richmond. All bring good reports from Grant. Say he is giving them lively work. Also good from Sherman, who is driving Gen. Johnston onto Atalanta [sic] in haste.

[*May*] *24.*

Capt. Everett & Cutting went outside with a squad last night to work en-
larging the Stockades. Hope they will have a good time working for the
Confeds. in the hot Sun. Rather *aiding* & *abetting* the Confe. Gov^t. taking
the place of a Confed. Soldier & be sent to the front to fight.

[*May*] *25.*

About 500 more prisoners came in today from "Army of the Potomac"
captured 12th & 14th inst. "Bull Pen" (as our lot is called) is getting sufficiently full for Comfort. Must now be about 14000 on 12 Acres of ground.

[*May*] *26.*

Our *family* have now increased to about 15000.

[*May*] *27.*

Excitable day around Camp. The Keeper of the prison mistrusted (or
had been informed) of the intention of the prisoners to make a break by
tunnelling & undermining the Stockade, caused search to be made and found
a number of tunnels completed. The plan was to undermine the Stockade,
make a break, bush it over, secure the 4 Guns, overcome the Guard, secure
sufficient provision and make for our lines. Daring procedure but anything
for liberty.

[*May*] *29.*

About 900 more prisoners came in today from "Army of the Potomac."
All reports are that our Army is doing well; undoubtedly a strong push for
Richmond this time. May they succeed & bag all the ringleaders of this
damnable rebellion is my prayer.

[*June*] *3.*

Another hard rain today. Everything wet. Took a severe cold last night,
Blanket, Tent (Shanty) and ground being so wet. It's enough to kill a
castiron Man.

[*June*] *23.*

Another man shot for being over the "Dead Line." 400 or 500 more prison-
ers came in today captured at Petersburgh. Have now over 24.000 in the
"Bull Pen." Very hot today. Diarrhea better & feel better generally, thank
God.

[*July*] *1.*

The Main Excitement today is moving into the new addition to the camp.
About six Acres enclosed & detachment above 48 move, taking at least half
our number, leaving us a chance to breathe again.

[*July*] *5.*

Nothing new. All waiting for the 7th inst. Expecting to leave according
to all reports; Lincoln having issued a Proclamation to that effect. Said to

have been published in the "Herald" of 10th of June, that Exchange must commence the 7th and conclude the 27th of July, that the prisoners must be released.

[*July*] *10.*

Another Sunday, but should not know it only by the "Diary." Reported that six of the ringleaders of the "Raiders" that have been on trial, are to be hung tomorrow. They undoubtedly deserve it.

[*July*] *11-12.*

Very prominent indications that some one has got to stretch hemp, as they are now erecting a Gallows. About 5 o'C P.M. the Culprits were brought in and handed over to the Camp to be dealt with as they saw fit & at about ½ past 5 o'C. they ascended the Scaffold and were launched into eternity all at one time. Before ascending the Gallows one made a break for sweet life, which created a general stampede, but was soon taken and brought back to suffer the penalty. One rope broke but was soon readjusted and he then followed the rest.

[*July*] *28.*

Nothing new.

About 1000 prisoners came in from Sherman's Army just at night, report being captured two or three Miles from Atlanta.

[*August*] *27.*

All excitement expecting to start for home in a few days sure, but I manage to keep quiet.

[*September*] *7.*

None left during the night but five detachments are now going out and the whole Camp perfectly crazy with excitement. We hope & pray it may come our turn tomorrow.

[*September*] *9.*

Some left during the night, high numbers containing old prisoners. More have left during the day & *they say* "Plymouth Brigade" is to go tomorrow.

[*September*] *12.*

Arrived at the branch near Savannah about 7 o'C. A.M. and changed cars for Charleston, arriving at C. about 4 o'C. P.M. and were marched about a mile to the old race course for the night.

[*September*] *13.*

Pleasant night but very cold. No rations given out, consequently went *to bed* hungry. Found on the ground all the Yanks that had left before us, except about 1400 that were left at Savannah. Many Union people here especially among the females, who would take pleasure in distributing Eatables among us if the scamps (Rebs.) would allow.

[*September*] *14.*

Little fresh beef & 3 Hard tack issued today, about enough for one good meal.

[*September*] *15.*

Everybody hungry. Smaller rations issued than yesterday. Hunger staring us all in the face. May the curses of the Almighty rest upon the leaders of this damnable rebellion. Amen.

[*September*] *16.*

Small bit of beef left & ½ a hard tack for breakfast. About as hungry after breakfast as before. Sharp canonadeing down town during the night and continued to-day.

Little more beef just come in & no fire to cook it. Many are Eating it raw.

[*September*] *19.*

Rain last night. Woke up lying in two inches of water; nice time if a man did n't care what he said.

[*September*] *20.*

Five months this day since capture. Hardest five months ever experienced. Shower today, got our "Shabang" a little better arraigned so as to keep partially dry. No sign of Exchange. Our Gov^t. must fear our votes this fall, consequently intend keeping us until after election.

[*September*] *27.*

More Shells at night, than in the day time.

It must disturb their dreams somewhat, to have one of those large Shells come down through the top of the house and explode.

[*October*] *3.*

Rainy day. Everything damp. Many of the boys taking the oath of allegiance to this Southern Confederacy, thereby making themselves worse off. Their gut gets the best of their loyalty, very follish fellows.

[*October*] *4.*

Rations are very short, but my loyalty is longer so far; may come to it through Hunger, but in that case don't consider it binding on a Man.

[*October*] *5.*

"Still live" and have our being, but not much more. Great many are taking the Oath, to get out, but none for me, I thank you, at present. Butler & the Niger all powerfull to keep us here.

[*October*] *9.*

Very cold last night, couldn't sleep, so cold. Such weather will come tough on me, I am afraid, but must make the best of it.

Singular there is no exchange. Don't see what our Gov^t. mean by treating men in this way. Great mistake.

[*October*] *10.*

Very chilly morning & not much to Eat. Rations cut down to merely enough to keep life up, five Spoonsfull of meal & little Salt, & one pint of Flour for 24 hours.

[*October*] *11.*

Pleasant but cold, this morning. No signs of Exchanges, fear we have got a cold winter job. If I stand it through I shall be prepared for anything in way of hardship or any other boot.

[*October*] *14.*

I was in hopes to have made this day's record within our lines, but fate seems otherwise and as my "diary" has run out, I must depend upon memory hereafter. Nothing new today. No meat issued, but a little Molasses instead, poor substitute.

Got aboard of Boat under the old Flag Dec.10./64 and a happier event I never realized. Thank God for sparing my life to once more return to Freedom.

Laid in the diary was this newspaper clipping:

DEATH OF LIEUTENANT JAMES BURTON

Lieut. James Burton, late of Co. F, One Hundred and Twenty-second Regiment, New York Volunteers, died at the Voorhees House yesterday afternoon, at 4 o'clock, of consumption, from which disease he has been suffering for a long time.

Lieut. Burton, in 1862, in answer to the call for more troops by President Lincoln, entered the army as Lieutenant in the One Hundred and Twenty-second, in which capacity he served, sharing in the battles and hardships of that organization till he was captured at Plymouth, North Carolina, and taken to Andersonville, where he endured the horrible treatment given our prisoners in that infernal prison pen for a period of nine months. The affect of this treatment, added to a hereditary disposition to consumption, completely prostrated Mr. B., who though he afterwards joined his regiment and did his duty, the disease had taken too firm a hold on his system, and has at last caused his death. Mr. B. was a generous and social man, and was highly esteemed by all who knew him. The funeral services will take place from the Voorhees House on Thursday morning at 9 o'clock. The remains will be taken to Cazenovia for interment.

One month and three days before the surrender of Lee's army at Appomattox on April 9, 1865, the Assistant Secretary of War in the Confederate Government, John A. Campbell, former Justice of the Supreme Court of the United States, handed a report to the Secretary of War, John C. Breckinridge. The document is cool, quiet, and grave in tone as it makes its recital of conditions in a ghastly chaos. "There is anarchy in the opinion of men here, and few are willing to give counsel." The first year of the war volunteers filled the army ranks, then conscription took the able men between eighteen and thirty-five years of age, these shifting until in February of '64, "the population between seventeen and fifty were made subject to call." Meantime, the armies diminished, General Preston reporting "over 100,000 deserters scattering over the Confederacy," the crime has lost its stigma, the criminals "shielded by their families and by the sympathies of many communities." The earlier unity of the seceded States was gone. "The States of North Carolina, South Carolina, Georgia and perhaps others, have passed laws to withdraw from service men liable to it . . . and these laws have the support of local authorities."

The report is written in a smooth, Spencerian script covering three and a half large sheets of official stationery, signed at its close by J. A. Campbell, with his notation on the back of the sheet, "This letter was handed to General Breckinridge the day of its date." It could be truly, in its patience and dignity under awful stress, a psalm of desolation. The full text reads:

Confederate States of America,

WAR DEPARTMENT,

Richmond, Va.   March 6th   1865

Genl J C Breckinridge
Secretary of War
Sir,

The present condition of the country requires in my opinion that a full and exact examination be made into the resources of the Confederate Government available for the approaching campaign, and that accurate views of our situation be taken. It is not the part of statesmanship or of patriotism to close our eyes upon them.

1.   The most important of these, is the state of the finances. This Department is in debt from four to five hundred millions of dollars. The service of all of its Bureaux are paralyzed from the want of money and credit. The estimates for this year amount to $1.048.358.275.^{57}/100. This only includes an estimate of six months for the Commissary department and excludes £135.000 Sterling required for the Nitre and Mining Service. These being

included the estimate would be $1.338.858.275^{57}/100$. The currency is at the Treasury valuation 60 to 1 as compared with coin, and when the small stock of coin in the Treasury is exhausted, and the sales of which now control the market, no one can foretell the extent of the depreciation that will ensue. It is needless to comment on these facts.

2.   Second only to the question of finance, and perhaps of equal importance, is the condition of the armies, as to men.

In April 1862 the revolutionary measure of conscription was resorted to. The men between 18 and 35 were then placed in service. The eventful campaign of 1862 compelled the addition of the class of men between 35 and 40 to the call of April. The campaign that terminated in July 1863 with the loss of Vicksburg and the disaster at Gettysburg, made a call for the men between 40 and 45 necessary. In February 1864 the conscription act was made more stringent, and the population between 17 and 50 were made subject to call. At the same time the currency was reduced one third, and heavy taxes were laid.—In October 1864 all details were revoked.

The casualties of the war cannot be accurately ascertained, but enough is known to show that no large addition can be made from the conscript population. Genl Preston reports "that there are over 100.000 deserters scattered over the Confederacy—that so common is the crime, it has in popular estimation lost the stigma which justly pertains to it—and therefore the criminals are every where shielded by their families and by the sympathies of many communities."

The States of North Carolina, South Carolina, Georgia and perhaps others, have passed laws to withdraw from service men liable to it under existing laws, and these laws have the support of local authorities. I think that the number of the deserters is perhaps overstated, but the evil is one of enormous magnitude, and the means of the Department to apply a corrective have diminished in proportion to its increase.

3.   I do not regard the slave population as a source from which an addition to the army can be successfully derived. If the use of slaves had been resorted to in the beginning of the war for service in the Engineer troops and as teamsters and laborers, it might have been judicious. Their employment since 1862 has been difficult and latterly almost impracticable. The attempt to collect 20,000 has been obstructed and nearly abortive. The enemy have raised almost as many from the fugitives occasioned by the draft, as ourselves from its execution. Genl Holmes reports 1500 fugitives in one week in North Carolina. Col Blount reported a desertion of 1210

last summer in Mobile; and Governor Clark of Mississippi entreats the suspension of the call for them in that State.—As a practical measure, I cannot see how a slave force can be collected, armed and equipped at the present time.

4.   In immediate connection with this subject is that of subsistence for the army.

This has been attended with difficulty since the commencement of the war in consequence of the want of efficient control over the transportation and the deficiency of funds. There were abundant supplies in the country at that time, and the transportation was fully adequate, but these were not under control.

The Treasury has never answered the full demands of the Commissary department with promptitude.

These difficulties were aggravated when the currency became depreciated and prices were determined by Commissioners, so as to lighten the burden on the Treasury, and without reference to the market.

They have been still more aggravated by the subjugation of the most productive parts of the country, the devastation of other portions, and the destruction of railroads. Production has been diminished, and the quantity of supplies has been so much reduced that under the most favorable circumstances, subsistence for the army would not be certain and adequate.

At present these embarrassments have become so much accumulated, that the late Commissary General pronounces the problem of subsistence of the Army of Northern Virginia in its present position insoluble, and the present Commissary General requires the fulfilment of conditions not unreasonable but nearly impossible.

5.   The remarks upon the subject of subsistence are applicable to the clothing, fuel, and forage requisite for the army service, and in regard to the supply of animals for cavalry and artillery. The transportation by railroad south of this city is now limited to the Danville road. The present capacity of that road is insufficient to bring supplies adequate to the support of the army of Northern Virginia, and the continuance of that road even at its existing condition cannot be relied on. It can render no assistance in facilitating the movement of troops.

6.   The Chief of Ordnance reports that he has a supply of 25.000 arms. He has been dependent on a foreign market for one half of the arms used. This source is nearly cut off. His workshops, in many instances have been destroyed, and those in use have been impaired by the withdrawal of de-

tails. He calls loudly for the withdrawal of men from the army to reëstablish the efficiency of some of them.

There is reason to apprehend that the most important of the manufactories of arms will be destroyed in a short time, and we have to contemplate a deficiency in arms and ammunition.

7.   The foregoing observations apply to the Nitre and Mining Bureau, and the Medical Department is not in a better condition than the other Bureaux.

8.   The armies in the field in North Carolina and Virginia do not afford encouragement to prolonged resistance. Genl Lee reported a few days ago the desertion of some twelve hundred veteran soldiers. Desertions have been frequent during the whole season, and the morale of the army is somewhat impaired. The causes have been abundant for this. Exposed to the most protracted and violent campaign that is known in history; contending against overwhelming numbers; badly equipped, fed, paid and cared for in camp and hospital; with families suffering at home, this army has exhibited the noblest qualities. It sees everywhere else disaster, and defeat, and that their toils and sufferings have been unproductive.

The army of North Carolina can scarcely be regarded as an army. Genl Johnston has at Charlotte less than 3000 dispirited and disorganized troops, composed of Brigades that are not so large as regiments should be.

Genl Hardie has a mixed command, a small portion of it is probably efficient. The troops from the Tennessee army have not arrived, and we cannot hope that they will arrive in good condition.

9.   The political condition is not more favorable. Georgia is in a state that may properly be called insurrectionary against the Confederate authorities. Her public men of greatest influence have cast reproach upon the laws of the Confederacy and the Confederate authorities, and have made the execution of their laws nearly impossible. A mere mention of the conditions in Tennessee, Missouri, Kentucky, Western Virginia, the line of the Mississippi, the seabord [sic] from the Potomac to the Sabine and North Alabama is necessary. North Carolina is divided and her divisions will prevent her from taking upon herself the support of the war as Virginia has done.

With the evacuation of Richmond the State of Virginia must be abandoned. The war will cease to be a national one from that time. You cannot but have perceived how much of the treasure of the hopes and affections of the people of all of the States have been deposited in Virginia and how much the national spirit has been upheld by the operations here. When this exchequer becomes exhausted, I fear that we shall be bankrupt, and that the public spirit in the South and South Western States will fail.

It is the province of statesmanship to consider of these things. The South may succumb, but it is not necessary that she should be destroyed. I do not regard reconstruction as involving destruction, unless our people should forget the incidents of their heroic struggle and become debased and degraded. It is the duty of her Statesmen and patriots to guard her in the future with even more care and tenderness than they have done in the past.

There is anarchy in the opinions of men here, and few are willing to give counsel, still fewer are willing to incur the responsibility of taking or advising action. In these circumstances, I have surveyed the whole ground, I believe calmly and dispassionately. The picture I do not think has been too highly colored. I do not ask that my views be accepted, but that a candid enquiry be made with a view to action.

I recommend that Genl Lee be requested to give his opinion upon the condition of the country, upon a submission of these facts, and that the President submit the subject to the Senate or to Congress and invite their action.

Very Respectfully
Your Obdt Servt.
J A Campbell
A.S.W.

and invite their action.
Very Respectfully,
Your Obdt Servt.
J A Campbell
A S W

Closing lines of John A. Campbell's masterly understatements pointing toward collapse of the Confederacy, March 6, 1865. Clerk wrote document, Campbell signing

The surrender of Lee's army had been an event of elation and wild joy through the North, five days before the death of Lincoln. The farewell address of General Robert E. Lee to his army, the manuscript with Lee's signature, is naturally one of the high treasures of the collection. Among other incidental and related items is an "EXTRA DISPATCH" issued in St. Louis, exultant with headlines and exclamation points topped with a spread eagle flaring "E Pluribus Unum" from its beak and above the printed outcry: "Glory to God in the Highest: Peace on Earth, Good will amongst men." There was an air of anticlimax about the escape, flight and pursuit of Jefferson Davis.

Head Qr Army N Va,
April 10 1865

General Order No 9

After four years of arduous service, marked by unsurpassed courage and fortitude the Army of Northern Virginia has been compelled to yeild [sic] to overwhelming numbers. I need not tell the survivors of so many hard fought battles who have remained steadfast to the last, that I have consented to this result from no distrust of them. But feeling that valor and devotion could accomplish nothing that would compensate the loss that would attend the continuance of the contest, I determined to avoid the useless sacrifice of those whose past services have endeared them to their countrymen. By the terms of the agreement Officers and men can return to their homes and remain until exchanged. You will take with you the satisfaction that proceeds from the consciousness of duty faithfully performed, and I earnestly pray that a merciful God will extend to you His blessing and protection. With unceasing admiration of your constancy and devotion to your country, and a grateful remembrance of your kind and generous consideration of myself, I bid you an affectionate farewell

R E Lee
Genl

Since consequences are pitiless, since passions let loose follow courses unimagined beforehand, there was an aftermath of the cold war and the later war. Many were the paradoxes of reconciliation and what was termed reconstruction. Amid the travesties of justice was the case of Dr. Samuel A. Mudd, tried and convicted by a Military Commission that affronted and violated Anglo-Saxon legal procedure. The verdict of time is that he was no conspirator in a plot to assassinate President Lincoln, and that in setting a broken bone for the assassin of Lincoln he was loyal to the Hippocratic oath in performing a medical service for a man in pain whom he didn't know. To the lonely little coral isles called Dry Tortugas sixty-five miles west of Key West went Dr. Samuel Mudd under life sentence. Around the Fort

Head dr. Army. N. Va.
April 10ᵗʰ 1865.

General Order No 9.

After four years of arduous service, marked by unsurpassed courage and fortitude the Army of Northern Virginia has been compelled to yield to overwhelming numbers. I need not tell the survivors of so many hard fought battles who have remained steadfast to the last, that I have consented to this result from no distrust of them. But feeling that valor and devotion could accomplish nothing that would compensate the loss that would attend the continuance of the contest, I determined to avoid the useless sacrifice of those whose past services have endeared them to their countrymen. By the terms of the agreement Officers and men can return to their homes and remain until exchanged. You will take with you the satisfaction that proceeds from the consciousness of duty faithfully performed, and I earnestly pray that a merciful God will extend to you His blessing and protection. With unceasing admiration of your constancy and devotion to your country, and a grateful remembrance of your kind and generous consideration of myself, I bid you an affectionate farewell.

R. E. Lee
Genl

R. E. Lee's farewell address to the Army of Northern Virginia

Jefferson prison ran a deep moat, filled by the sea, holding ten man-eating sharks. When the yellow fever broke out, it took convicts and guards, soldiers and prisoners, alike. The last of the army surgeons died. Then they accepted the services offered by Dr. Mudd. The officers still alive gave him authority. He had all casements enlarged to let in the air. He toiled night and day with an intelligence and a fidelity that was a pleasant surprise. When the epidemic had passed Fort officers signed a pardon appeal to President Andrew Johnson, who on February 8, 1869, signed the final and unconditional paper for Mudd's release, which latter document is here. Also here are two letters of Mudd to his wife, "My darling Frank," one to a brother, and one by his brother to "Frank."

Fort Jefferson Dry Tortugos
Fla. Oct. 21st 1865

My Dear Jere,

Since I wrote you last, we four & another prisoner under a life sentence, recently arrived, have been locked in a room every night closely guarded & not allowed to leave the door during the day without being accompanied by a guard. This is said to be owing to a rumor or information which the Govt. is in possession of, that a plot or plan is originating, either at Havana or New Orleans to rescue us from this place. The Nation certainly is growing mad to believe in such nonsense; & we the victims of its Credulity, feel greatly the Sting caused by the Sensationist & Political Intriguers hostile to our well being.

No man can say naught against the Conduct of either of us up to the present, other than my individual effort to get away, and I plead my apprehensions—the insecurity of life, the humiliation of being guarded by an ignorant, irresponsible & prejudiced negro Soldiery, before an Enlightened People as a justification. We are now guarded entirely by negro soldiers & a few white Officers a skins difference.

You will please quietly enquire concerning these foolish reports, so injurious to us, & know what orders if any, that have recently eminated [sic] from the War Department regarding our future imprisonment. We are of the opinion that these rumors were gotten up purposely to have an excuse to treat us with more rigor & hardship. The only way such a thing could be possible, would be by capturing the Fort, which could only be effected by a large fleet & land force, and then only by starving it out. I recd. no advice or council until it was to[o] late. Could we have had the White Regiment, the 161st N.Y.V. to guard the place no thought of leaving should have have been harbored for a moment

I recd. a letter, some letter paper, scapulas, beads, stamps & etc a few days ago, from Cousin Ann. I am truly sorry I did not receive such letters earlier. Should you see her, inform, that I will not be able to answer for some days, owing to the restrictions under which I am at present placed.

I also recd. a letter from Frank. I have heard there would be restrictions placed over our correspondence, so be careful what you write.

Give my love to all; I will not be able to write as often, owing to my altered position. I am very well, hoping the Circumstances that led me to make the foolish attempt to extricate myself from this woeful place, may be ameliorating I am most truly & devotedly Yours &c

Saml A Mudd

N. B. Write me soon & let me know wheather [sic] my attempted escape will have a tendency to prolong my stay here, or likely to lessen the influence of friends. I have done nothing more than any other man would under similar circumstances. There is no man living, but would free himself from such a place at the present time, had he the power, I am resolved not to leave this place unless released by proper authority.

Balto   April 12th   1867

Dear Frank

To day I've been able to see Ridgely & he says he can do nothing until after he sees Reverdy Johnson, & learns from him what bills were passed by congress, that would have a bearing on Sams case. The Senate will adjourn tomorrow, and he will be here the first of next week—he also stated Chase had now been assigned to this Circuit, & would be here the first of next month, & he would see him and again make the application for the writ, as there is now no doubt as to his jurisdiction, under the decision of Chief Justice Lorner & says he thinks he now will have no excuse for not issuing it, I have; gotten back the letter of Capt Henry which was stolen from Ridgely in Washington—Henrys letter is sworn to—he gives a conversation he had in Washington, with Gen Hunter in which Hunter states he nor the Court never believed Sam had any thing to do with the killing of Lincoln, but was the victim of his own timidity. Iv left the letter with Mr Carter the Editor of the Boto Gazette, this morning he told me he would examine it & let me know tomorrow if he thought it best to publish it if so he would do it & comment on it. If he advises to do so I will go over to Washington on Tuesday & get the Editor of the Intelligencer to publish it also—it Clearly proves, that Hunter believed—Sam was innocent of any conspiracy. I will urge the matter & do all in my power to procure poor Sams release & when I come down next Satturday, will give you my views of what can be done

Mary Clare will go down to Dr Blandford on Tuesday. I will not leave here until Satturday morning. As I will be a widower for three or four days. How is Bess getting on farming, has done any plowing & finished stripping Job tell Mr Bess I hope he has his Pig fat for I will certainly call on him for it at Easter I suppose he will be able to give me Beets & beans & peas also. Can you not have a s[t]uffed ham. I am tired of Balto meet, does Andrew & Lilly go to school, tell Andrew if Lilly knows more than he does, I wont give him one thing, but will give Lilly something pretty. Love to Lilly & Children

Yor Brother

Jere

Mary Clare is very well   ⎱
but anxious to get down home ⎰

Ft Jefferson Fla. Nov 7th 1867

My Darling Frank,

I recd yours of the 22nd Oct. last night. Also a letter from Key West relative to my case, containing the opinion of the Lawyer (in my case)— which is far from being pleasing. I have been so inured to hardships, that this fresh surprise, hardly awakens more than the natural feelings of revenge of wrongs inflicted and suffered. I shall leave here to explain the contents of the letter, believing him more competent to give it a proper version. I am however lead to hope for satisfaction & redress at the hands of our Most Worshipful President, the very cause & source of all my miseries. It is a strange disease that is cured by its cause. If poison sickens, take a little more, & it will cure—(that is), by killing. This is the remedy held out to me. I do not wish to increase your present trials and difficulties by the nar-ration of gloomey forebodings—but I must calmly state that I look forward with no degree of hope. ×××× Those who have sent me here, knowing the outrage they have committed, against me, will be the last to sanction my release. A letter was recd. from Mr. Ford the last mail stating the Articles had all safely come to hand—so Lilly will soon [have] recd her desk. I shall send yours by the first safe opportunity, that presents. How I am grieved I can't do more. The only anguish I suffer is in regard to you & our little children. I have grown accustomed to imprisonment & it no longer gives me pain. My soul though sometimes burn[s] with vengence [sic] when I think of the authors. You spoke of Pa's proposal to break up housekeeping &

live with him another year. This, although kind in him would render you far more unhappy & miserable. You would feel far greater dependence, moreover the children would ever be a source [of] anxiety & trouble Try therefore to remain where you are at present, but learn from the past to prepare better for the future & not be incommoded by a set of worthless hands. Sell off all stock except that which is actually needed for you own use & which it costs to keep. You did not state the bargain that had been made by Pa with those Parties for the rent of the place. How it was to be worked wheather [sic] you furnished any of the means &c. Give me full particulars when you write again. Bear up bravely against present adversities & I am in hopes God from whom all Governments proceed, will bring order out of the Present Confusion & allow justice once more to prevail. Say something kind to each of the children from me. Tell Andrew he must learn fast & write to me. Try to give him ambition to learn ~~with-out~~ not [to] create disgust or dislike to books &c. Hoping this may find you & family—Dear Pa Ma & all well I am as ever devotedly   Yrs

Sam.

Fort Jefferson, Florida
Jan. 1st 1868

My Darling Frank.

To day, being New Year, I will begin it by dropping you a few lines to let you know that I am spending the day soberly & thoughtful of you & little ones. I sometimes fancy I can see the dear little creatures coming in with chattering teeth & little *snotty noses* shivering with cold. I have felt great concern to know how you are provided with fuel & fire. Since the darkies have been turned away. Jere in his last told me he had been down though did not state wheather [sic] he had obtained any one to see to affairs during the winter. Your last letter led me to a different conclusion which the one preceding was calculated, had I not seen through the myth. Any one would judge from the former that my release was immediate—all that had to be done was to present the petition & etc. with the long list of Hon. Names to obtain the desired boom. Your last postpone the happy day four months longer—planting time. I can't see there is so much virtue in Honorable Names & letters—or even for meritorious services rendered. These are hard things to overlook. I have no doubt saved dozens of lives & thousands worth of property to the nation & can say from my inmost heart that I have never so much desired the death of an individual—yet you with me & the children are suffering for a crime which I am sure never entered our brains. This is justice I would like to see visited upon those who have so cruelly wronged me, that they may be brought to a sense of their guilt & may atone for their crime I have seen mention of the action of the Medical Confraternity in my behalf, but of what use, if it will not secure my release. My pride is not elevated by seeing my name paraded in the News-papers as deserving the clemency of the Government for the services I have rendered. Why don't they take up the case & prove my innocence & con-found my infamous calumniators. This would be doing the world a service, besides relieving the injured—I don't say satisfy.

My Darling Frank you ask me to write something cheering? Nothing would afford me more pleasure than to be able to comfort & console you in your present unhappy & helpless condition. So long as the Government is controled [sic] by men without souls & less honesty I can [not] promise you nor myself anything. The Spirit of infidelity pervades the whole Coun-try. This is not only in regard to God, but to the laws & the Constitution of the Country. They are materialists & think only of self gratification—exult-ing in the ruin & misery they cause others. I have had no means except by reading to arrive at the truth of our political woes. The soldiers are a very ignorant class generally & there is no one here in civil life who is capable of advising. The Officers I rarely have anything to say to. You can now judge of the facilities I have of acquiring knowedge, even upon the most unimportant matters. The Gentleman whom I have been expecting down— has not made his appearance. I will be prepared to undergo his bread & water administration upon his arrival. I think I have acted wisely. I shall certainly not make any statement—until I am placed right before the law. The only comfort or consolation I can give you, is, that I am well with a very good prospect of living until planting time. You are in a situation to know more than myself, consequently you should look to those better in-formed & receive cheer. If you believe all that is told you I am sure you ought not to despond on my account. Two Companies of soldiers have been ordered from here to New Orleans & will leave upon the first steamer that arrives. The two remaining Companies have orders to be in readiness to move, but their destination is not known. From what I have heard & can judge this Post will soon be guarded by negro troops—perhaps early in the Spring. Owing to the damp and unhealthy condition of the Fort, the Com-mandant has recommended that the Garrison & Prisoners be removed to one of the Islands near & erect temporary sheds &c to shield us from the heat of the sun & rain. The truth is beginning to be manifest.

Tell Lilly Pop has nearly completed her little work box. It is made of mahogany & inlaid with crab wood. Three little leaves representing a branch is inlaid in the corners of the top—a fancy piece in the centre with the enetials [sic] of her name in German letters engraved & inlaid, which looks quite nice. I have the sides yet to finish. I have several little crosses made of crab wood which I will send to be distributed among you all. We received the box & barrel of Potatoes in good order. There is no objection to our receiving anything. The jug of whiskey was a great treat to us—it lasted us over a week—so you can judge our moderation. Maj. Andrews has given us permission to receive anything our friends chose [sic] to send us not excepting whiskey. Remember me to dear Pa & Ma & family to all of our houshold—kiss our darling little children & tell them Pop loves them with all his heart, & they must be good & learn their little lessons well & learn to write to Pop—Wishing you my precious, Frank and all a happy New Year—I am devotedly   Yours   husband

Sam

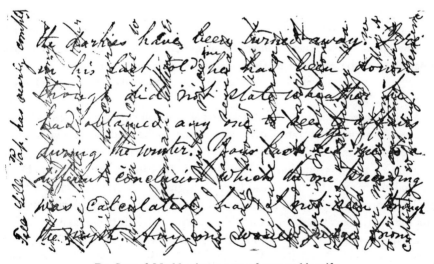

Dr. Samuel Mudd criss-crosses a letter to his wife

From a ciphered telegram of Jefferson Davis as late as April 24, 1865, the derivation can be made that he believes the war has not yet come to an end.

Decoded message reads: "The hostile government reject the proposed settlement, **and** order active operations to be resumed in forty-eight hours from noon today"

Charlotte N C

April 24, 1865

The hostile government reject the proposed settlement, and order active operations to be resumed in forty eight hours from noon today [1]

(Signed)   Jefferson Davis

Many were the myths of the aftermath. Rumors, exaggerated reports, interesting morsels of fabricated tales, came to be widely believed, came into common talk as having really and truly happened. This was so with relation to the assassination of Lincoln and the capture of Jefferson Davis by Federal troops. We may read here a telegram to Secretary Stanton from P. T. Barnum, once known as the world's greatest showman, offering money for the "petticoats" garb in which it was reported Jefferson Davis had tried to escape capture. We may also read a letter in which Jefferson Davis, long afterward, gives his version. We may also in another letter read his persuasive account of how and why he had at no time any hand in a plot to take Lincoln's life as alleged by the Confederate Government clerk and diarist J. B. Jones.

[1] The code words used in this message are "Come Retribution"—but two full pages would be required to explain the method of deciphering the letter.

— Original Telegram —

AMERICAN TELEGRAPH COMPANY.

No. _____
June _____

TERMS AND CONDITIONS ON WHICH THIS AND ALL MESSAGES ARE RECEIVED BY THIS COMPANY FOR TRANSMISSION.

In order to guard against and correct as much as possible some of the errors arising from atmospheric and other causes appertaining to telegraphy, every important message should be REPEATED by being sent back from the station at which it is to be received to the station from which it is originally sent. Half the usual price will be charged for repeating the message, and while this Company in good faith will endeavor to send messages correctly and promptly, it will not be responsible for errors or delays in the transmission or delivery, nor for the non-delivery of REPEATED MESSAGES, beyond TWO HUNDRED times the sum paid for sending the message, unless a special agreement for insurance be made in writings, and the amount of risk specified on this agreement, and paid for at the time of sending the message. Nor will the Company be responsible for any error or delay in the transmission or delivery, or for the non-delivery of ANY UNREPEATED MESSAGE, beyond the amount paid for sending the same, unless in like manner specially insured, and amount of risk stated hereon, and paid for at the time. No liability is assumed for errors in cipher or obscure messages; nor is any liability assumed by this Company for any error or neglect by any other Company over whose line this message may be sent to reach its destination; and this Company is hereby made the agent of the sender of this message to forward it over the lines extending beyond those of this Company. No agent or employee is allowed to vary these terms, or make any other or verbal agreement nor any promise as to the time of performance, and no one but a Superintendent is authorized to make a special agreement for insurance. These terms apply through the whole course of this message on all lines by which it may be transmitted.

CAMBRIDGE LIVINGSTON, Sec'y.   145 BROADWAY, N.Y.   **E. S. SANFORD, Pres't**

Send the following Message—subject to the above Conditions:

To _Hon Edwin M Stanton Secty of War_
GIVE ADDRESS IN FULL

Washington C & DC

I will give three hundred dollars to Sanitary
commision or Freedmens association for the
petticoats in which Jeff Davis was caught

P. T. Barnum

Words _14_   Operator's Check.

☞ *Please write your Address under the Signature.* ☜

Barnum offers five hundred dollars for petticoats

33 Camp St N.O.,
11th May 1876

My dear Crafts,

I have received your two very welcome letters and have not sooner replied, for two reasons, first I have been very busy, and second it is painful to me to realize, as I must, in discussing questions of the sectional war, that my early and ever dear friend, is not in accord with me.

My Father was a revolutionary soldier, and as you see by the name he gave me, a friend of Thomas Jefferson, and an adherent to the states rights doctrine. I grew up in that faith, and could no more conscientously [sic] have abandoned it, than I could have deserted a friend when surrounded by foes.

I sent to you the March No. of the Historical papers, and felt sure you could appreciate the truths and would do justice.

The diary of one Jones I have not seen, but suppose the poor devil after having fed on the Confederacy until it went down, then framed his story anew so as to gain admission to other pastures. As a Soldier and a Lawyer, you will see how little credibility is to be given to his tale of the proposition to assassinate Presid^t Lincoln. Would anyone making such a proposition send it through the Adjt. Genls. Dept., where he (Jones) only could have seen it. If so sent, it would not have been referred to me, but to the Secty. of War. Would any man who ever filled that office, have sent it to me. Yet these are the preliminaries to his falsehood, that I returned it without rebuke. Where was that man of stainless reputation as well in the old army as that of the Confederacy, Adt. Genl. S. Cooper, when a proposition to be employed for assassination was sent to him? Most lies have some grain of truth in them, and this one has an atom. Col. Alston of Genl. Morgan's staff, at the time when it was attempted to implicate me in the murder of Mr. Lincoln, published a statement which was copied in many papers of the time, it was substantially to this effect, that an officer of Genl. Jno. H. Morgan's command, had sent to *me*, not to the War office, a letter offering his services to go secretly and assassinate Mr. Lincoln, and that I had sent the letter to the War office, with an endorsement, ordering the officer to be arrested, and brought before a court Martial. That the officer was arrested, and would have been tried but for events which rendered it impossible. I do not know where that published letter is, nor do I recollect the circumstances further than as above written. The other story, of what I said to Breckinridge on receipt of the news of Lincoln's death is an equally

bald falsehood. Breckinridge was not with me, but in the conference with Genl. Sherman at Raleigh, and sent to me the telegram announcing the death of Mr. L. The news was to me very sad, for I felt that Mr. Johnson was a malignant man, and without the power, or generosity which I believed Mr. Lincoln possessed. The telegram was handed to Mr. Johnson, an eminent citizen of Charlotte N.C. He read it aloud to some persons there assembled, and I passed into the house to which I had been directed, on riding into the town.

The despatch was handed to me immediately after I had dismounted in front of the door, it was from Gen. Breckinridge, then in Raleigh, where he received the information from Genl. Sherman. So much for the particulars intended to confirm the fiction. One who was there present, has published an account of the incident, which, I believe, is mainly correct. He says that when I handed the telegram to Mr. Johnson, that I remarked this is sad news, and that the crowd called for the reading of the telegram, that when it was read, someone shouted and that I checked it, with remarks of sadness. The fact was, that without any personal regard for Mr. Lincoln, I considered him a kind hearted man, and very much to be preferred by us to his successor Mr. Johnson: but had it been otherwise nothing could have made me willing to adopt assassination as a means to be employed. This I trust all who ever knew me personally must believe, without asseveration or proof. Though several attempts were made to assasinate me during the War; though I was warned by a letter from Philad. that a desperado had been released from the Pa. penitentiary and sent to Montgomery Ala. for that purpose; though a man who waylaid me and shot at me, when riding in the suburbs of Richmond, and who by many circumstances was believed to be an emissary bribed with gold, found on his person, to commit the odious crime, yet neither I, or those associated with me, believed Mr. Lincoln to be particeps criminis. For the rest I will only say, it is not possible for me to think as favorably as you do of Messrs. Stanton, Seward, & Genl. Sherman; but I am glad that one whose opinion I respect so much as I do yours, entertains the conclusions you state.

It would be a great pleasure to me to see you, and you would be welcome among my friends. Like reasons to those formerly given, will prevent me from going to the West Point, at the "Centennial" meeting. With affectionate regard & pleasant memories, I am your friend

Jefferson Davis

C. J. Wright.

Beauvoir Harrison Co. Miss
April 8th, 1878.

Dear Friend,

I have just received your of the 2nd & 4th insts. together with the Chicago Tribune which you enclosed to me. I thank you for the affectionate zeal you manifest in my behalf. Mrs Davis is now in Memphis & I have not the advantage of availing myself of her recollection of events. So as you ask me to answer at once I can only give you at this time my own recollections to be filled out as soon as I may with what I may learn from her.

As has been heretofore stated our little encampment was surprised by the firing across the Creek, being a combat of the Federal brigade with the other. It was then as stated so dark that the troops did not recognise each other. My coachman waked me up & told me there was firing across the Creek; as I had lain down fully dressed, I immediately arose, stepped out, & saw some cavalry deployed at large intervals advancing upon the Camp: It was not light enough to distinguish any thing distinctly, but the manner of the movement convinced me that it was not by the marauders who were expected, but by troopers; and I stepped back so to inform my wife. She urged me to leave them believing that troops would not injure them but that I would be in danger by remaining. She threw over my shoulders her own Waterproof cloak and a shawl also, and sent her servant girl, a colored woman[,] with me as if going to the Branch for water. There were no sentinels around the tents, but a horseman advanced towards me, ordered me to halt & dropped his carbine on me. I instantly threw the shawl & cloak off, so as to be unencumbered & answering his demand for a surrender with a defiance, advanced towards him. My wife seeing this for I was still very near to the tent, ran after me & threw her arms around my neck; I then turned back, led her to the tent—& passed around to the rear of it, to a fire which was burning there. The colored woman picked up the cloak & shawl and returned with them to the tent. All statements not in keeping with this, are *false*. Some time elapsed after this before I saw Col Pritchard, he afterwards told me that he was sent in pursuit of the wagon train, that he had no expectation of finding me with it and did not know for three hours after that *I* was in the camp—which time he has however now reduced to "ten minutes"! With the addition the purpose of which is evident, that he also thus early learned, that I was "disguised when captured." The pillage of the Camp commenced immediately & my servants, who were preparing some breakfast for my children had it snatched from the fire when it was partly cooked & *this* was the thieving which provoked my angry language

to Col Pritchard when he at length came, & told me he was the Commanding Officer. I cannot with any accuracy answer your inquiry as to how much was lost, by the members of the party at that time. I only know that the pillage was general, rapidly & expertly executed—for example—My horse was seized, the Waterproof cloak strapped behind the saddle (similar to the one Mrs Davis threw over my shoulders, which I had been in the habit of wearing in Richmond) was taken from the saddle, the saddle taken from the horse, one girth taken off, saddle blanket & one rein of the bridle, so that the horse & his equipment were soon in different places, even down to the minute divisions I have stated. When I noticed this I remarked— "You are an expert set of thieves" One of the men with admirable coolness laughingly replied—"You think so! Do you?" I have no recollection of Col Pritchard even having proposed to "divide our supplies" but I do remember that Mrs Davis had some little delicacies such as were needed for her children, and that she complained to Col Pritchard of their seizure & that he promised to have all requisite supplied when we got to Macon. 'Tis *quite* absurd for him, now to pretend that they were necessary for an issue of provisions to a Brigade—and I also remember that they were never replaced but that myself & family & staff when on the ship were served at a second table & provided only with the coarsest food. As to his report of a conversation with me, in which he said the garments worn by me when captured were not particularly adapted to rapid locomotion or the use of fire arms— I can only regard it as an attempt to bolster up the falsehood he may have vauntingly told at some other time to Genl. Wilson or another, & will only add that if he had perpetrated such insolence he would have received an answer he could not have forgotten. Though minute in describing the expedition and the Transport ship on which my wife & children were held in captivity, after I had been immured in fortress Monroe, Col Pritchard only gives the result, of a Waterproof Cloak and a black woolen shawl, omitting putably as unimportant the fact that the trunks of my family were broken open & robbed of every article tempting to the sight, including the clothes of my infant daughter, photographic albums, medals, &c &c &c. One of these albums, by the assistance of an honest man in New York, was traced to Iowa, where a personal friend of mine recovered it, though many of the most valued family portraits had in the meantime been extracted from it. With a cool assurance, which is really laughable, a man in New York who acquired one of the medals, wrote to me sending photographs of the front and reverse and asking me to give him its history! I weary of these disgusting details, to men like yourself it must be a mortification to know that your countrymen have behaved so meanly. So far as I know, never in the annals of civilized war did a Commanding Officer treat a prisoner of high rank among his own people in a manner so little in accordance with the usages of a soldier and the instincts of a gentlemen, as Col B. D. Pritchard treated me while in his power. Yet had he limited himself to his official report or had he afterwards stated only the truth I should not probably have thus recorded his meanness and dishonesty.

Truly your friend,

Jefferson Davis

P.S. . . . Not only were my horses taken as loot, but also two, which were the property of my Wife, and those of all the gentlemen who were with our party, some of whom were paroled soldiers riding their own horses, and acting as helps to my Wife and children before I joined them. Col. Pritchard announced his purpose to take my saddle horse, & said he would like to say he had my horse after he went home, &c &c.

Truly,

To C. J. W.   J. D.

Albert Hunt, a craftsman in charcoal, was at the headquarters of General Grant on March 27, 1865, and made this sketch of Lincoln from life. Some may prefer the photographs taken a few days later in April. Others will value this interpretative sketch. The questions rise: Has the President and Commander in Chief been reading the newspaper on his left leg or is he going to read it or is he saying he knows more about the war than the newspaper can tell him? And his unduly large hand at his right ear indicates he is listening for what? It is conceded he was a supremely sensitive listener and did Mr. Hunt wish to convey the impression that the listening was improved by a hand placed forninst the right ear—or could it be that Mr. Lincoln is about to scratch his head back of the ear? Of these matters we know only that Mr. Hunt with his charcoal did the best that was in him. On the floor back of the chair we can see the gripsack or satchel holding Mr. Lincoln's nightgown, change of shirt, and accessories. Draped vaguely over a barrel is Mr. Lincoln's shawl. Not far from his right elbow on a shelf is what Mr. Hunt purports to be General Grant's large flask. The hat, historically, is probably more accurate than Mr. Lincoln's very neat and dapper boots. Presumably the artist presented his charcoal portrait to Mr. Lincoln who gave it to Mrs. Lincoln who promptly presented it to the Negro coachman, eventually landing in the collection of Major William H. Lambert, from which it passed to the Barrett Collection.

The later and bearded Old John Brown of Osawatomie, Kansas (*left*). Slaves and cabin (*below*). Negro family coming into Union lines (*below left*)

10. Americana: A Span of Years, 1834-1886

Wherein are rescued from obscurity and oblivion various antique letters and prints bearing on The American Way of Life—

1   1834

Lieutenant Jefferson Davis in Arkansas writes Sarah Taylor "by *dreams* have I been lately almost crazed for they were of you," and "your letter tonight . . . I have kissed it often."

2   1839

Ulysses S. Grant, a seventeen-year-old cadet at West Point, writes a droll and boyish letter to a cousin in Ohio.

3   1842

A country journal burlesques the barn-dance caller.

4   1848

Zachary Taylor, having seen Whig soldier and Democrat soldier fight side by side to lie buried in the same grave, asks why Whigs and Democrats should hate each other or be "Ultra" party men.

5   1853

Robert E. Lee, West Point Commandant, writes his "dear Son" of the conduct of life and the purity and nobility of a dying woman.

6   1857-1859

John Brown in one letter reports his preparations for a shooting war in Kansas and in a second letter writes terrible and ruthless words inviting a young man to join a cause and die a martyr.

7   1857-1859

John Brown on the day he was hanged wrote two wills, this being the second one, proved and accepted in court.

8   1861

A Kansas pioneer vividly reports a devastating snowstorm.

9   1861

Braxton Bragg in St. Louis writes his wife that having been appointed Brigadier General in the Confederate Army, "You will be astounded to hear I am off without seeing you."

10   1861

Briefly and thankfully Stonewall Jackson accepts appointment as Brigadier General.

11   1862

General Earl Van Dorn writes from Arkansas to his Sister Emily of combat, deaths, disasters, hopes, enclosing love to his wife Carrie and kisses to his "dear little daughter," enclosing also $400, half for Emily, half for Carrie.

12   1863

Former President Franklin Pierce writes to New York Governor Horatio Seymour his detestation of President Lincoln lacking dignity and a sense of duty.

13   1863

Gen. John A. Rawlins and his Emma write of their mutual passion and coming marriage—and their horror of U. S. Grant's hard drinking.

14   1864

Walt Whitman, poet and companion, writes of Lincoln, of wounded men, of men become "wrecks and phantoms," of money needs.

15   1864

Mosby writes Sheridan that since Sheridan's men have been hanging and shooting captured Mosby men, he, Mosby, has already hanged and shot captured Sheridan men, and will go on keeping the score more than even.

16   1871

Horace Greeley briefly, abruptly, and peremptorily nails a lie and leaves it lay.

17   1882

Frank Sanborn writes a lecture giving an awesome portrait of John Brown, fanatic root-and-branch revolutionary.

18   1883

The indurated warrior William Tecumseh Sherman replies refusing to write for a charity sale a sentence, "The pen is mightier than the sword."

19   1886

William Tecumseh Sherman recalls marching men, remembering particularly how and when he cut the wires so no orders could be telegraphed stopping his march from Atlanta to the Sea.

Potters spin a wheel which moves neither forwards nor backwards yet moves both ways at once, therein copying the revolution of the universe. On this wheel as it revolves they make pottery of every shape and no two pieces are alike, though they are made from the same material and with the same tools. Men and animals too are in the same case.

—HIPPOCRATES

I   1834

Fort Gibson, Dec. 16, 1834

Tis strange how superstitious intense feeling renders us but stranger still what aids chance sometimes brings to support our superstition. dreams my dear Sarah we will agree are our weakest thoughts, and yet by *dreams* have I been lately almost crazed for they were of you and the *sleeping* immagination [sic] painted you not such as I left you, not such as I could live and see you, for you seemed a sacrifice to your parents desire the bride of a wretch that your pride and sense equally compelled you to despise, and a creature here, telling the ondits of the day at St Louis said you were "about to be married to a Doctor McLeannin" a poor devil who served with the Battallion of Rangers possibly you may have seen him—but last night the vision was changed you were at the house of an Uncle in Kentucky. Capt McCree was walking with you when I met you he left you and you told me of your father and of yourself almost this same thought that I have read in your letter to night, Kind dear letter. I have kissed it often and it has driven many mad notions from my brain. Sarah whatever I may be hereafter I will ascribe to you, neglected by you I should be worse than nothing and if the few good qualities I possess shall under your smiles yield a fruit it will be yours as the grain is the husbandman's.—It has been a source productive of regret with me that our union must seperate [sic] you from your earliest and best friends, a test to which the firmness of very few are equal, though giddy with passion or bouant [sic] by the hope of reconciliation there be many who brave it. from you I am prepared to expect all that intellect and dignified pride brings. the question as it had occurred to you is truly startling your own answer is the most grattifying [sic] to me, is that which I should [have] expected from you, for as you are the first with whom I ever ought to have one fortune, so you would be the last from whom I would expect desertion. When I wrote to you I supposed you did not intend soon to return to Kentucky. I approve entirely of your preference to a meeting elsewhere than at Prairie-du-Chien and your desire to avoid any embarrasments might widen the breach made already cannot be greater than my own. did I know when you would be at St. Louis I could meet you there. At all events we meet in Kentucky. Shall we not soon meet Sarah to part no more? Oh! how I long to lay my head upon that breat which beats in unison with my own. to turn from the sickening sights of wordly duplicity and look in those eyes so eloquent of purity and love. do you remember the "hearts ease" you gave me. it is bright as ever how very gravely you ask leave to ask me a question. My dear girl I have no secrets from you have a right to ask me any question without an apology. Miss Bullitt did not give me a guard for a watch but if she had do you suppose I would have given it to Capt McCree. But I'll tell you what she did give me, a most beautifull and lengthy lecture on my and your charms the which combined once upon an evening at a "fair" in Louisville as she was one of the few subjects of conversation we had apart from ourselves on that evening you can. & I have left you to guess what beside a desiribility to your charms constituted my offence. the reporters were absent and the speech I made is lost.

Pray what manner of message could la belle Elvin have sent you concerning me? I suppose an attempt to destroy harmony. I laughed at her demonstrations against the attachment existing between myself a subaltern of Dragoons, but that between you and J is not fair game it is robbing to make another poor but no: She is too discerning to attempt a thing so difficult and in which success would be valueless "Miss Elizabeth one very handsome; lady" Ah! Know what did you put that semi colon between handsome and lady for? I hope you find in the society of the Prairie enough to amuse if not to please. The griefs over which we weep are not those to be dreaded, It is the little pains the constant falling of the drops of care which wear away the heart. I join you in rejoicing that Mrs. McCree is added to your society. I admire her more than anyone else you could have had. Since I wrote to you we have abandoned the position in the Creek Nation and are constructing quarters at Fort Gibson. My lines like the beggars days are dwindling to the shortest span. Write to me immediately my dear Sarah, my betrothed. No formality is proposed between us.

Adieu Ma chere tres cheri amie adieu au Revue

Jeff

To Miss Sarah K. Taylor
  Prairie du Chien
    W. T.

2   1839

Spelling, punctuation, and capitalization follow the original of this letter of young "U. H. Grant."

Military Academy
West Point N.Y.
Sept. 22d 1839

Dear Coz.

I was just thinking that you would be right glad to hear from one of your relations who is so far away as I am so, I have put asaid my Algebra and French and am going to tell you a long story about this prettiest of places West Point. So far as it regards natural attractions it is decidedly the most beautiful place that I have ever seen; here are hills and dales, rocks and river; all pleasant to look upon. From the window near I can see the Hudson; that far famed, that beautiful river with its bosom studded with hundreds of snow ~~white~~ sails. Again if I look another way I can see Fort Putnan frowning far above; a stern monument of a sterner age which seems placed there on purpose to tell us of the glorious deeds of our fathers and to bid us remember *their* sufferings—to follow their examples. In short this is the best of all places—the *place* of all *places* for an institution like this. I have not told you *half* its attractions. here is the house Washington used to live in—there Kosisuseko used to walk and think of *his* country and of *ours*. Over the river we are shown the duelling house of Arnold, that *base* and *heartless* traiter *to* his country and his God. I do love the *place*. it seems as though I could live here ferever if my friends would only come too. You might search the wide world over and then not find a better. Now all this sounds nice, very nice, 'what a happy fellow you are' you will say, but I am not one to show fals colers the brightest side of the picture. So I will tell you about a few of the *drawbacks*. First, I slept for two months upon one single pair of blankets, now this sounds romantic and you may think it very easy. but I tell you what coz, it is *tremendeus hard*. suppose you try it by way of experiment for a night or two. I am pretty shure that you would be perfectly satisfied that is no easy matter. but glad am I these things are over. we are now in our quarters. I have a spleanded bed and get along very well. Our pay is nomonally about twenty eight dollars a month. but we never see one cent of it. if we want any thing from a shoestring to a coat we must go to the commadant of the post and get an order fer it or we cannot have it. We have tremendous long and hard lessons to get in both French and Algebra. I study hard and hope to get along so as to pass the examination in January. this examination is a hard one they say, but I am not frightened *yet*. If I am successful here you will not see me fer two long years. it seems a long while to me. but time passes off very fast. it seems but a few days since I came here. it is because every hour has it[s] duty which must be performed. On the whole I like the place very much. so much that I would not go away on any account. The fact is if a man graduates here he [is] safe fer life. let him go where he will. There is much to dislike but more to like. I mean to study hard and stay if it be possible. if I cannot—very well—the world is wide. I have now been here about four months and have not seen a single familier face or *spoken* to a single lady. I wish some of the pretty girles of Bethel were here just so I might look at them. but fudge! confound the girles. I have seen great men plenty of them. let us see. Gen Scott. M. Van Buren. Sec. of War and Navy. Washington Irving and lots of other big bugs. If I were to come home now with my uniform on. they way you would laugh at my appearance would be curious. My pants sit as tight to my skin as the bark to a tree and if I do not walk *military*. that is if I bend over quickly or run. they are very apt to crack with a report as loud as a pistol. my coat must always be buttoned up tight to the chin. it is made of sheeps grey cloth all covered with big round buttons. it makes me look very singular. If you were to see me at a distance. the first question you would ask would be. 'is that a Fish or an animal'? You must give my very best love and respects to all my friends particularly your brothers. Uncle Ross & Sam'l Simpson. You must also write me a long letter in reply to this and tell me about every thing and every body including yourself. If you happen to see my folks just tell them that I am happy, *alive* and *kicking*.

I am truly your cousin
and obediand servant

McKinstrey Griffith
U. H. Grant

N.B. In coming on I stopped five days in Philidelpha with my friends they are all well. Tell Grandmother Simpson that they always have expected to see here before. but have almost given up the idea now. they hope to hear from her often. U. H. Grant

(On side of sheet) My very best respects to Grandmother Simpson. I think often [of] her, I put this on the margen so that you may remember it better. I want you to show this letter and all others that I may write to you, to her

(On margin of second page) I am going to write to some of my friends in Philadelphia soon when they answer I shall write you again to tell you about them &c. &c. remember and write me very soon fer I want to here much

(On margins of envelope sheet) I came near forgetting to tell you about our demerit or "black marks" They give a man one of these 'black marks' for almost nothing and if he gets 200 a year they dismiss him. To show how easy one can get these a man by the name of *Grant* of this state got *eight* of these "marks" fer not going to Church today. he was also put under arrest so he cannot leave his room perhaps fer a month, all this fer not going to Church. We are not only obliged to go to church but must *march* there by companys. This is not exactly republican. It is an Episcopal Church

Contrary to the prediction of you and rest of my Bethel friends I have not yet been the least *homesick* no! I would not go home on any account whatever. When I come home in two years (if I live) they way I shall astonish you *natives* will be *curious*. I hope you wont take me for a Babboon

Addressed to:
> Mr. McKinstrey Griffith
> Bethel Clermont Co.
> Ohio

Closing lines of letter of seventeen-year-old Grant at West Point

3   1842

From the *Winchester* (Scott Co., Ill.) *Battle Axe*, February 26, 1842

BALLS.—As Balls are all the rage in these parts, we publish from an exchange paper, for the benefit of our dancing friends, "a new cotillion, and how to dance it. First couple forward, wheel and fore—second couple, ditto—alumode at the corners—nose-your-nose—gentlemen cross hands—ladies kiss over—right and wrong—pussey—lemonade all-first couple dance round the whole posse comitatus—second do.—third do.—fourth do.—bob your cocoa-nuts and then go to roost."

4   1848

We have seen hereinbefore in the handwriting of Lincoln, and signed by him and E. D. Baker, the sentence: "He lied in his heart when he told General Taylor he was not an ultra whig." Now we have from General Taylor himself a short straightaway answer on the meaning of the term "ultra Whig." In an issue of the *Carrollton* (Greene County, Illinois) *Gazette* of October 21, 1848, in the lower right-hand corner of the front page are the paragraphs:

Anecdote.—The following anecdote of General Taylor is related by the Staunton (Va.) Spectator. It is perfectly characteristic of the man:

The old hero was asked on one occasion, by a lady, what he meant in saying he was not an ultra Whig. His reply was—"Madam: I have been called upon to pass through three wars since I joined the army. In the war of 1812, I saw both parties represented on the battle field, and even in my little command at Fort Harrison, they stood shoulder to shoulder. I saw the Whig and the Democrat lie down in the swamps of Florida, and in the morning rise up to their posts of duty; and again I saw them rise not up, but together lie in the embrace of death!—I have seen the Whig and the Democrat again, side by side, on the banks of the Rio Grande. I saw them both stand together at the cannon's mouth at Monterey—and both looked up to the same star-spangled banner. The Whig and Democrat spread the same tent upon the sand banks at Vera Cruz, and together marched to the halls of the Montezumas at their country's call.—And, at last, I have seen the Whig and Democrat returning home, with constitutions broken and health impaired, TO DIE—and seeing these things, *I could not find it in my heart to proscribe men for mere political differences.*

1853

                                        WestPoint 4 May 1853

My dear Son

I have rec^d your affectionate letter of the 31st & thank you Sincirely for
the love & Consideration you feel & express for me. The affection of my
children, their welfare and prosperity, is all the pleasure I expect or Care
for in this world, and my only desire is to deserve the first, promote the
Second, & do my duty to my Country & God. When I Can no longer do
any of these, I no longer wish to live. You therefore See that much of my
pleasure depends upon you. If you feel the affection for me you profess,—
and I believe; be Careful of every thought word & act that may give me
pain. Do not be Satisfied with *wish*ing & in*tend*ing right, but *do* it. All
would do right if easy or agreeable, but because it is not, it is done by few.
Be one of those few. Have that Command of yourself, that will enable you
to defy the tempter & scorn the Sinful pleasures he offers. Let your pleasure
be in doing good. Keep before you the example of your dear G^d Mother.
Remember how she laboured for others. Remember her Care & love of you.
Prove yourself a worthy descendant of one of the purest beings in the
World. Her entire want of Selfishness so Conspicuous throughout her life,
was equally distinguished in her last moments. On Saturday night when told
by the D^r that she was dying, & asked if she had any message for her
daughter, she took no thought of herself but only thought of the distress
of her she so much loved, & said, "Oh how terribly she will be shocked
when she hears this"! She was always ready for the Summons & happy to
meet her God. Seeing that your younger Sister Could not restrain her grief
and fearing she was repining at her departure, She turned to her & Said,
"Why do you weep So Annie". She left a letter for me prepared before her
last Sickness, full of affection & interest, which the grave Could not diminish,
for your G^d father, your Mother & yourselves. May you die the death of
the righteous—& may your last end be like hers! I have rec^d a very gratifying letter from your Sister. Mine to her announcing the Sad news was for
Some Cause late in reaching her. Although it was overwhelming at first,
Miss B— wrote me she was quite Composed & resigned. I hope you were
able to get to See her Saturday. It would be a Comfort to you both. You
must Cherish your love for each other, & Stand always ready to relieve and
assist your Sisters & brothers. Rob & Mildred are very well and very good.
They can hardly realize their loss, though at first were much distressed.

Wm. H. Fitzhugh Lee

West Point. 4 May 1858

My dear Son —

I have received your affectionate letter of the 3d — + thank you sincerely for the consideration you feel & express for him. The affection of my Children, their love & sympathy, is all the pleasure I expect to enjoy for in this world.

Opening part of a letter of R. E. Lee to his son, William H. Fitzhugh Lee.

Your brother spent Saturday ev^e with me as usual. It was muster & Inspection day, & my daily duties were much augmented. But at night when the little people had retired, we had a quiet talk together. His grief is deep and strong, but notwithstanding he has maintained his position in every Class & been present at every duty, except drawing monday. (He rec^d the Sad intelligence at 1 P.M.) afternoon, when he was too blinded by his tears to guide his pencil. He said he should write to you Sunday—I have no news to tell you, & you know I have little time for writing. I endeavour to take Rob a short ride every ev^e before parade & Send Eliza to walk out with Mildred. They go to school as usual & are very well & very good

I remain your devoted
father
R E Lee

Wm H. Fitzhugh Lee

6   1858-59

Materials collateral to the Lincoln life and personality, touching on men and events strictly in the gaze of Lincoln, these from time to time were added to the Barrett Collection. In the storm tides rocking the nation the figure of old John Brown rose. We have one essence of the man at sixty years of age writing from Peterboro, New York, February 24, 1858, to young F. B. Sanborn at Concord, Mass. Here we have Brown the bearded elder inviting the youth into lawless adventure of danger, crime, tumult and probable death on the gallows.

Mr. Morton has taken the liberty of saying to me that you feel ½ inclined to make a common cause with me [wrote John Brown]. I *greatly rejoice at this;* for I believe when you come to look at the *ample field* I labour in; & the rich harvest which (not only this entire country, but) the whole world during the present & future generations *may reap* from its cultivation: you will feel that you are out of your element until you find you are in it; an entire Unit. What an inconceivable amount of good you might so effect; by your *counsel, your example, your encouragement, your natural, & acquired ability;* for active service. And then how very little we can possibly loose [sic]? Certainly the cause is enough *to live for;* if not to [die?] for. [Where Brown here left out a word, the inference is that the word he meant was "die." And the old man went on in his invitation to the youth to join him in death for a cause.] . . . But my dear friend if you should make up your mind to do so I trust it will be wholly from the promptings of your own spirit; after having *thoroughly counted* the cost. I would *flatter no man* into such a measure if I could do it ever so easily. *I expect nothing* but to "endure hardness"; but I expect to effect a mighty conquest even though it be like the last victory of Samson. I felt for a number of years *in earlier life:* a steady, strong, desire to *die:* but since I saw any prospect of becoming a "reaper" in the *great* harvest I have not only felt quite willing to *live:* but have enjoyed life much; & am now rather anxious to live for a *few* years more.

Closing part of letter of John Brown to Frank B. Sanborn

Five months earlier Brown wrote from Fremont County, Iowa, to young Sanborn at Concord, Mass., mentioning money and supplies to be sent to him, and acknowledging a check received. Brown has "194 Carbines, about 3300 Ball and Cartridges," and miscellaneous guns and revolvers, for the war he is to start. Brown's assumed name, for his shadowy purposes, is Jonas Jones Tabor, and his mail should be so addressed. "I paid out $550. on a Contract for 1000 superior Pikes as a cheap but effectual weapon to place in the [blank] of entirely unskilful & unpracticed men: which will not easily get out of order; & require no Ammunition." The blank space for the omitted word naturally means *hands.* And by "entirely unskilful & unpracticed men" Brown means Negro slaves. Brown is aware *"wise* Military men may ridicule the idea," adding, "I take the whole responsibility of that job."

Tabor, Freemont Co., Iowa, Oct. 1st. 1857.

F. B. Sanborn Esqr.
Concord, Mass.
My Dear Sir

Two days since I received your very kind letter of the 14ᵗʰ Sept: also one from Jas. Hunnewell Esq. saying he had sent me $72.68 Seventy Two Dollars & Sixty Eight Cents through P. J. Jackson Esqr. of Boston, for both which I am very glad. I can not express my gratitude for your earnest & early attention to my wants & those of my family. I regret that Mr. Hunnewell did not at once send me either a Check, *or a Draft* on New York, or Boston: as it will probably be One Month or more before I can realize it: & I have not the means of paying my board bill here; not having as yet received any thing from Mr. Whitman towards balance of $500 nor heard from him. If I get the money from Mr. Hunnewell & from Mr. Whitman it will answer my present wants *except* for the *secret service* I wrote about. I have *all the Arms* I am likely to need: but am destitute of Saddle Bags or Knapsacks, Holsters, & Belts. Have only a few Blankets; have no Shovels or Spades: no Matttocks: but 3 or 4 Axes (Ought to have 100.) & am nearly destitute of Cooking utensils. *The greater part* of what I have just named, I must do without till another Spring at any rate. I found here One Brass field piece complete, & One damaged Gun carriage with no Limber, with some ammunition suitable for it, some 70 to 75 old damaged U S Rifles, & Muskets, One Doz old Sabres, some Powder & Lead, (*enough for present,* weight not known,) I suppose sent by *National Comm.* Also One Doz. Boxes & Barrels Clothing, Boots &c. with 3 Hand Grist Mills sent to Nebraska City, from some source. I also got from Dr. Jesse Bowen of Iowa City: One old Waggon which broke down with a light load on the way: also 9 full sized Tents, 3 set Tentpoles (additional,) 11 pair Blankets, & 3 Axes, sent there by National Comm. Also from Mr. Hurd I got an order for Fifty Dollars worth of Tents Waggon covering, Ropes &c, at Chicago: which was paid me. I find 194 Carbines, about 3300 Ball Catridges, all the Primers; but no Iron Ladles. This I believe with the teams & Waggon I purchased, will give you a pretty correct idea of the stuff I have. I had a Gun & pair Pistols given me by Dr. Howe: & some 3 or 4 Guns made for experiment by Mr. Thayer: & a little Cannon & carriage as one of them, one nice Rifle by the manufacturing Co. at Worcester. I had also a few Revolvers, common Guns, & Sabres left on hand that I took on with me in 1855. While waiting here, I & my son have been trying to learn a little of the arts of *Peace* with Col F who is still with us. That is the Scool I alluded to. Before I reached here I had written particularly to friends in Kansas saying I wanted help to meet me here *& to wait for me* should I be detained on the way. I also aranged with Mr. Whitman in regard to it in Chicago. He sent One Man with $150. $40. of it he kept, & went immediately back. From that time I send you copies of some of the correspondence between Kansas & me; as rather essential to give you a correct idea of things in connection with my statements yet to be made. When I got on here I immediately wrote Mr. Whitman & several others what was my situation, & wants. He Mr. Whitman has not written me at all since what I send. Others have written as you will see. I wrote the Man Mr. Whitman sent amonong the rest; but yet no word from him since what I now send. As to the "policy" of voting on Monday next I think Lane hit his mark at the Convention of Grasshoppers—if never before. I mean "an escape ~~through~~ *into* the filth sluice of a prison." I had not been able to learn by papers or otherwise *distinctly* what course had been taken in Kansas till within a few days; & probably the less I have to say the better. I omited above to say that I paid out $550 on a Contract for 1000 superior Pikes as a cheap but effectual weapon to place in the [hands?] of entirely unskilful, & unpracticed men; which will not easily get out of order, & require no Amunition. They will cost handles & all complete a little short of One Dollar each. That contract I have not been able to fulfil, & *wise* Military men may ridicule the idea; but "I take the whole responsibility of that job"; so that I can only get them. On hearing that Lane had come into Nebraska, I at once sent a young man with a line saying I had been hurt & was exceedingly anxious to see him early in Sept. To this he sent me no reply unless Redpaths letter be one. I am now so far recovered from my hurt as to be able to do a little & foggy *as it is:* we "do not give up the Ship." I will not *say* that Kansas watered with the tears & blood of my Children: shall *yet be Free* or I fall. I intend at once to place the supplies I have in a secure place: & then to put myself, & such as may go with me where we can get *more speedy communications;* & can wait until we know better *how to act;* than we now do. I send this whole package to you thinking Concord a less offensive name just now than Boston; at this end of the route. I wish the whole conveyed to my friend Stearns & other friends at Boston as old Browns last report. Untill further advised, I wish all communications directed to Jonas Jones Esqr. Tabor, Freemont Co, Iowa *outwardly* & I hope you will all write often. I had forgotten to say that day before Yesterday one single man alone with no team whatever, came from Lane to have me

start at once for Kansas as you will see by copies. He said he had left **Ten**
fine fellows about 30 miles back. The names he gave me were all strange
to me as well as himself. Tabor folks (some them) speak rather slitingly
of him not withstanding that he too; is a General   Oct. 3d,/57

Yours covering Check is this moment to hand & will afford most season-
able relief. Express goes to K. to see how land lies at once. You will hear
again soon

Yours most truly

J. Brown

7   **1859**

I John Brown a prisoner now in the prison of Charleston Jefferson
County Virginia—do hereby make and ordain this as my true last will and
testament—

I will and direct that all my property, being personal property, which is
scattered about in the States of Virginia and Maryland should be carefully
gathered up by my executor herein-after appointed—and disposed of to the
best advantage—and the proceeds thereof paid over to my beloved wife,
Mary A. Brown.

Many of these articles, are not of a war like character, and I trust as to
such and all other property that I may be entitled to ~~and I ask~~ that my
rights and the rights of my family, may be respected—

And lastly I hereby appoint Sheriff James W. Campbell, executor of *this*
my true last will hereby revoking all others

Witness my hand & seal this 2nd day of December 1859

John Brown Esq
Seal

Signed sealed and
declared to be the
true last will of
John Brown, in our
presence, who at
tested the same
at his request, in
his presence and in
the presence of each other
  John Avis
  Andrew Hunter

Codicil—I wish my friends James W. Campbell sheriff, and John Avis jailor, as a return for their kindness, each to have a Sharpe rifle, of those belonging to me, or if no rifle can be had, then each a pistol—

Witness my hand & Seal this 2nd day of December 1859

John Brown Esq
Seal

Signed, sealed and
and [sic] declared to be a
Codicil to the last will
& testament of John Brown
in our presence who attested
the same, at his request in
his presence and in the
presence of each other
  Andrew Hunter
  John Avis

<u>51</u>

John Brown's Will
& Codicil

1859 Dect 19th Will and
Codicil proved by the oaths of
John Avis & Andrew Hunter.
Order to be recorded.
  Teste
  T A Moore: C. C.
Recorder Will Book
No. 16 page <u>143</u>

8   1861

From the *Aurora of the Valley* Newburg and Bradford, Vt., February 23, 1861:

Topeka, K. T., Feb. 3d, 1861

MR. EDITOR:—Twice, already, has the Kansas winter been declared finished. But this morning, the mercury was 120 degrees below its maximum reach in July. A mild winter was hoped for, and consequently predicted. Almanac makers need not try their art here. About three-fourths of the winters will be mild.

But the exceptional one will give no notice of a visit. The snow is from one to three feet deep. A snow storm on the prairies is not interesting, but terrible, only. The traveler has no fence, field, no tree, no forest, no hills or mountains to point his way. The wind is too fickle to be trusted, though too constant in one respect. Instead of a succession of puffs and blasts, it is the gale upon the seas, continuous, merciless, freezing. Unending is the stream of snow, coming from nowhere, and hurrying, uselessly, to the same locality. One grows dizzy and drunk, while gazing at the impatient, racing snow-flood. Add to all, the gloom of a twilight day, and the despair of black night, and Dante is vindicated in making the third circle of Hell—a realm of snow and sleet, and Milton, (who seems the child-poet Dante, returned to earth,) in raising the idea to the sublime horror of frozen fire.

The wet earth and the crop of corn are made sure by this, now snowy abyss. But it will be hard upon the people.

The short grass dried and cured in the sun, was sufficient for the stock, so long as they could get it, and thousands depended on it to keep their stock, except for three or four weeks. The fodder laid up, is being eaten up. Already cattle have died—mostly estrays, which no one would feed. It is pitiful to see the poor, patient, obedient oxen. A multitude of teams were upon the prairies when winter set in. First came the snow. Then it melted just enough to cover the country with ice. Five dollars was the prize [sic] for shoeing oxen; but there was no money to do it, even at rational prices. The ice disappeared, and left the roads mud, frozen into sharp points, which wore the feet of the oxen almost to bleeding. I saw twenty-five pairs crippling and hirpling along, of a single morning, trying to reach the southern counties with supplies for the destitute. Then came these great snows. All transportation is upon wagons. One man was eleven days in reaching this place, from Atchison, 46 miles. Many began to leave part of their loads that they might be able to reach their families with a little. To see the drivers is proof enough of the condition of those at home. They are but half clad. One man was seen passing through this town with his ox-team, mearing [sic] shoes, but no stockings, and the snow twenty inches deep. Many, from scarcity of hay, are compelled to feed their oxen with relief meal, from their wagons. Men have swapped off two pairs of reduced cattle, for one pair smaller than either of the two, but in condition to draw their loads. Many men have been frostbitten. Mr. Pomeroy has a small hospital at Atchison, for their comfort and cure. The amount of suffering in the thinly settled prairies, cannot be known till Spring. But we almost fear to know. For example, what will be this winter's history of that German family where the father was sick and his wife walked 44 miles to Atchison in the deep snow, for relief? Be assured that the people of Kansas, having had so much assistance in '56, are a good deal humiliated to receive aid again so soon. Some are so proud that they deny and distort the facts. Such are generally men with money, and speculators. But these need not fear. For population will return. This is, in many respects, the most beautiful country in all this world. There are a good many disagreeable days of wind and soot. But the evenings of these days, as Miss Bremer says of the evenings of Cuba, are paradisiacal. Something enchants. The emigrant may get homesick. A short visit to the old home generally effects a cure. The faults of the land are forgotten, and the fascination endures.   Yours truly,   A.M.

9   1861

St. Louis Hotel. Mo.
7th March. P.M.

My dearest Wife—

You will be astounded to hear I am off without seeing you. At 11 o'c this morning I received by telegraph, notice of my appointment as Brigadier General in the Confederate Army and order to proceed to Pensacola and assume command. What this means, you know as well as I do, but it is so sudden and unexpected it finds me unprepared. At first I concluded to run over tonight, but then no one would meet me, and I could not get to you. So I concluded after seeing my friends to give up my happiness to duty. *I shall leave tomorrow for Pensacola*—from there I will let you know what I think. You know how unprepared I am for any such move. My wants must be supplied by purchase here, and you must send by Towson all that you think I may require from home.

Tell Towson to close up all my business, as far as he had orders, and bring with him the other accounts. I can settle them by letter. I enclose drafts for Ribbeck, Eng^d and Vaush [?] Noel, Cooper. If I should owe them any more I will settle when the bills come. I also enclose a draft to George Guion to pay pew rent. All these Towson can deliver for you. After he has done all this he can take charge of my baggage, including swords & belts. Such. and come on to Pensacola. He must stop a day in New Orleans, see Co^l Westmore, get his orders, draw his pay and Travelling expenses from Capt. Winnemore for going to Baton Rouge and join me. Just as soon as you can join me he shall come back for you.

Machmont [?] must get along as best he can, and rely on Tom if he has trouble.

What is to become of all this I do not see except war. Mr. Lincoln says he will not recognise our government, and if he does not we must take the Forts in our limits; To do that is war, and when it commences it will rage from one end of the country to the other. God grant us a safe deliverence. Our cause is just, and we must triumph I deplore the necessity, but neither you nor I could wish me out of it. Come what will I must be in it. Mr. Taylor speaks of going over with me. General Van Dorn is here and applies for service under me.

Pray for me, dear Wife, and accept the ardent love of

Y^r. Husband,

Braxton Bragg.

10   1861

Head Quarters 1st Brigade
Camp near Winchester
July 8th, 1861.

Sir,

Your letter informing me that I have been appointed a Brigadier General in the Provisional Army in the Service of the Confederate States has been received, and the appointment thankfully accepted. The oath of office is herewith transmitted.

Very respectfully your Obdt Servt
T. J. Jackson.
Brig. Genl P.A.C.S.

Hon L. P. Walker
  Secretary of War

11   1862

Other accounts than the one here by a commander in the field give more complete details on the battle of Pea Ridge, Arkansas, March 6-8, 1862. Major General Van Dorn later made brilliant cavalry raids, and it was a great loss to the Confederate forces when at his headquarters desk at Spring Hill, Tennessee, he was shot and killed by a personal enemy.

Van Buren, Arkansas,
March 11th 1862

Dear Sister Emily

Please pardon me for a long silence—I have been sorely "bedeviled" by all sorts of things. This position brings a thousand and one troubles and annoyances, and ones time is seldom his own. It was my duty however, to

write to you in *addition* to the natural promptings of affection, and I
should not have neglected it. but to tell you the truth I have been *unable*
until now to send you any money and *waiting* to get some to send you has
been the chief cause of my not writing. I hope sincerely that you have not
been *seriously* in need of it, though I am afraid that you have been. I now
enclose you two hundred dollars for Carrie and two hundred dollars for
you and Libbie which I hope will be sufficient for a month or six weeks
when I hope to be able to send you more. I send you the money for Carrie
as I am not sure that she is with you or in Alabama. If she is not with you
I will ask you to send it to her, if you please. Tell her I have been unable
to send it to her before and that I have been unable to write to her or to
any one since I left Pocahontas, I have been travelling on horse back from
forty to fifty miles a day and have been actively employed in moving the
army to the attack of the enemy. I have fought a great battle which lasted
two days. I did not succeed in entirely routing the enemy, though I took
two of his batteries, drove him from the field and slept on our arms on the
scene of action—having taken more than two hundred prisoners and killed
and wounded about fifteen hundred or two thousand. The loss of Gen^{ls}
McCulloch and McIntosh and the taking of Col. Herbert threw my right
wing into utter confusion. Prudence dictated to me not to hazzard [sic]
another days fighting and I withdrew with tears in my eyes—the first time
in my life I ever was compelled to fall back from an enemy. My eleventh
battle! On the 6th we drove one Division of the Army before us for twelve
miles—the 7th the main attack was made at 10 O'Clock A.M. and Continued
with great fury until after dark. The 8th we fought from day light until
about 10 O'Clock A.M. During the night the enemy had taken a new position stronger than the first, and my men were then unequal to the task of
driving him from it. Hungry for two days—without sleep—and ammunition
nearly exhausted and leaders Killed. I could not risk another battle. We had
driven the enemy from every position and had not lost an inch of ground—
but—I was compelled to give up the attempt to Conquer him *completely*.
We were not *defeated* in battle, but defeated only in our *intentions* to drive
him from Arkansas back to his den. I shall prepare again and give him
another trial soon.

Please tell my dear Carry to write to me if she is with you, and if she is
still in Alabama write me word of it. I shall start back to Pocahontas in a
few days, or as soon as I can reorganize the army. I will place it under command of Genl Price to march it and then go myself to Pocahontas to prepare the other Corps for the field by the Mississippi near Beauregard, who

has written to me to come to his assistance. You will hear of active times soon from this section of country. I shall try to make it a hot place for the Yankees. I will write as often as I can but you may imagine that I have but little time for writing letters of affection I am going day and night and am beset all the time by officers &c &c. Please then do *your* part of the correspondence and do not be too exacting of me. Kiss my dear little daughter for me and tell her that I love her more than all the world, and that I feel so proud to hear that she is as good as she is beautiful. She must write to me often, *often*. I think of her continually. And she must not think that I have forgotten her because I do not write. I am too much wearied in mind and body to do much else at night but to lie and *think* of those far away whom I love. Kiss her for me a hundred times and my boy too if he is with you, and my wife also. God bless them all and God bless you and yours. Send Earl to me to learn the Art of War in the field. I will try and get him a Cadetship in the Army. Send him to me. I will take good care of him.

Believe me my dear Sister Emily to be as ever your affectionate and loving brother

Earl

12   1863

Concord N.H.
Apr 15, 1863

My dear Sir.

Your note addressed to me at this place was forwarded to Andover Mass where I have been confined by a severe cold for several days. Altho the authenticity of the order had been asserted in various papers, still I could not believe that it was genuine and hence I hesitated to reply to your question. On my arrival here last Eve'g I found that the question was relieved from all doubt.

I enclose an extract from the order now on the files of the Adjt Genl of this State and have only to add that upon it Lt Edgerly has been dropped from the rolls. I can hardly realize now that such an act could be authenticated by a public record and above all that the President of the United States could have so far forgotten his duty and his dignity as to assail with false charges coupled with vulgar epithets more than 32000 of the most worthy citizens of New Hampshire. But here is the language, now a matter of record.

Despotism like this would be bad enough under the direction of intelligence & decency. What it is now I have no language to express.

Yr friend,

His Excellency   Franklin Pierce
    Horatio Seymour
        Albany, N.Y.

P.S. I enclose a curious order for the dismissal of a Lieutenant of your 42ⁿᵈ Volunteers.

Back page
                    Hon. Franklin Pierce.
                    Concord, N. H.
                    April 15, 1863

Political
Enclosing discharge of
Lieut. Edgerly.

Will you acknowledge the reception of this. Some letters written by me have never reached their destination.

13   1863

Hd. Qrs. Mil. Div. of the Miss.
Chattanooga, Tenn. Nov. 16 1863.

My dearest Emma.

Your letter imprisoning thoughts beautiful in conception and fettered in language of fitting comeliness of date the 31st Ult. was duly received and read with all the avidity and interest its own merit and my love for its charming authoress inspired and for the unspeakable pleasure thus derived. Many thanks to that soft southerly breeze and Moonlight-jewelled night that induced my dearest Emma to write it. You desire to know whether I will visit you by the 1st of Janry. I had hoped & still hope to be able to do so by that date, and had I written last evening as I came near doing I should have said the probabilities were all in favor of my doing so. Today however matters have changed and the necessity of my presence here made almost absolute, by the free use of intoxicating liquors at Head Quarters which last nights devellopements showed me had reached to the General commanding. I am the only one here (his wife not being with him) who can stay it in that direction & prevent evil consequences resulting from it. I had hoped but it appears vainly his New Orleans experience would prevent him ever again indulging with this his worst enemy; Thus dearest Emma you see that that would come so near ending forever our talk of an engagement so near that you had partly turned to leave me, stands now between us and an early meeting. Even now the thought pains me that on the occasion alluded to I lowered myself as a man in your esteem, and you blamed me for the position I then assumed. I tell you my dearest Emma, unless the blighting shadow of intemperance had hung like a pall over one's pathway all his life and shaded the consummation of his fondest hopes and made him from its continuous presence feel to ask himself the question, and to die a drunkard? he can poorly appreciate my feelings on this subject. You failed to understand me, for had you not, though your lips moved by a woman's pride, refused my request, in your heart you could have condemned me never. I have run out on paper a train of thought that I wish I had not, for it can only be the parent of sadness, and if my spirits were not in gloom this evening I would re-write this letter to leave it out. You ask me to tell you all my troubles. Were I with you I would do so, but with the pen I would fail to make you understand them, and to be candid dearest my troubles are not very serious, the one most so is that of which I have here written & which threatens to extend the time beyond that named for my coming to you, this however I shall try and obviate by persuading the General to send for his spouse, if she is with him all will be well & I can be spared. the next most serious one, is how little of home comforts and present social enjoyments I have to offer in lieu of all I invite you from. You are now agreeably and lovingly situated exempt from domestic cares, in circumstances of comfort if not of affluence, with friends, with music and company and all the attendant enjoyments of social life. All these you leave, and for what, well I need not write it here. Of my family and circumstances you have been fully and truthfully advised, and being so advised have consented to be my wife and make me happy, and dearest Emma let me here assure you that this consent you shall never have cause to regret. So will I ever demean myself toward you, as to preserve the sweetness of your disposition, your amiability of manners, your personal charms and all that makes you the most lovely and beautiful of women down to the latest period a kind Providence may permit us to walk together along the flowery slopes of time. I have not a good Photograph of my little ones or I would send it. Yours I have not as yet received. Col. Wilson has been appointed a Brig. Genl., his stars will never illuminate a curved [?] path. He will have a cavalry command. Col Duff desires to be remembered to you. Write me often your letters are all read & re-read over and over again & again. Dont say you feel sad ever. I desire to feel, you at least (of all I love) are happy for on your happiness depends that of my children and my own. This letter does not altogether please me, for the reason I fear there are some things in it may make you feel badly. Would that I were with you to night that I might tear it up and tell you all that is in it, how sincerely I love you, how long the time seems since we parted, and how distant appears the first of January when I expect to meet you in your northern home in all your beauty and loveliness. You will try and look beautiful then, wont you dearest! Do you think you will view yourself in the mirror & wonder if you are as lovely & charming as I shall expect to find you, say dearest.

Trusting I have not in this alienated your affections in the slightest as I am sure I have not I must bid you a kind good night.

Your own

Jno. A Rawlins

To Miss M. E. Hurlbut

What I have said of the General is strictly confidential.

Emma Hurlbut came home from a ball to once more read the foregoing letter. The dancing party had been gay and exciting. She is still in the flush of its excitement, the waltzes, the polkas, the schottisches. Taking up John Rawlin's letter again, she writes in pencil between the lines her endearing and passionate answers. It could have been a letter she would have sent him had she dared. It could be her diary entries for the evening. At times she breathes in some lover's code or pet name without giving any clue to the reader who doesn't have their private signal system.

Once more in the welcome solitude of my own room I can hold – – & liberty to think of, write to & hold sweet commune with my hearts best beloved, my dear John. How delightful it is after the gayeties & confines of a large party to be alone, to muse on the past and dream of – – dreams of the future. The hour is late, it is the hour at which you are wont to bid me good night in that land of beauty & flowers. O my darling could you only have heard me, how much I could impart to you, that my pen cannot portray – I wonder where you are tonight. Are you fallen in the arms of morpheus, dreaming of the one, who loves you so dearly or are you angered with the [?] & neverending labors of the dept. Would that you were here in my pretty quiet room away from all the dangers & horrors that now sorround you. How my heart aches at the thought of the perils, which you may pass through ere we meet again. [?] of fires & battles & victory to the Union forces. O [?] God grant that you may pass safely through all & that our meeting be not far distant. With what deep joy I look forward to that blissful time when I shall welcome you to my own fireside & proudly present you to my dear parents. It was with the deepest regret that I heard of his again yielding to the temptation, that the poisonous serpent is again encircling him in his deadly folds. How can he in his high position holding the lives of 10,000 in his hands & when so much depends on him, how dare he do any thing that would render him incompetent or unfit for the important duties of his position, it is truly honorable if you can try, you turn stop the destruction which threatens him, it is your duty to ~~to do so~~ remain with him. What mean you by the words: I lowered myself as a man in your esteem and you blamed me for the position I assumed. [?] No my conduct that night, when I refused the sin (which openly showed the influence of your words the high esteem & love I have for you [– – – – –] for you. If this is my one thing more – – – – another that I love him & – – – it is you. – I acknowledge that my foolish pride for an instant misled my better judgement & for which I was sorry. O how – – – – – – then I knew you and with that a – – – – – – – – – – high minded-being you are. O how passionately I loved you then. Again you think of your circumstances, dear John, I am not in affluence, I have a comfortable home, kind friends & tender parents who would always have me with them, if such a thing were possible.

I counted to – – your believe I had you for yourself alone – – for your – – – worth. – – Is not home where the heart it? – – – – – It matters not how humble the home may be in which you place me. I shall be happy, cheered – – by your love & the – – – – of the little darlings – – whom – – I belong to & you, to take to my bosom & dear John, a life time of devotion shall prove you how – – – – is my – – – from you.

I am pleased to hear of the promotion of CGn.W. I prophecy for him a – – – career.

My compliments to Col. Duff.

14   1864

During the period of his volunteer service Walt Whitman sought contributions of money to be used for the soldiers in his care. The following is from the original of a rough draft of a letter written by Whitman in war time: he is a "wound dresser," going among stubs of men in hospitals, visiting "wrecks and phantoms":

for J P Kirkwood
   44 Union Square
   New York City

I forget whether I wrote to you acknowledging the receipt of the $10 sent for the wounded and sick, 1st Feb. It came safe also the $5 you sent some ten days since. My dear sir your contributions are very very welcome. They go to the direct sustenance, cheer and comfort of special cases of wounded and sick. I have now been over a year on the wounded. I find that personal application with entire sympathy, tact and insight, are the only means effectual in hospitals—every case wants some peculiar adaptation—to some, some little article purchased—many the tender hand and word, oft repeated, never slacks up, till danger is past.

Some while prostrated are out of money and too proud to speak of it. To these a little gift or two or three—to some a little tobacco is a great treasure. Anything like beggars or deceivers, are very rare indeed. I don't meet one a fortnight. The soldiers are nearly altogether young American men of decent breeding, farmers sons ordinarily educated, but well behaved and their young hearts full of manliness and candor. Their condition makes deepest attachments under their sufferings and wounds often brought right to the bitterness of death. Some indeed one feels to love deeply and they return it with interest.

I have lately been down to the front on a short tour through the Army; part of the time being in camp among the men, (I know a great many soldiers in the ranks) and visit the division hospitals. The hospitals in the field are at present thin—the main cases are here. The condition of the Army the past winter has been surpassingly good (go on with acc't) the talk here is that Grant is going to make things hop in this region presently. The idea is that the means of railway transportation between here and the southwest are to be increased to the extremest practical degree, so that he can swing large bodies to and fro, with unprecedented dispatch, and have the use of the Army, in either quarter, at a few days' notice. We hear he [Grant] thinks it indispensable that we should smash Lee and the Richmond junta this summer though more for our prestige than for any practical need of Richmond as a locality. I can assure you from personal knowledge that the Army of the Potomac is in splendid condition, physically and in soul—it has now the fibre of the most veteran troops, one of the historic armies. It is very youthful. I think well of Meade. He is very cautious and con-

Refugees leaving the old homestead (*above left*). A canvas pontoon bridge (*above right*). Federal camp at Johnsonville, Tennessee (*below left*). Three "Johnnie Reb" prisoners (*below right*). (*Barrett Collection stereographs*)

Joseph Holt (a Brady photograph)

Thomas J. (Stonewall) Jackson, August 10, 1855

Henry W. Halleck

Major General Thomas J. (Stonewall) Jackson

Ulysses S. Grant

Lieutenant John S. Mosby

scientious, yet very alert, (would be perfect if he fused those qualities with the lightning of audacity and venturing all when it was worth it but he has not that dangerous but necessary crowning merit, Napoleon's).

I make no calculations on the course and result of the ensuing summer campaign, except that I believe it will be vehement. Meantime we are liable at any moment to have an incipient caving in of the South, parts of it like North Carolina but the shrewd ones here still reckon on a desparate fight of the Richmond junta, ferocious, carrying things with as high hand as ever the ensuing year.

I see the President often. I think better of him than many do. He has conscience and homely shrewdness—conceals an enormous tenacity under his mild gawky western manner. The difficulties of his situation have been unprecendented in the history of statesmanship. That he has conserved the government so far is a miracle. The difficulties have not been the south alone. The north has been and is yet honeycombed with semi-secesh sympathizers ever ready to undermine—and I am half disposed to predict that after the war closes, we shall see bevies of star-straps, two or three of our own Major Generals shot for treachery, and fully deserve their fate. I write this in hospital having leisure here. I am sitting by the side of a soldier of the 6th Maine—he had his leg amputated lately.

The sick are coming in pretty freely here, poor wrecks and phantoms— a sign of action, as they are breaking up the field hospitals. One's heart bleeds for them. Every day I am among them as usual. I desire you, if you have any friends able to send me aid, and that feel to do so that you would show them this letter, as I would like more means. It shall be sacred.

15   1864

Nov 11th 64

Major General P. H. Sheridan
Commanding U. S. forces in the Valley
General.

Some time in the month of September during my absence from my command, six of my men, who had been captured by your forces, were hung & shot in the streets of Front Royall by the order & in the immediate presence of Brigadier General Custer. since then another captured by a Col. Powell on a plundering expedition into Rappahannock was also hung—a label affixed to the coat of one of the murdered men declared "that this would be the fate of Mosby & all his men." Since the murder of my men not less than seven honored prisoners, including many officers of high rank, captured from your army by this command, have been forwarded to Richmond, but the execution of my purpose of retaliation was deferred in order as far as possible to confine its operation to the men of Custer and Powell. Accordingly on the 6th inst. seven of your men were, by my order, executed on the Valley pike, your highway of travel. Hereafter any prisoners falling into my hands will be treated with the kindness due to their condition unless some new act of barbarity shall compel me reluctantly to adopt a course of policy repulsive to humanity.

Very respectfully
Your Obt Serv—
Jno S. Mosby
Lt. Colonel

Colonel Mosby warns General Sheridan about shooting affairs

16 1871

NEW YORK TRIBUNE

New York, Oct. 30, 1871.

Sir:

In reply to yours of the 25th inst., I see no reason to say more than that the United States should scrupulously keep faith with *all* who have sustained them in trouble without asking whether they be rich or poor.

Your assumptions that the Rich alone own bonds and that the poor alone pay the debt are lies.

Yours,

Horace Greeley.

W. B. Loubbere, Esq.
Omaha, Neb.

17 1882

Twenty-four years had passed in the life of Frank B. Sanborn since John Brown was hanged and we have here the manuscript of a remarkable lecture Sanborn delivered on John Brown. In one of his earliest talks with John Brown, in 1857, as Sanborn wrote it, John Brown said to him: "I believe in the Golden Rule, and the Declaration of Independence. I have always been delighted with the doctrine that all men are created equal; and to my mind it is like the Savior's command, 'Thou shalt love thy neighbor as thyself.' How can we do that unless he is equal with ourselves? Rather than have the doctrine fail in the world or in these States, it would be better that a whole generation, men, women and children, should die a violent death."

On this, Sanborn, the convinced revolutionary abolitionist, commented: "It was his fixed opinion, in support of which he gave his own life and that of those brave sons. . . . Who now boasts that he helped hang John Brown? The last man that did so was Wilkes Booth, the assassin of Lincoln, who five years before had stood among the armed band that guarded the scaffold at Charleston. The execution of Brown and the slaying of Lincoln were deeds of the same nature, and sprang from the same accursed root; it was slavery that demanded the sacrifice in both cases. They marked the

New-York Tribune.

New York, Oct. 30, 1871.

Sir:

In reply to yours of the 25th inst., I see no reason to say more than that the United States should scrupulously keep faith with all who have sustained them in trouble without asking whether they are rich or poor. Your assumption that the Rich alone own bonds and that the poor alone pay the debt are lies.

Yours,

Horace Greeley

N. B. Louvere, Esq.,
Omaha, Neb.

Horace Greeley's handwriting—some legends say it was undecipherable beginning and the end of that bloody contest from which our great nation came forth strengthened and purified; and each of these victims was as blameless as the other. Both had caused human blood to flow, Brown, in a few slender streams on the prairies of Kansas, and the hillsides of Virginia; Lincoln on a thousand fields of battle. But both should be held guiltless of bloodshed, because the objects for which they contended were worth more than the costly price paid for them."

18   1883

We can run our eyes over a letter of William Tecumseh Sherman in 1883. The managers of an auction for charity have asked him to write a letter to be sold to the highest bidder, the specific request being that the grizzled old warrior shall inscribe in the letter a line, "The pen is mightier than the sword." He reports straightaway he can do no such thing, and, "You and I have seen the day when a good and Great man ruled this Country, Lincoln, who wielded a powerful and prolific pen, yet had to call to his assistance a million of flaming swords."

Headquarters Army of the United States
Washington, D.C., Sept. 6 1882

James Van Norden, Esq.
Brooklyn. N Y.
Dear Sir.
Your long letter of Sept 4 is received, and as you say my Autographs with the official heading may have a Value in an affair of Charity I send you a few more to add to those previously sent. I prefer not to make scraps of sentimental writing to be sold. When I write any thing I want it real and connected in form—as for instance in your quotation from Lord Lytton's Play of Richelieu, "The pen is mightier than the sword." Lord Lytton would never have put his signature to so bare a sentiment. Surely I will not. There was a prefix or qualification. "Beneath the Rule of men entirely great The pen is mightier than the sword." Now this world does furnish

not often present the condition here presented. "Men entirely great" are very rare indeed. And even Washington who approached greatness as near as any mortal found good use for the sword *and* the pen, each in its proper sphere. You and I have seen the day when a good and Great man ruled this

Country, Lincoln, who wielded a powerful and prolific pen, yet had to call to his assistance a million of flaming swords.

No, I cannot subscribe to your naked sentiment, The pen is mightier than the sword, because it is not true.

Rather in the Providence of God, "there is a time for all things," a time when the sword will cut the Gordian Knot, and set free the principles of Right justice, bound up in the meshes of hatred, revenge and tyranny, that the pens of mighty men like Clay, Webster, Crittenden and Lincoln could not disentangle.

Wishing you all success in your Charitable work, I am

With respect, yr Friend,
W. T. Sherman

Warrior W. T. Sherman declines to write "the pen is mightier than the sword"

19   1886

From "5th Avenue Hotel New York, December 22, 1886," W. T. Sherman writes to R. U. Johnson, Esq. of the *Century Magazine:*

I adhere to my former conclusion not to attempt a Magazine article on any war event. I do not profess the skill or patience of an historian, but only to be a witness before the Great tribunal of the world, of scenes which I have witnessed or events in which I shared. Of these I have testified fully in the two volumes of Memoirs.

Also, he points out, there is now available the *Personal Memoirs* of U. S. Grant. Later in this long letter he is saying:

True, many an orator in his safe office at the North had proclaimed his purpose to cleave his way to the sea. Every expedition which crossed the Ohio River in the early part of the war headed for the sea, but things were not ripe till the Western Army had fought, and toiled, and labored down to Atlanta.

He credits Grant, Thomas, Lincoln—but not Rawlins, whose measure he takes—and Mr. R. U. Johnson certainly would have liked it for a magazine article.

I had been acquainted with Genl Jno. A. Rawlings [sic], Genl Grant's "Chief of Staff" from the beginning of the War. He was always most loyal & devoted to his Chief, an enthusiastic patriot, and of real ability. He was a neighbor of General Grant in Galena at the breaking out of the war, a lawyer in good practice, an intense thinker and a man of vehement expression: a soldier by force of circumstances rather than by education or practice yet of infinite use to his Chief throughout the war and up to the hour of his death as Secretary of War in 1869. . . .

Mr. Lincoln was the wisest man of our day and more truly and kindly gave voice to my secret thoughts and feeling when he wrote me at Savannah from Washington under the date of Dec 26. 1864 "When you were about leaving Atlanta for the Atlantic Coast I was anxious if not fearful; but feeling that you were the better Judge and remembering 'nothing risked, nothing gained' I did not interfere. Now the undertaking being a success, the honor is all yours, for I believe none of us went further than to acquiesce; and taking the work of General Thomas into account, as it should be taken, it is indeed a Great Success. Not only does it afford the obvious and immediate military advantages, but in showing to the world that your army could be divided, putting the stronger part to an important new service, and yet leaving enough to vanquish the old opposing force of the whole, Hood Army, it brings those who sat in darkness to see a great light. But what next? I suppose it will be safer if I leave General Grant and yourself to decide."

So highly do I prize this testimonial that I preserve Mr. Lincoln's letter, every word in his own hand writing unto this day; and if I know myself I believe on receiving it I experienced more satisfaction in giving to his over burdened and weary soul one gleam of satisfaction and happiness than of selfish pride in an achievement which has given me among men a larger measure of fame than any single act of my life. . . .

General Rawlings was enthusiastically devoted to his friend in the Western Army, with which he had been associated from Cairo to Vicksburg and Chattanooga, and doubtless like many others at the time, October 1864, feared that I was about to lead his comrades in a "wild goose chase," not fully comprehending the objects aimed at, or that I on the spot had better means of accurate knowledge than he in the distance. He did not possess the magnificent equipoise of General Grant, nor the confidence in my military sagacity which his chief did, and I am not at all surprised to learn that he went to Washington from City Points to obtain an order from the President or Secretary of War to compel me with an army of sixty five thousand of the best soldiers which America had ever produced to remain idle when an opportunity was offered such as never occurs twice to any man on earth. General Rawlings was right according to the lights he possessed and I remember well my feeling of uneasiness that something of the kind *might* happen, and how free and glorious I felt when the magic telegraph was cut which prevented the possibility of orders of any kind from the USA coming to delay or hinder us from fulfilling what I knew was comparatively easy of execution and was sure to be a long stride toward the goal we all aimed at—Victory and Peace from Virginia to Texas. He was one of the many referred to by Mr. Lincoln who sat in darkness, but after the event saw a great light. . . .

I am sincerely your Friend,

W. T. Sherman

INDEX

INDEX